Symbolic Interaction and Cultural Studies

Symbolic Interaction

and Cultural Studies

Studies

Edited by Howard S. Becker

and Michal M. McCall

The University of Chicago Press
Chicago & London

HOWARD S. BECKER is MacArthur Professor of Arts and Sciences and professor of sociology at Northwestern University. Among his many books is *Writing for Social Scientists,* also published by the University of Chicago Press. MICHAL M. MCCALL is associate professor and chair of the department of sociology at Macalester College.

THE UNIVERSITY OF CHICAGO PRESS, CHICAGO 60637
THE UNIVERSITY OF CHICAGO PRESS, LTD., LONDON
© 1990 by The University of Chicago
All rights reserved. Published 1990
Printed in the United States of America
99 98 97 96 95 94 93 92 91 90   54321

Library of Congress Cataloging-in-Publication Data
Symbolic interaction and cultural studies / edited by Howard S. Becker
  and Michal M. McCall.
      p.   cm.
    Papers originally prepared for the 1988 Stone Symposium
sponsored by the Society for the Study of Symbolic Interaction.
    Includes bibliographical references.
    Contents: Introduction / Michal M. McCall and Howard S. Becker
— Social interaction, culture, and historical studies / John R. Hall —
The good news about life history / Michal M. McCall and Judith
Wittner — Studying religion in the eighties / Mary Jo Neitz — Why
philosophers should become sociologists (and vice versa) / Kathryn
Pyne Addelson — Art worlds : developing the interactionist approach
to social organization / Samuel Gilmore — Symbolic interactionism in
social studies of science / Adele E. Clarke and Elihu M. Gerson — Fit
for postmodern selfhood / Barry Glassner — People are talking:
conversation analysis and symbolic interaction / Deirdre Boden.
    ISBN 0-226-04117-4 (alk. paper). — ISBN 0-226-04118-2 (pbk. : alk.
paper)
    1. Symbolic interactionism—Congresses.   2. Culture—Congresses.
I. Becker, Howard Saul, 1928–   .   II. McCall, Michal M.   III. Society
for the Study of Symbolic Interaction.   IV. Stone Symposium (1988 :
Chicago, Ill.)
HM291.S8878   1990
306—dc20   89-48060
                                                     CIP

Contents

Acknowledgments

We wish to thank the several organizations that made this volume possible by contributing to the support of the conference at which these papers were originally presented: the Gregory P. Stone Foundation, the Midwest Sociological Society, and the College of Arts and Sciences, the Center for Interdisciplinary Research in the Arts, the Center for Urban Affairs and Policy Research, and the Department of Sociology, all of Northwestern University.

1 Introduction

Michal M. McCall and
Howard S. Becker

The papers in this volume were originally prepared for the 1988 Stone Symposium, sponsored by the Society for the Study of Symbolic Interaction; they are presented here in the order in which they were given at that meeting. The authors had the following assignment, more or less in these words: tell about work being done in your substantive *outline* area of cultural studies; say what the tradition of symbolic interaction *for* thought and research has to tell other people who do such work; say *papers* what the other people who work in your area have to tell those of us who are symbolic interactionists; and illustrate your points and arguments with examples from your own work (all the authors had in fact recently done empirical studies of the topics they were to discuss). The assignment assumed that symbolic interactionists have not taken full advantage of work done in related fields that would be useful to their own projects, and that other people in cultural studies would be glad to know, and find useful, some of what symbolic interactionists take for granted as working ideas and procedures.

Most of the authors are sociologists, and many of them—Clarke, Gerson, Gilmore, Glassner, McCall, Neitz, and Wittner—have worked within the symbolic interactionist tradition. Others of the authors have been more loosely identified with that tradition. Boden, a well-known conversational analyst, makes her affinity with symbolic interaction explicit here. Although familiar with symbolic interaction theory, Hall has worked primarily in the area of cultural history. Addelson, a feminist philosopher, has found interactionism sufficiently useful to want to bring it to the attention of her disciplinary colleagues as well as to make the links between philosophy and sociology clearer to sociologists.

AUDIENCES

As a result of the assignment and the mixed disciplinary affiliations of the authors, the papers address themselves to several audiences from several subject matter positions, with all the risks and

1

potential confusions that entails. Most confusing, perhaps, and certainly the most numerous, are the papers that speak to symbolic interactionists from within that same tradition but from another content area. North American sociology is organized around content areas, not around methodological and conceptual approaches. Thus, there are sociologies of art, science, religion, and knowledge, into which the symbolic interaction approach has been incorporated, but symbolic interactionists have not developed a general approach to cultural studies.

Furthermore, practitioners of symbolic interaction research and thinking often have little in common beyond their common possession of certain "sensitizing concepts," their inductive approach to empirical research, and their adherence to the faith that the proper object of that research is "the natural world of every-day experience" (Blumer 1969:148). They may know very little about what other symbolic interactionists are doing in content areas other than their own.

Rather, individual interactionists have arrived at positions on general theoretical questions by solving the problems of working with the specific data of their content specialties. So, for instance, symbolic interactionists create an approach to epistemology by dealing with problems created by such specific subject matter as scientific texts. But, as a group, symbolic interactionists seldom bring their solutions together to develop a more general approach through comparisons of the findings specific to their subject matters. The annual Stone Symposium is one occasion for such a comparative, intellectual exchange.

Most of the papers in this volume, then, tell symbolic interactionists, in one way or another, what their colleagues in related areas are up to. (The detailed bibliographies following the separate papers will help interested readers follow up these introductions.) Neitz, for instance, describes a body of work on religion which other interactionists should see as crucially related to the problems of identity and personal change they study in other milieus. Gilmore describes the symbolic interactionist tradition of research on the arts, and Clarke and Gerson do the same for science studies.

Boden and Hall bring news from other areas of sociology, and from other methodological and theoretical approaches. Boden speaks to symbolic interactionists from the flourishing specialty of discourse analysis. She renders an important service by making the connections between the two apparent, in order to make them more useful to each other than they have been in the past. Hall, discussing historical research, shows how concepts adapted from work by historians as various as Braudel and Kubler can be put to work in interactionist thinking, as well as the way findings from specific studies in cultural history can help solve our own research problems.

Other papers bring interactionists news of work on topics symbolic interactionists share with workers in other disciplines, particularly the papers by McCall and Wittner and by Glassner. McCall and Wittner focus on a method—the gathering of life histories—that has provoked much argument and raised many basic analytic problems in a variety of fields in the humanities and social sciences. They bring discussions from both sides of the fence to bear on these questions, demonstrating concretely what each has to offer the other. Their paper, in its use of long quotations arranged in dialogue form, exemplifies some of the problems and solutions they discuss. Glassner uses a frankly postmodern approach to understand the social nature of the human body, an area to which sociology has given scant attention (although see Yonnet 1985).

Addelson's paper brings a different kind of news to interactionists. She reports on her efforts to construct a feminist ethic—an "ethic of respect" as contrasted with the "traditional" (patriarchal) ethic of "rights" (property)—based on Blumer's injunction to "catch the process of interpretation from the standpoint of the acting person." She thus shows a more practical connection between philosophy and sociology than many interactionists would be aware of.

What is Symbolic Interaction?

Symbolic interaction is a sociological tradition that traces its lineage to the Pragmatists—John Dewey and George Herbert Mead, particularly—and to sociologists of the "Chicago School"—Robert E. Park, Herbert Blumer, Everett C. Hughes, and their students and successors. We can summarize its chief ideas, perhaps oversimply, this way:

> Any human event can be understood as the result of the people involved (keeping in mind that that might be a very large number) continually adjusting what they do in the light of what others do, so that each individual's line of action "fits" into what the others do. That can only happen if human beings typically act in a nonautomatic fashion, and instead construct a line of action by taking account of the meaning of what others do in response to their earlier actions. Human beings can only act in this way if they can incorporate the responses of others into their own act and thus anticipate what will probably happen, in the process creating a "self" in the Meadian sense. (This emphasis on the way people construct the mean-

ing of others' acts is where the "symbolic" in "symbolic interaction" comes from.) If everyone can and does do that, complex
joint acts can occur. (Adapted from Becker 1988:18; see also
Blumer 1969:10.)

These ideas have furnished the basis of thousands of fieldwork (ethnographic) studies in such areas as community, race, class, work,
family, and the sociologies of art, science, and deviance. Symbolic interaction is an empirical research tradition as much or more than a
theoretical position, and its strength derives in large part from the
enormous body of research that embodies and gives meaning to its abstract propositions.

What Is Cultural Studies?

We use the term *cultural studies* to refer to the classically humanistic disciplines which have lately come to use their philosophical, literary, and historical approaches to study the social construction of
meaning and other topics traditionally of interest to symbolic interactionists, disciplines to which, in turn, social scientists have lately
turned for "explanatory analogies" (Geertz 1983:23) as they "have
turned away from a laws and instances ideal of explanation toward a
cases and interpretations one" (ibid.:19). The term is most closely
identified with work carried on, since 1964, at the Centre for Contemporary Cultural Studies at the University of Birmingham in England.
The main features of cultural studies, according to scholars associated
with the center, are "its openness and theoretical versatility, its reflexive even self-conscious mood" (Johnson 1986–87:38), and its critical
(or "engaged") approach to its primary objects of study: working class
and youth subcultures, the media, language, and the social relations of
education, the family and the state (S. Hall 1980).

Perhaps because cultural studies is self-consciously non-disciplinary,
and has resisted theoretical orthodoxy (ibid., 1980) and methodological
codification (Johnson 1986–87), it has engaged many of the important
intellectual currents of the last twenty-five years, in a way that symbolic interaction has not. Among them: the revolution in literary criticism; the "new social history" movement; the "complex Marxism"
of Lukacs, Goldman, Walter Bènjamin, and the "Frankfurt School";
the structuralisms, both the structural linguistics of Levi-Strauss and
Barthes and the Marxist structuralism of Althusser and Gramsci; the
feminisms (Weedon 1987; S. Hall 1980); and the poststructuralisms,

developed in and from the work of Derrida, Lacan, Kristeva, Althusser, and Foucault (Weedon 1987:19; S. Hall 1980; Johnson 1986–87).

Symbolic interactionists, like many other social scientists, have for the most part not been very attentive to these major intellectual currents represented in cultural studies. But, as the humanities and social sciences have approached one another in recent years, a lively discourse has grown up along the border. The intention of this volume is to bring symbolic interactionists into that conversation, both as listeners and speakers.

THE BORDER: TOPICS AND METHODS OF MUTUAL INTEREST

A number of major topics are addressed by workers in both traditions. Their interests converge most generally on the problem of meaning. Under that broad heading they find much of mutual interest in such topics as the nature of knowledge, our experience of our own lives and the lives of others, the relation between individual experience and action and the workings of social structures, the self and subjectivity, language and discourse. Both groups are interested, as well, in such concrete subject matters as art, science, education, and religion.

Empiricism

The great strength of the symbolic interaction approach to meaning is that it is empirical. The ultimate interactionist test of concepts is whether they make sense of particular situations known in great detail through detailed observation. You answer questions by going to see for yourself, studying the real world, and evaluating the evidence so gathered. Symbolic interaction takes the concrete, empirical world of lived experience as its problematic and treats theory as something that must be brought into line with that empirical world (Blumer 1969:151).

Addelson argues, on just these grounds, that philosophers must become sociologists (by which she means symbolic interactionist sociologists) because symbolic interactionism is empirical and, therefore, gives better accounts of human nature, human action, and of human group life than traditional philosophy does. She applies this reasoning in a nice example of how the interactionist emphasis on process helps solve the traditional philosophical problem of rules and rulebreaking. She quotes Blumer: "It is the social process in group life that creates and upholds the rules, not the rules that create and uphold group life," and goes on to say that if this is true, it is the social process and not the rules that must be understood and conceptually analyzed and clarified to answer the question, "What is morality?"

Symbolic interactionists typically find that meaning is constructed in the *process of interaction*, and have always insisted that process is not a neutral medium in which social forces play out their game, but the actual stuff of social organization and social forces (Blumer 1969). Society, for them, *is* the process of symbolic interaction, and this view allows them to steer the middle course between structuralism and idealism John Hall recommends in his paper.

For symbolic interactionists, process is not just a word. It's shorthand for an insistence that social events don't happen all at once, but rather happen in steps: first one thing, then another, with each succeeding step creating new conditions under which all the people and organizations involved must now negotiate the next step. This is more than a theoretical nicety. It makes theoretical room for contingency, another point many workers in cultural studies want to emphasize (Turner 1986). Nothing *has* to happen. Nothing is fully determined. At every step of every unfolding event, something else *might* happen. To be sure, the balance of constraints and opportunities available to the actors, individual and collective, in a situation will lead many, perhaps most, of them to do the same thing. Contingency doesn't mean people behave randomly, but it does recognize that they can behave in surprising and unconventional ways. The interactionist emphasis on process stands, as Blumer insisted, as a corrective to any view that insists that culture or social structure determines what people do.

Neitz's discussion of religious conversion shows the utility of such a view for a variety of problems of interest to cultural theorists. Earlier analyses looked for the conditions that led people to be converted, but had no language to describe the back-and-forth, shifting character of what went on when they did. Such "instantaneous" theories of conversion failed to see the importance of the events that lead up to conversion and, perhaps more important, the events that follow conversion, reinforcing and solidifying what might otherwise be a momentary whim. The new research, according to Neitz, sees conversion as a process and, for that reason, can turn to symbolic interaction and its concern with process for help in understanding the fluid relationships between religious and social structures today.

Although much of the work in cultural studies, and particularly at the Centre for Contemporary Cultural Studies, has been accused of being too theoretical, it has also been empirical, right from the start.

Unlike symbolic interactionism, though, cultural studies has not been willing, or able, to privilege empirical work over theory: "we had no alternative but to undertake a labour of theoretical definition and clarification at the same time as we attempted to do concrete work in the field" (S. Hall 1980:25).

Nor have empirical workers in cultural studies identified themselves as fieldworkers as thoroughly as symbolic interactionists have. Indeed, in Stuart Hall's words, "the tension between experiential accounts and a larger account of structural and historical determinations has been a pivotal site of Centre theorizing and debate ever since" Paul Willis's ground-breaking ethnographic work in *Learning to Labour* (ibid.:24). "While sharing an emphasis on people's ability to make meaning, critical theorists concerned with cultural production" differ in important ways from symbolic interactionists: their ethnographies are more "openly ideological" and they are more overtly concerned with locating human agency in social structure:

> Both approaches emphasize human agency and the production of meaning and culture, but the critical production theorists ground their work on a moral imperative, [on a] "political commitment to human betterment." Moreover, the critical production theorists recognize the power of structural determinants in the sense of material practices, modes of power, and economic and political institutions. Unlike the more voluntaristic [symbolic interactionists and ethnomethodologists], the critical ... theorists remain accutely aware that, as Marx notes, "while men [*sic*] make their own history, they do not make it just as they please." Their recent work has focused in different ways on the need for a theory that will recognize both human agency and the production of knowledge and culture and will at the same time take into account the power of material and ideological structures. This dialectic between individual consciousness and structural determinants has led them to seek more developed theories of ideology, hegemony, and resistance, and to the development of what has been called "critical ethnography." (Weiler 1988:12–13)

Willis himself recognizes the "profoundly important methodological possibility" in fieldwork—"that of *being surprised*, of reaching knowledge not prefigured in one's starting paradigm" (1980:90), but argues there is "no truly untheoretical way in which to 'see' an 'object.'" To "remove the hidden tendency towards positivism" in fieldwork research, he suggests that the "theoretical organization of the starting-out position should be outlined and acknowledged in any piece of research"; that fieldworkers "add to the received notion of the 'quality' of the data an ability to watch for inconsistencies, contradictions and misunderstandings" and "make theoretical interpretations of them"; and that they recognize their "reflective relationship to their subjects" (ibid.:90–92).

McCall and Wittner also address these issues, emphasizing how studies in the social sciences have tended to take the point of view of dominant social groups and thus have failed to create knowledge about matters considered important to less powerful people. Aware of the "key insight of advanced semiology," that "narratives or images always imply or construct a position or positions from which they are to be read or viewed" and that "realist" texts "naturalise the means by which positioning is achieved" (Johnson 1986–87:66), they challenge other fieldworkers to ask, Where have we positioned ourselves as researchers? From what position have we viewed the subjects of our research? How has our realistic, documentary style of representing social life naturalized our own authority?

Culture Production and Reproduction

Cultural studies is, in important ways, the result of Marxist critiques of economism and of the realization that "cultural practice and cultural production are not simply derived from an otherwise constituted social order but are themselves major elements in its constitution" (Williams 1981:12). Much of their best work has focused on the production of knowledge in educational institutions. Early work concerned social and cultural *reproduction*—that is, the reproduction of class structures and of class cultures, knowledge, and power relationships in schools. However, much of this work on reproduction "did not get inside the school to find out how reproduction went on" (Apple 1985:20). According to Weiler, furthermore, it was based on "the underlying view that students are shaped by their experiences in schools to internalize or accept a subjectivity and a class position that leads to the reproduction of existing power relationships and social and economic structures" (Weiler 1988:6).

Later work, by critical ethnographers like Paul Willis, "demonstrated that rather than being places where culture and ideologies are imposed on students, schools are the sites where these things are produced" (Apple 1985:26). By opening up the black box of education, critical ethnographers revealed that education is a system of production as well as reproduction. Furthermore, they discovered that students aren't simply shaped by their experiences, but actively "assert their own experience and contest or resist the ideological and material forces imposed upon them" (Weiler 198811).

The importance of these critical ethnographies to symbolic interaction is the suggestion, carried forward in education, that ethnography must be consciously ideological and can be both "transformative," that is, can "help create the possibility of transforming such institutions as schools—through a process of negative critique" (Brodkey 1987:67), and "empowering" so long as it rests upon the assumption that "each person [has the] ability to understand and critique his or her own experience and the social reality 'out there'" (Weiler 1988:23).

Recent work in the sociology of science, reported on in the paper by Clarke and Gerson, makes related points, demonstrating that the organization of scientific work creates and shapes the knowledge we accept as "scientific." Treating science as the work people do, rather than as a privileged window on reality, lets us see science as continuous with the rest of human experience. This empirical approach coincides with the philosophical critique of scientism made in the name of pragmatism by Rorty (1979) and others.

Social Worlds and Institutional Ethnography

Many sociologists have criticized symbolic interaction theory for being too focused on the "micro" aspect of society, on face-to-face interaction as opposed to the "macro" structural level of society. Gilmore, basing his argument on empirical work in the sociology of art, shows how the idea of social worlds helps bridge the micro-macro gap, making the insights of interactionism more useful to workers in cultural studies.

Symbolic interaction emphasizes collective action. One special version of this has proved useful: the idea of a "world," a more or less stable organization of collective activity. This idea has been used extensively in the sociologies of art and science (Kling and Gerson, 1977, 1978; Shibutani 1955; Becker 1982; and P. Hall 1987) but it can, in principle, come into use anywhere people are connected through their joint involvement in a task or event of a repetitive kind. Wherever social events happen routinely, we can expect to find a world.

Gilmore argues that the concept of social world, as developed and used by symbolic interactionists, allows for the kind of movement back and forth between "micro" and "macro" levels, between structure and culture and individuals, which has come to seem more important in cultural studies. Gilmore suggests that the idea of social worlds of-

fers a solution to Marxists who want to stop talking about the reflections of the economic base in the cultural superstructure and instead
look at how human agents produce culture. "World" does the work of
a good concept. It tells you what to look for, what ought to be there to
find in the phenomena we study. Then you can either find what you
were told would be there or know that you have a new and interesting
theoretical problem, because something that ought to be there wasn't
there after all.

Dorothy E. Smith has recently proposed an alternative way of bridg-
ing the micro-macro gap, which she calls institutional ethnography. A
feminist methodology, Smith's is compatible with the concerns of the
critical ethnographers. Specifically, although it is careful to try to understand the everyday world from the point of view of the people who
live in it, institutional ethnography also recognizes that knowledge of
"the extralocal determinations of our experience does not lie within
the scope of everyday practices" and must, therefore, "be the sociologist's special business" (1987:161).

> Our point of entry was women's experience of the work they
> did in relation to their children's schooling. We would begin by
> asking women to talk to us about this work. The resulting ac-
> counts would provide a wealth of descriptive material about
> particular women's local practices. There is nothing new socio-
> logically about this procedure. While feminism has brought
> new sensitivities and a new scrupulousness to open-ended in-
> terviewing, it is our uses of material that have been distinctive.
> And here we are trying something different again. Standard so-
> ciological analysis uses some method of coding and interpret-
> ing such accounts to order the interview materials in relation
> to the relevances of the sociological and/or feminist discourses.
> These enable the interviews to be sorted into topics typical
> of the study populaton. In such a process, the standpoint of
> women themselves is suppressed. The standpoint becomes that
> of the discourse reflecting upon properties of the study popu-
> lation. Characteristics of the study population become the ob-
> ject of the knower's gaze.
>
> We sought a method that would preserve throughout the
> standpoint of the women interviewed. To do so we worked
> with a sequence of stages in the research. We were concerned
> to locate women's work practices in the actual relations by
> which they are organized and which they organize. This meant
> talking to women first. Women's accounts of the work they
> did in relation to their children's schooling would then be

examined for the ways in which they were articulated to the social organization of the school. That scrutiny would establish the questions and issues for the second stage of research, interviewing teachers and administrators in the schools. Our strategy would move from particular experiences to their embedding in the generalizing social organization of the school. It would preserve a perspective in which we could look out from where we are, from where our respondents are, onto the larger landscape organizing and containing their daily practices. (Ibid.:182–183)

Self, Body, and Subjectivity

The idea of *the self* in the simple symbolic interaction version emphasizes the existence and profound consequences of the interior dialogue through which society is incorporated into the individual. Blumer explained this idea through an exegesis of George Herbert Mead's thought:

> In declaring that the human being has a self, Mead had in mind chiefly that the human being can be the object of his own actions. He can act toward himself as he might act toward others. . . . This mechanism enables the human being to make indications to himself of things in his surroundings and thus to guide his actions by what he notes. . . . The second important implication of the fact that the human being makes indications to himself is that his action is constructed or built up instead of being a mere release. Whatever the action in which he is engaged, the human individual proceeds by pointing out to himself the various conditions which may be instrumental to his action and those which may obstruct his action; he has to take account of the demands, the expectations, the prohibitions, and the threats as they may arise in the situation in which he is acting. His action is built up step by step through a process of such self-indication. The human individual pieces together and guides his action by taking account of different things and interpreting their significance for his prospective action. (Blumer 1969:79–81)

This stripped-down notion of the self builds society into every empirical analysis, in the form of all those others present in the situation of action to whom the actor pays attention. Most importantly, it recognizes people's ability to check their activity and reorient it on the basis of what's going on around them, rather than responding automatically to stimuli, impulses, or the dictates of a culture or social organization. A classic example of the utility of such a view of the self is Lindesmith's (1948) study of opiate addiction, which emphasizes the crucial importance of the self-process in understanding how addicts learn to see themselves as needing opiates to function normally.

Feminist theorists have criticized the dualism of Western culture and thought, especially the classic dualisms of nature/nurture and mind/body, and this criticism can reasonably be leveled at symbolic interactionists who often (though not always, see Becker 1986:47–66) leave out bodies, the biological component of human experience. Addelson criticizes Mead for this, and the fault is there to criticize. Interactionists have largely left the body and physical experience out of the self. Glassner now shows us one way to avoid this dualistic error and deal with bodies as well as minds when we talk about the self. He takes advantage of the insights of feminists and postmodernist thinkers to import a cultural-economy argument into the interactionist concept of the self. (See, also, Yonnet, 1985.)

Another critique of the symbolic interactionist self is implicit in Boden's paper on discourse analysis. Following Althusser (1971), cultural studies has replaced the "conscious, knowing, unified rational" *self* with the *subject* of discourse. In this account, "[t]he 'I,' the seat of consciousness and the foundation of ideological discourses, [is] not the integral Cartesian centre of thought but a contradictory discursive category constituted by ideological discourse itself" (S. Hall 1980:33).

> The political significance of decentering the subject and abandoning the belief in essential subjectivity is that it opens up subjectivity to change. . . . As we acquire language we learn to give voice—meaning—to our experience and to understand it according to particular ways of thinking, particular discourses, which pre-date our entry into language. These ways of thinking constitute our consciousness, and the positions with which we identify structure our sense of ourselves, our subjectivity. Having grown up within a particular system of meanings and values, which may well be contradictory, we may find ourselves resisting alternatives. Or, as we move out of familiar circles, through education or politics, for example, we may be exposed to alternative ways of constituting the meaning of our experience which seem to address our interests more directly. . . . This process of discovery can lead to a rewriting of personal experience in terms which give it social, changeable causes. (Weedon 1987:33)

custronergies

Discourses

The various critical, feminist, and poststructuralist theories that
have so profoundly influenced cultural studies have made discourse—
talk and text—the site of meaning, social organization, power, and
subjectivity. In this view, social structures and social processes are organized by institutions and cultural practices such as the law, the political system, the church, the family, education, and the media, each
of which is "located in and structured by a particular discursive field"
or discourse. Following Foucault, discourses are defined as "ways of
constituting knowledge, together with the social practices, forms of
subjectivity and power relations which inhere in such knowledges and
the relations between them" (ibid.:108). A discourse both constitutes
the "nature" of the "subjects" it "seeks to govern" and subjects its
speakers to its own power and regulation (ibid.:108, 119). Powerful discourses are based in institutions and realized in institutional practices.
"Yet these institutional locations are themselves sites of contest, and
the dominant discourses governing the organization and practices of
social institutions are under constant challenge" (ibid:109).

> Much feminist discourse is, for example, either marginal to or
> in direct conflict with dominant definitions of femininity and
> its social constitution and regulation. Yet even where feminist
> discourses lack the social power to realize their versions of
> knowledge in institutional practices, they can offer the discur-
> sive space from which the individual can resist dominant sub-
> ject positions . . . [and] resistance to the dominant at the level
> of the individual subject is the first stage in the production of
> alternative forms of knowledge or where such alternatives al-
> ready exist, of winning individuals over to these discourses and
> gradually increasing their social power. (ibid: 110–11)

In this volume, Boden introduces symbolic interactionists to discourse analysis, suggesting studies of the social production of culture
and cultural products, especially science but also social science itself,
as discourse: talk and text. Her analysis shows that the details of ordinary conversation, analyzed with the tools of conversational analysis,
constitute the process of mutual adjustment of lines of action called
for in Blumer's theory, and thus are integral to the understanding of
organizational activity at every level. McCall and Wittner suggest that
symbolic interactionist might well imitate other social scientists, especially anthropologists, who have begun to pay attention to their own

discourse, looking critically at their own "central task, in the field and thereafter"—that is, writing—and at the contextual, rhetorical, institutional, genre, political and historical contexts which "govern the inscription" of cultural accounts (Clifford 1986:2, 6).

CONCLUSION

The above thoughts suggest the variety of uses to which the audiences these papers address can put these materials. We hope that interactionists will learn from each other to cross subject matter boundaries in search of ideas and examples. We hope that noninteractionist sociologists will see how the symbolic interaction tradition, consisting of both theoretical ideas and detailed research findings, can contribute to their own work. And we hope that workers in cultural studies will find, in the ideas and results of this sociological tradition, as yet a largely unused resource, much to use and integrate into their own traditions.

REFERENCES

Althusser, Louis. 1971. "Ideology and Ideological State Apparatuses," in Althusser, *Lenin and Philosophy, and Other Essays*, translated by Ben Brewster (London: New Left Books), pp. 121–173.

Apple, Michael. 1985. *Education and Power*. Boston: Ark Paperbacks.

Becker, Howard S. 1982. "Culture: A Sociological View," in Becker, *Doing Things Together* (Evanston: Northwestern University Press), pp. 11–24.

———. 1986. "Consciousness, Power, and Drug Effects," in Becker, *Doing Things Together* (Evanston: Northwestern University Press), pp. 47–66.

———. 1988. "Herbert Blumer's Conceptual Impact." *Symbolic Interaction* 11 (Spring, 1988): 13–21.

Blumer, Herbert. 1969. *Symbolic Interactionism: Perspective and Method*. Englewood Cliffs, N. J.: Prentice Hall.

Brodkey, Linda. 1987. "Writing Critical Ethnographic Narratives." *Anthropology and Education Quarterly* 18 (June): 67–76.

Clifford, James. 1986. "Introduction: Partial Truths," in James Clifford and George E. Marcus, editors, *Writing Culture* (Berkeley: University of California Press), pp. 1–26.

Geertz, Clifford. 1983. *Local Knowledge*. New York: Basic Books.

Hall, Peter. 1987. "Interactionism and the Study of Social Organization," *Sociological Quarterly* 28:1–22.

Hall, Stuart. 1980. "Cultural Studies and the Centre: some problematics and problems," in *Culture, Media, Language: Working Papers in Cultural Studies, 1972–79* (London: Hutchinson in association with the Centre for Contemporary Cultural Studies, University of Birmingham) pp. 15–47.

Johnson, Richard. 1986–87. "What is Cultural Studies Anyway?" *Social Text* 16: 38–80.

Kling, Rob, and Elihu M. Gerson. 1977. "The Social Dynamics of Technical Innovation in the Computing World." *Symbolic Interaction* 1:132–46.

———. 1978. "Patterns of Segmentation and Interaction in the Computing World." *Symbolic Interaction* 2:24–33.

Lindesmith, Alfred. 1948. *Opiate Addiction*. Bloomington, Ind.: Principia Press.

Rorty, Richard. 1979. *Philosophy and the Mirror of Nature*. Princeton: Princeton University Press.

Shibutani, Tomatsu. 1955. "Reference Groups as Perspectives." *American Journal of Sociology* 60:562–69.

Smith, Dorothy E. 1987. *The Everyday World as Problematic: A Feminist Sociology*. Boston: Northeastern University Press.

Turner, Victor. 1986. *The Anthropology of Performance*. New York: PAJ Publications.

Weedon, Chris. 1987. *Feminist Practice and Poststructuralist Theory*. London: Basil Blackwell.

Weiler, Kathleen. 1988. *Women Teaching for Change: Gender, Class, and Power*. Granby, Mass.: Bergin and Garvey.

Williams, Raymond. 1981. *The Sociology of Culture*. New York: Schocken Books.

Willis, Paul. 1977. *Learning to Labour*. Westmead, England: Saxon House.

———. 1980. "Notes on Method," in *Culture, Media, Language: Working Papers in Cultural Studies, 1972–79* (London: Hutchinson in association with the Centre for Contemporary Cultural Studies, University of Birmingham), pp. 88–95.

Yonnet, Paul. 1985. "Joggers et marathoniens," in Yonnet, *Jeux, modes et masses* (Paris: Gallimard) pp. 91–140.

2

Social Interaction, Culture, and Historical Studies
John R. Hall

The pendulums of sociology reached their zeniths in structuralism and formal theory some time ago. In the last twenty years positivism, abstracted empiricism, and what C. Wright Mills mockingly called "grand theory" have been supplanted by historical sociology and grounded theories; at the same time, culture has begun to receive its due. Formal theory has lost ground in large part because it tends toward reductionist explanations of social action and fails to incorporate the contingent character of action that is foundational to historicity. The renaissance in the sociology of culture, on the other hand, has come about because theorists of diverse persuasions, from neo-Marxism to structuralism, have come to see culture as something of a missing link. These trends have converged recently in the expropriation from historical studies of the label "cultural history." Yet despite the increased use of the label, both historians and sociologists have much to gain by considering what it means to study culture historically.

This is no easy task, since the sociological approaches to history are diverse (Skocpol, 1984; Hamilton, 1987). The other side of the problem stems from the healthy controversies that currently abound about culture (Peterson, 1979; Wuthnow et al., 1984; Mukerji and Schudson, 1986; Johnson, 1986–87; Wuthnow, 1987; Wuthnow and Witten, 1988). Even if we cannot resolve the controversies about culture in advance, it seems to me that the study of history represents a decisive basis for sorting out sociological approaches to culture. This is so because histories of culture are particularly vulnerable to the charge that they invoke idealism, an essence, *geist,* or spirit that animates the surface events of history. There would be no point to avoiding the Scylla of the structuralism that has been discredited in recent years (e.g., by Bourdieu, [1972]1977; cf. Denzin, 1985), only to sail into the Charybdis

I wish to thank the other participants at the 1988 Symposium for the Study of Symbolic Interaction, as well as Wendy Griswold, Michele Lamont, and the editors of the present volume, for their comments, which I hope and believe helped me clarify certain issues.

of idealism, a whirlpool that has been marked on the sociological charts since the beginning of the twentieth century.

Avoiding problems of structuralism and idealism in approaching cultural history seems most feasible within one broad sociological perspective—the cluster of approaches that focus on meaning, action, symbols, and the interactive, unfolding and historically contingent character of social life. Interpretive sociology, symbolic interactionism, phenomenology, hermeneutics, and ethnomethodology taken together I will call (to be as generic as possible) the social interaction perspective. They may differ in their methodologies, empirical foci, theoretical projects, and conceptual terminologies, but they all eschew both structuralism and idealism, because they all force analysis into the realm of the lifeworld, where neither structure, social forces, symbols, nor ideas have lives of their own, but must come into play as proximate realities (cf. Blumer, 1969: 22).

Yet to say that the social interaction perspective offers the best hope of doing cultural history does not suggest either that the procedures are clear-cut or that problems of historiography are resolved a priori. To the contrary, precisely because the perspective admits to human agency and the historicity of knowledge, it brings to the fore problems that might be sidestepped in a more objectivist framework. In order to sketch a consistent approach to the tough case of cultural history, I want to consolidate the insights of the social interaction perspective around key problems of historiography. After briefly describing the social interaction perspective, I will consider four central problems of cultural history that need to be addressed. First, definitions of culture, series, and sequence as key concepts offer an initial basis for specifying an interactionist model of cultural history. Second, there is a need to clarify the nature of the historical object (sometimes [Weber, 1949] called the "historical individual") and how it is constituted in historical analysis. Finally, we need to consider the nature both of sociological explanation and of historical explanation, and the roles they might play in the study of cultural history. I thus will use the social interaction perspective as a tool for clarifying analysis of culture, and the boundaries and working relationships between history and sociology.

THE DILEMMAS OF HISTORY AND THE SOCIAL INTERACTION PERSPECTIVE

The key problem historians always have faced is how to define the subject matter. On the empirical level there are all those events, great and small. Do they all constitute history equally, or are some events more important than others? Is history simply the set of events themselves, or do these events somehow manifest deeper (or higher but, at any rate, hidden) forces? At the level of historical analysis, these questions translate into the problem of "selection" (see, e.g., Atkinson, 1978): How is the historian to choose among manifold events? Which events, when their connections are shown, bring to light the patterns of history that are otherwise lost in the detail? How, for example, is the Russian October Revolution to be accounted when most Muscovites had no direct experience of it at the time, and indeed at least one man died believing it to be a Leninist propaganda story?

For modern historians coherent answers to these sorts of questions first came from the nineteenth-century German historiographer Leopold von Ranke. Searching for a rigorous way to "tell what actually happened" yet match events with the master trends of history, Ranke proposed a "scientific" history that focused on political and religious elites as representing the cutting edge of societal change. In this neat (but wrong-minded) solution, Ranke solved the problem of selection with the presupposition that the history of elite groups defines the overall pattern.

Once the concept of elite is broadened, Ranke's solution for historiography remains influential in some quarters (e.g., Himmelfarb, 1987). But even by the end of the nineteenth century, the Rankean position had given ground to two broad reactions that remain important to this day in the "new" historiography. These reactions can be characterized most concisely by their conceptions of temporal relativity. On the one hand, practitioners in the now-famed *Annales* school injected relativity into the historical equation by the device of placing all events on multiple scales of objective time. Some phenomena—ecological history, social history, the history of mentalities—came into focus on centuries-long scales of objective time, changing only slowly, but forcefully, as the tides rise and fall. By contrast to the long term, the events in Ranke's history of elites, for *Annales* scholars like Fernand Braudel ([1966]1972: 27), represent only short-term "surface disturbances, crests of foam that the tides of history carry on their strong backs." Still, in Braudel's grand vision, all events on the multiple scales of time are linked together in the single matrix of objective time (Hall, 1980).

For the social interaction perspective, it is the alternative to Braudel, a subjectivist revision of Rankean historiography, that holds more promise. In the subjectivist critique, objective time is simply an observers' convention for mapping events, while historical processes themselves may involve discontinuous leaps across objective time and decisively different subjective and social orientations toward the temporal flux of events. Time, in short, is subjectively and socially constructed, and it is meaningful action and interaction that give time its shape (Leyden, 1962; Kracauer, 1966; Kellner, 1975; Hall, 1980; Maines, Sugrue, and Katovich, 1983).

The question remains, of course, whether the subjectivist rejection of objectivist historiography can deliver on a viable alternative approach. It would take too much of a digression here to consolidate systematically the interaction perspective's approach to historiography. But at least I can make my presupposition explicit: it is that the work of people like Wilhelm Dilthey, Georg Simmel, Max Weber, and George Herbert Mead converge in the social interaction perspective, and that this perspective offers a distinctive and coherent approach to historiography. Dilthey (1976) cut past objective time by focusing on the biography as the fundamental unit of historical analysis. Both Simmel ([1905]1977) and Weber (1949, 1977) tried to reconcile historical causation and social action. Mead (1956) sought to account theoretically for emergent meaningful action in relation to institutionalized meaning through the device of subjective temporality.

Granted the differences in terminology and methodological strategies, these scholars share a focus on social and individual meaning, on action and interaction, on the lifeworld as the arena of causation, and on historicity as a basic element for social theorizing (cf. Blumer, 1969: 49). Together these elements mark the social interaction perspective as distinctive in its recognition of a world that is humanly made and remade anew. Action is always episodic and existential, but typically it is carried out with the hubris of socially constructed reality that portrays the widespread as unique and the ephemeral as enduring. The precarious plausibility of this world, it is not too much to say, is accomplished by "ignoring practices" that establish the social construction as real (Wendy Griswold, personal communication; Berger and Luckmann, 1966).

Formulating the perfect abstract epistemology and ontology for interactionist cultural history along the lines just described would be an empty exercise if it failed to inform historians' work. Historians have to be practical people, for they face a world of many events and only fragmentary information (Shiner, 1969). Because both historians and interactionists are justifiably suspicious of abstract solutions, I will address the formal problems of cultural history by way of some recent empirical studies that show the possibilities and challenges of cultural history for the social interaction perspective.

FROM CULTURAL PROBLEM TO SERIES AND SEQUENCE IN CULTURAL HISTORY

Culture, counterposed to society and social action, may be understood as the (1) "knowledge" and recipes, (2) humanly fabricated tools, and (3) products of social action that in turn may be drawn upon in the further conduct of social life.[1] I do not mean to be contentious in offering this deceptively simple and broad definition. I have sought to avoid an "idealist" definition by recognizing both ideas and artifacts (cf. Mukerji, 1983) as culture. Oddly enough, the tendency toward a narrower, "symbolic" definition of culture comes from two directions, first from some cultural sociologists themselves, who may want to carve out their own bailiwick, and also from some structuralists, who may think that limiting culture to ideas and beliefs will make it easier to discount arguments about its salience.

We all live in the "prison house of language" (the term of Jameson, 1972), and we had best remember that such distinctions finally are analytic ones, while reality is a seamless manifold concatenation of "action," "culture," and "structure." When Japanese corporations organize morning aerobics, so long as Grateful Dead fans wear tie-dyed T-shirts, and until fast-food restaurants disappear from interstate highway interchanges, we had best recognize culture as involving not only symbols and ideas, but also social practices in relation to self, others, and material objects. Nor should we understand culture as limited to matters of taste (Gans, 1974). Instead, I want to underscore the relevance of cultural analysis to understanding phenomena as diverse and seemingly distant from "high" and "popular" culture as organizations, wars, and economies.

To study culture historically, then, involves the identification of some cultural patterns or artifacts, either material or symbolic. These may be traced as to their origins, their consequences, their creation and incorporation into unfolding, contingent interaction, and other aspects that involve temporally emergent qualities. Take, for example, *Gone from the Promised Land* (Hall, 1987). I chose as its subtitle "Jonestown in American Cultural History." The implicit claim is that the quest for a promised land in Jim Jones's Peoples Temple was born out of deep cultural connections to established currents in American history. In another study, Viviana Zelizer (1979) has identified a puzzle about the early nineteenth-century United States: why was there ideological resistance to acceptance of life insurance compared to other forms of insurance? The puzzle offers occasion to bring to light cultural taboos about attaching monetary value to human life that inhibited acceptance of life insurance. With this backdrop, Zelizer is able to identify the strategies adopted in the insurance industry to counter the cultural taboos.

Jonestown's mass suicides don't seem very American, and we don't experience insurance as a pressing cultural issue. Nevertheless, the examples of Peoples Temple and of life insurance offer more general lessons about studying culture historically, for one of the problems of cultural analysis turns on how to identify the stuff, and these examples illustrate a strategy. We are used to being told that "structure" (even if it lacks a consensus definition) has real substance, while culture somehow is ephemeral and "soft"; no wonder, the structuralist critics rave, that cultural methods tend toward the qualitative; we can't really pin down culture, so we are reduced to metaphor and poetics.

True enough, culture does not always have the relatively discrete boundaries that the person, the organization, the nation-state are supposed to have; nor is it always rationalized like foreign trade balances and survey research questions. Indeed, some of the more interesting puzzles about culture have to do with the ephemeral ways it pops up in unexpected locations, like some Hydra crossed with a chameleon. Precisely because normative culture channels perceptions of the world, the cultural bases of practical activity often are buried in routines. Under these circumstances, anomalies, "problems," disjunctures identified by social actors—those breaches of the normatively organized world—offer points of entry into cultural analysis because they represent situations in which actors have collided with some cultural recipes and knowledge, tools and practices. The "problem" for particular actors—be it reaching the promised land or selling life insurance—can become a window through which the cultural historian can identify otherwise latent cultural elements and their connections to one another.

Such are the tough sorts of cases. Yet for all the critics' lamentations, culture is not always so difficult to identify, and though its history may not be any easier to trace than any other history, it is hardly latent. Much culture, both symbolic and material, is codified, organized, stored, and packaged for easy retrieval and use, hence "structured" (cf. Wuthnow, 1987). We need think only of the medieval Christian mass, laboriously copied by monks, to recognize an early example of "mass" culture. Through the wonder of the symbolic activities of writing and notating music, Christian worshipers across old Europe could experience what counted as the "same" liturgy on a given day of worship (for a musical history, see Georgiades, [1974]1982).

Following one of Max Weber's lines of analysis, we must recognize the drift toward the rationalization and routinization of culture through industrialization and the consolidation of the mass media. Culture now often comes mass produced and distributed in discrete, bounded packages; witness the book, the film, the compact disk, the videotape. Even when cultural distribution depends more on the continuing practices of people in an "art world" (Becker, 1982), those practices may be sufficient to insure a relative degree of coherence of cultural material over time. At one end of a continuum we might find actors in the "same" play night after night on a Broadway run; at the other, a painter treating a range of subjects, working within a well-defined genre for a relatively known audience, or jazz musicians using the format of "standard" tunes as a vehicle for improvisation. The general point here is this: sometimes, as with Jonestown and with life insurance taboos, culture may be latent, and difficult to bring to light. But often culture obtains an explicit character over time through the repetitive actions of those who enact, display, or use it. Under these conditions, the possibility of tracking culture historically differs little from the possibility of tracking "social structure." If anything, the opportunities are greater, for the archives of culture often are more centralized and richer than, for example, the archives that might bring to light voting patterns or family structures.

Given the archival storage of certain cultural materials, perhaps the most established approach to cultural history takes a particular cultural genre or form and traces such things as its origins, its diffusion, its collapse, and subsequent revivals. A "classic" recent example is Edward Berlin's (1980) study of ragtime music from its origins in American vaudeville and minstrel music, to the heyday of player-piano music (when middle-class parents feared for its devilish effects on their children), to its eventual subsumption within jazz during the 1920s. In a similar vein, Wendy Griswold (1986) has explored the cultural origins of Elizabethan theater genres of city comedy and revenge tragedy. Then asking why, during the centuries that followed, these plays were revived on the London stage in some eras and not others, she has been able to explore relationships between cultural institutions, historical circumstance, and the meanings of theater productions for socially constructed audiences. A similar, but more "material," study concerns the American motel; Warren Belasco (1979) finds that the highway landmark is not just a hotel at the edge of town, but really stands in a direct line of descent from tourist courts, cabins, and private camp-grounds that were established in response to the upper-middle-class's turn-of-the-century fling with "gypsying" in the automobile. To men-tion another, more familiar example, Lynn Hunt (1984) has used a va-riety of visual, written, and statistical archival materials to trace the birth of ideology during the French revolution as a new basis of politi-cal culture.

Studies of ragtime music, Elizabethan theater, the motel, and changes in political culture might seem of a different order than inves-tigations of the cultural resistance to life insurance and the cultural origins of Peoples Temple's quest for a "promised land." Yet the differ-ences have more to do with the degree of latency of the cultural history than with process. A general model of cultural history may be derived from the social interaction perspective as a way of conceptualizing all of the examples I have noted. The work of George Herbert Mead offers a point of departure.

For the purposes of understanding history, one of Mead's core ideas has to do with the distinction between the social symbol and indi-vidual meaning. According to Mead, the social symbol is shared, and it is in part on the basis of socially shared symbols that the actor faces a situation and formulates actions. Individual meaning, however, is uniquely established through the contextualization of social symbols during the formulation of action in relation to private thought and the perceived gestures of others. For all his emphasis on the act, Mead (1956: 180, 253–54) acknowledged that much life is socially patterned by institutions and routines that control conduct. Moreover, in a way that is seldom acknowledged today (but see Strauss, in Mead, 1956: ix, xiv), Mead (1956: 187–88), like Alfred Schutz (1970), treated the actor as rationally weighing alternative stratagems in relation to particular-istic problems and goals, be they emotional, instrumental, aesthetic. These aspects of Mead's ideas suggest that we can understand culture as received symbols, recipes, and products that actors draw on by way of grappling in emergent meaningful ways with situational "prob-lems." In similar ways, Bourdieu ([1972]1977) notes the regulated im-provisational nature of habitus, and Swidler (1986) writes of culture as a "tool kit." Such terms offer a remarkable parallel to the work of George Kubler (1962), the structuralist historian of material culture. Paralleling Mead, Kubler treats artistic and craft actions as directed to cultural "problems."

For example, spatial perspective in painting has been convention-al-ized by various devices of size, shape, and lighting to solve the "problem" of representing three-dimensional space on a two-dimensional surface. Baxandall (1972: esp. 94–102, 124–28) has argued that solutions to the Quattrocento artists' problem of perspective were informed by close ties to the Italian commercial quest for measurement precision. As a result of these ties, the artists used a receding grid that offered a basis for sizing objects proportionately and aligning their edges with vanishing points. However, objects tended to be represented in a set of planes parallel to the canvas, and it was not until the seventeenth century that the plane convention was dropped in favor of true recessional perspective (Wölfflin, [1915]1950: 73ff.).

Turning to a quite different problem, before machines set the rhythm of industrial production, the Protestant ethic established a configuration of personal consciousness that converged in an elective affinity with the capitalist problem of work discipline. The Protestant, serving God in a "calling," would work on the basis of an inner-worldly asceticism that rationalized labor as a predictable commodity (Weber, [1905]1958; cf. Thompson, 1967).

To the degree that recipe "solutions" to "problems" become socially shared and transmitted over time, we may speak of institutionalized culture. In large part, then, the study of cultural history initially depends on the identification of new cultural patterns, their connections to social life, their persistence, and changes. Along with patterns, changes, and their timing, issues of explanation and interpretation also may be addressed.

Kubler recognizes that cultural solutions over time may change, through processes such as invention, variation, drift, and discard. Two concepts from Kubler's work—series and sequence—seem especially useful for charting these processes. Both share one overarching feature: they center on repetitive patterns of social action as directed to the solution of some cultural problem. Kubler (1962) describes a *series* as a closed class of equivalent items directed to some solution of a cultural problem. On the other hand, a *sequence* is "an open-ended, expanding class" of items "related to one another by the bonds of tradition and influence" that thus constitute "linked solutions" to an *emergent* cultural problem. We could consider as a series, for example, the Quattrocento paintings that employed the receding grid to represent perspective. Paintings of a continuous artistic tradition that broke away from planar sections toward receding perspective would constitute a sequence.

Of course these examples are material ones, and in general, Kubler was interested in material objects such as pottery, paintings, and sculpture, and how their creators approached both technical problems (such as incorporation of handles that would carry the weight of materials in a jug) and aesthetic problems (such as how to proportion the sizes of objects depicted in a painting to give a particular sense of perspective). In these terms, the members of a series always solve a problem in the same way based on the same culturally shared reasons, while in a sequence, the cultural problem itself shifts over time, as do the solutions, but the changes are connected to one another by the linked activities of their creators. By extension, as the example of the Protestant ethic suggests, the approach that Kubler used to describe material culture can be applied to other, more ephemeral cultural "problems" (such as legitimacy or salvation) and to more diffuse cultural "objects" (such as ethics and norms). The "solutions" may be directed to the demeanor of individuals, and their styles of interaction, as well as the cultures of groups and organizations, and their patterned relationships (Hall, 1988a).

The concepts of series and sequence offer a way of consolidating cultural history within the social interaction perspective, for they mark an underlying sociological unity of cultural process. The staff of Peoples Temple, no less than other social movement organizers, faced cultural problems ranging from ultimate goals to mundane matters of publicity and social control. Thus, we can ask, following Schutz and Mead, what culture did they draw on, and from what sources, in trying to solve their problems? On a more diffuse scale involving insurance companies facing cultural resistance based on economic, social, and religious taboos, Zelizer treats the process of legitimating life insurance in much the same manner, showing how what amounted to a public relations campaign sequentially shifted cultural meanings. For genres of aesthetic culture, like ragtime music and Elizabethan comedy, the concepts of series and sequence seem particularly easy to apply, and they work as well for the many false starts, innovations, and consolidation of solutions that mark the movement from tourist camps to tourist cabins, motor courts, and motels. Generically we may say that cultural history traces cultural problems and their solutions in serial and sequential patterns.

THE PROBLEM OF THE HISTORICAL OBJECT

From an objectivist viewpoint, it would be easy enough to leave the concepts of series and sequence behind, and get on to other matters. But many of the problems of objectivist history derive from tendencies to assume the facticity of objects of historical analysis as constituted prior to the observer's study of them, even if philosophical investigations suggest the reverse. Paul Veyne ([1971]1984), on the other hand, is careful to distinguish between human events as "true occurrences with man [sic] as the actor," and history as "an account of events." Sande Cohen (1986; cf. Carroll, 1980) recently offered a deconstructionist assault on the artificial coherence of historical accounts, by showing how to locate "transcendent" staging devices in historical discourses. Situated outside history, such devices render historical accounts plausible to readers by providing "history with continuity and discourse with meaning" thematized by "aboutness." A "history" of Nixon's Watergate crisis, for example, can only be narrated by telescoping events into a coherent story (Cohen, 1986: 74–76). In this light, any notion that the historical object is simply "out there," waiting for the historian to discover and describe it, seems a self-serving conceit.

Yet the interaction perspective pulls in two directions at once on the problem of the historical object, because it consistently looks to the construction of knowledge from the point of view of the actor. On the one hand, all actors themselves give shape to history through their meaningful constructions of events. On the other hand, since historians themselves are actors, it follows that a historical account is constituted according to the purposes of the historian constructing it. This relativism of the observer, in fact, is the position Mead (1938: 94) adopted, one taken up in greater detail by others more directly concerned with historical analysis (e.g., Weber, 1949; Aron, [1948]1961; Veyne, 1984).

Employing a neo-Kantian line of reasoning, Weber essentially adopted a strategy that acknowledged the values of the investigator as shaping the questions raised about events: "aboutness" was ultimately the product of the scholar's interests, as Cohen has argued. Against this sphere of values beyond rational adjudication, however, Weber counterposed a methodology of historical investigation that was to be informed by the ethic of science (Weber, 1946). Rather than acceding to the total relativity of value-driven inquiry, he sought to mark off from topical values the scientific ethic of investigation that pursues interpretation and causal explanation by attending to the interconnections of meanings and causalities in events themselves (Hall, 1984a). Following Heinrich Rickert, in a highly provisional way Weber (1949: 155) recognized that what he termed "primary" historical facts might be constituted in other ways than through the explanatory interests of the historian, as " 'historical individuals' in their own right."

At the opposite end of the continuum from Mead, Dilthey (1976: 208–45) was less concerned than Weber with the role of the historian in relation to the framing of a historical subject. Instead, Dilthey looked to the relativity of actors *in* history, and sought to provide historical accounts that reconstruct history from the points of view of interactive biographies. In Dilthey's perspective, it is at least in theory possible to identify historical objects that obtained their coherence in the interrelations of events themselves. Drawing on Weber and Dilthey, I will call these interrelated sets of events "intrinsic historical objects," insofar as they are linked in the conscious actions of human participants. Such objects are the province of *Verstehen*, or interpretive understanding, as an approach to history.

It would take us too far afield to consider *Verstehen* in detail. Still, difficult though the historian's task may be when it comes to understanding the meaning of events for participants, one red herring should be cast aside. In our terms, following Weber, *Verstehen* is an epistemological requirement of adequate explanation, not, as Dilthey would propose, some magical technique for apprehending "inner" states of subjectivity (cf. Oakes, 1977). Under this formulation, the historian is to make use of whatever evidence is available concerning the intentions of actors—diaries, recordings, accounts of witnesses, the "fit" of a hypothetical motive with other aspects known about the actor, and so forth. Such evidence is subject to the same rules of usage and argumentation as other evidence. On the basis of this sort of discourse, the historian is hardly likely to simulate the state of mind of a social actor, but it is at least in principle possible to consider and reject or tentatively accept a formulation about the actor's motives.

Despite other differences, Dilthey's approach shares Weber's (1977: 7–8) stricture that the subject matter of sociology proper ends at the bounds of meaningful social action (cf. Bendix, 1984: 30). When the stricture is applied in historical analysis of culture, the bounds of a particular cluster of meaning of an intrinsic historical object are defined by the subjective intentionalities of the actors themselves. This criterion only can be called into play in actual investigation, for it is impossible to specify on formal grounds whether an empirical complex of actions constitutes an intrinsic historical object. Indeed, as a primary task of the historian, *Verstehen* is directed toward apprehending the meaningful character of actions and their specific connections to other actions. Empirically, the task of the *verstehende* historian is synonymous with the epistemological problem of identifying and describing the intrinsic historical object.

With this understanding, it is possible to elaborate the concepts of series and sequence. Mead (1956: 131) is right to say that the same objects, for example, furniture, may be placed in different historical series by different individuals (e.g., their owners versus auctioneers) or even by the same individual at different biographical junctures. So it is equally possible for historians to create their own series and sequences; this is more or less Cohen's lament about "transcendent" staging devices. Yet in Weber's and Dilthey's terms, another possibility obtains. Insofar as a "problem" is addressed by one or more historical actors, and insofar as the solutions are, as Kubler says, "related to one another by the bonds of tradition or influence," then the actors' focus on the problem itself is the linkage *in* history that constitutes an intrinsic historical object, and in this case history is something other than merely a reflection of the historian's use of transcendent linking devices. Indeed, the linked activity in intrinsic historical objects seems presupposed by Mead's (1956: 261ff.) ideas of community and social institution.

In these terms and in principle, we may distinguish cultural histories of intrinsic historical objects, in which certain series and sequences result from the efforts of the actors under consideration, from cultural histories in which the series and sequences are the products of the "transcendent" staging devices of the historian—what might be called "extrinsic historical objects." To give substance to these distinctions let me comment on my study of Peoples Temple in more detail. It is true enough, as both Mead and Weber would maintain, that I wrote only one of a number of possible histories of Peoples Temple. I concentrated on the developmental history of the group and its relation to historical and contemporary culture. Another project might offer, for example, a social history of life in the temple for rank-and-file members. Still, either of these studies is premised on the idea that Peoples Temple represented an intrinsic historical object; in reference to that object, different narratives may develop and test plots (cf. Veyne, [1971] 1984) that crisscross one another. While these plot narratives may be contained within the Temple as an intrinsic historical object, it is possible that other plot narratives might transcend it, for example, in a history of "cults" in the United States that places the historical object into an extrinsic series of the historian's making.

My own goal was to treat Peoples Temple as an intrinsic object, and I therefore sought to explore the series and sequences that became salient in the the mindful interactions of participants themselves. To take fund-raising as an example, even if Peoples Temple used its monies for different purposes than those of Jim and Tammy Bakker, temple staff located the techniques of their efforts solidly in the cultural practices among Pentecostalist, storefront, and mass media religions. It is not just a sociological comparison that establishes connections between the temple and Oral Roberts; rather, temple staff faced a cultural problem and drew inspiration by participating in an intrinsic series that has been constituted through the living practices of a succession of evangelical religious movements that share a common culture (Hall, 1987: 84–88). Much the same holds for Jim Jones's practices of faith healing (Hall, 1987: 17–23).

Intrinsic sequences also connect Peoples Temple with broader currents of American cultural history. Connected by the "bonds of tradition and influence," as Kubler (1962) put it, Jim Jones and his staff not only replicated familiar cultural recipes; they also offered novel solutions linked to emergent cultural problems. Thus, the image of a "promised land" is not simply one that I chose as an evocative metaphor; rather, Jones himself worked with the image in ways that symbolized the quest of his religious social movement for redemption from the American society that he identified as classist and racist. But he hardly invented the term; to the contrary, he had "borrowed" it from his self-adopted mentor, Father Divine. Nor were the formulations of Divine and Jones entirely improvisational; instead, they resonated deeply with the aspirations of many of Jones's black followers in ways that connected with a cultural sequence dating back to antebellum days. The simple fact of the forced migration from Africa of blacks to become slaves in the United States constituted a legacy that has been met by a sequence of cultural solutions, from back-to-Africa movements spanning a hundred years, to internal migrations and Martin Luther King's "trip to the mountaintop" that prophesied the promised land in coming changes within the United States. For people like the black woman follower of Jones who said she'd always wanted to live in a black country, Peoples Temple's colony of Jonestown put new fire into the dying embers of an old dream of getting out of "Egypt" completely. Here, Jones succeeded in attracting followers in part because his program offered a new solution in a previously established and culturally linked sequence of black efforts to reach the promised land beyond their bondage.

It would be possible to consider intrinsic historical objects in similar ways in the case of life insurance taboos studied by Zelizer, in ragtime music, and in the genres of city comedy and revenge tragedy identified by Griswold. To cite just one example, Griswold (1986: 196ff.)

found that the patterns of revivals for the two genres differ substantially according to time period. City comedies were overrepresented in the eighteenth century and "declined during the nineteenth century," while revenge tragedies were overrepresented from the mid-1950s through at least the end of the 1970s (Griswold, 1986: 189). These sorts of patterns, Griswold has argued, result from theater producers identifying categories of plays that play well under certain conditions, or totally elude their audiences. Here, linked social actions flow from what the producers themselves identified as series, that is, particular genres of plays.

To be sure, not all cultural histories point to intrinsic historical objects as their subjects. Some, like Barrington Moore's (1984) study of privacy in different historical societies, and Pelikan's (1985) exploration of Jesus as a symbol in different contexts, have altogether different purposes. Broadly speaking, they are comparative. Despite the historical focus on culture, within the frame of the interaction perspective such studies would have to offer different rationales than the history of an intrinsic object. Other studies seem ambivalent in strategy. Hillel Schwartz's (1986) "cultural history of diets, fantasies, and fat," for example, offers vignettes of dietary and weight-reduction histories that might seem to stand for a unified cultural history; yet in practice, the connections between vignettes are not always intrinsic; that is, the historical actors sometimes placed themselves in widely disparate series and sequences. To the extent that this is the case, Schwartz really offers a "transcendent" narrative of a plot that extends beyond the boundaries of tradition and influence of the historical actors, hence, beyond any intrinsic historical object. His study thus raises questions about whether—and how—cultural history in the interaction perspective can deal with events as something greater than the sum of individual actions and interactions. These issues involve questions of sociological and historical causation.

SOCIOLOGICAL EXPLANATION OF CULTURE

The social interaction perspective stands at the precipice of historicism. Since all events are understood to be unique, some interactionists concern themselves largely with "thick description" and culturally centered interpretation (Geertz, 1973). Yet most interactionists assume that some sort of general sociological knowledge is possible. How to reconcile the unique with a sociological theory, that has been the methodological problem. Alfred Schutz and George Herbert Mead, and in ways Georg Simmel, offered what amount to essentialist models: since empirical diversity cannot be subsumed within theory without distorting it, the alternative is to offer a general model of processes that undergird *all* empirical realities. Thus, the "I" and the "me," Schutz's (1970) theory of relevance, Simmel's forms. Weber did not so much offer a general theory of interaction; instead he resolved the problem of empirical diversity by use of ideal types as benchmarks of comparison and as explanatory models. Each in his own way, Schutz, Mead, and Simmel also drew on typification, and despite the nuanced differences, there is no reason to think that essentialist models and ideal type analysis represent incompatible solutions. To the contrary, together they may comprise a distinctive interactionist approach to sociological explanation. To take up the question of sociological explanation, we need to be clear about one point: there is no need for the social interaction perspective to regard "structuralist" explanations with hostility. For all his concerns with symbols and interaction, Mead (1956: 284ff.) recognized that context conditions process, and that, for example, feudalism offers a different context than democracy or slavery. In his essays on topics like the metropolis and the significance of numbers for social life, Simmel (1950) identified what amount to structural dynamics that undergird interaction, much as Goffman has done in identifying the dramaturgical contexts that make role performances plausible. In these terms, the interaction perspective solves the problem of sociological explanation by treating structure not just as some skeleton characteristics that describe functionally equivalent aspects of different societies. Instead, structure itself is a culturally infused aspect of social reality that, if it is to have causal salience, either directly shapes the emergent practices of social actors (e.g., in the metropolis), or is "made present" by those actors. Weber sought to build this connection into his conceptual framework: when describing overarching "structures" of authority, ideal types of social organization, and economic forms, he insisted on "meaning adequacy" as a criterion of concept formation (1977: 13, 20), thus avoiding the false analytic distinction between micro- and macro-sociology. In the interaction perspective, sociological explanation must be mediated by understanding emergent meaningful action, even in the case of overarching social "structures."

With a provisional understanding that meaning and structure are intertwined, we can consider two alternative approaches to sociological explanation. In one approach, sociologists may attend to cultural history by application of a conceptual vocabulary. The vocabulary solves the historiographic problem of selection and offers a framework on which to drape the historical account. Thus, Meyrowitz (1985) is able to bring to light a new way of conceptualizing media effects on audiences by using the dramaturgical vocabulary of Goffman. Meyrowitz's specific explanations are open to debate, but he effectively argues in general that television creates a new set of stage relationships: both for people portrayed in the media and for the audience, the old frontstage-backstage division is blurred by the television cameras with their multiple angles, and by television content, superficial in depth but broad in its topical coverage. In this example, the conceptual framework itself makes possible an explanation of cultural change that could not easily be conceived in a framework more concerned with "variables" and their relationships.

The second approach to explanation within the interaction perspective depends on empirical or ideal types. Here there are several strategies, and in considering them, again we face the problem of what constitutes a series. Clearly, not all examples in a series are exactly the same, yet how are they to be conceptualized? For the historian, the problem is partly a pragmatic one: how to use general terms and concepts to discuss a myriad of examples that differ in details. Take musical genres, which capture the problem in a classic form. By now, no one doubts the historical existence of ragtime music, but our conception of it differs from the ones that held sway during its heyday, and any serious effort to identify ragtime's features—either by analyzing musical motifs or by assaying the comments of performers, critics, and audiences—runs into trouble. Berlin (1980) found no single historical lineage (sequence) that gave rise to ragtime, nor did he feel comfortable offering a definitive characterization of the music. Instead, ragtime appears to have been a label that some contemporaries invoked for a particular kind of player piano music, while for others, what mattered were lyrics or rhythm. Following Berlin's lead, the interaction perspective can shed light on the ephemeral nature of social truth by offering cultural histories of typification and labelling.

Yet such an approach is hardly adequate to the full problem of sociological explanation in cultural history. For all their oversimplification, descriptive types and models of average courses of action offer a shorthand way of summarizing historical processes roughly replicated over a wide number of cases. With Arthur Stinchcombe (1978: 6), we can understand the problem to involve the depth of analogies between social instances. It is not so useful to invoke a type or average if it lacks any meaningfully adequate basis for connection to parallel empirical paths of action. To talk of middle-class tastes in music makes little sense if class is an insufficient basis for identifying shared modalities of conduct.

One solution to the problem is to use the category of currency among actors themselves. Thus Belasco (1979) was able to describe the vacation practice of going "a-gypsying" in the new automobiles as a particular cultural phenomenon in the turn-of-the-twentieth century United States. As Berlin's consideration of ragtime shows, a term can easily obscure too much if it is taken as a narrow ritual or "thing." But Belasco describes gypsying as a range of improvisational activities within a general format, capturing cultural practices in terms that evoke the participants' understanding of them. So long as examples and empirical typifications consolidate and summarize diversity rather than distorting it, they offer a useful basis for charting the meaningful pathways of social interaction. Perhaps the best protection against their abuse is the forceful application of negative evidence (Lindesmith, 1947) to clarify the range of typicality, subtypes of empirical process, and affinities with other conceptual clusters.

An alternative procedure, followed by Griswold (1986), is somewhat more sensitive to Mead's argument that the historian gives meaning to any series in the first place. Thus Griswold created her own canons for the genres of Elizabethan revenge tragedies and city comedies. Not that she ignored the historically situated typifications of plays; to the contrary, she made good use of such data to establish each canon in terms of accepted characteristics of the genre. But studying revivals of the plays required an unambiguous set of cases, and Griswold (1986: 56) chose to exclude one revenge tragedy, *Hamlet*, "because its revival pattern has less to do with its characteristics as a revenge tragedy than with its membership in the elite circle of Shakespeare's best-known plays." Here, the intrinsic characteristics of a case give way to a rationale from sociological analysis—a hypothesis about the causes of the play's revival—that sets the range of typification.

Empirical typification—either actor-centered or analyst-centered—can offer a useful vehicle for exposition, but sociological explanation still faces the problem of empirical diversity. The classic solution is that of Max Weber. Rather than rely solely on empirical types or averages, Weber employed ideal types—what Guenther Roth (1976) calls "socio-historical models" to emphasize their continuities with empirical phenomena. Such types, Weber (1977: 20) freely admitted, lack historical concreteness and specificity, but by way of compensation, they obtain heightened precision "by striving for the highest possible degree of adequacy on the level of meaning." As both Schutz ([1932]1967) and

Mead (1956) have argued, and as Weber acknowledged, empirical social actors give meaning to their actions in unfolding, improvisational, and intentionally or unintentionally ambiguous ways. How to analyze social life in a way that respects its existential and emergent nature? Ideal types offer a way of working out unambiguous and coherent sociological models that differ from functionalist and abstract variable approaches by their capacity to reflect subjective and social temporality, and hence, meaning and meaningfully patterned social organization (Hall, 1984a); one way of thinking about them is to consider them as generic plots. Such clarified, meaningfully adequate typifications are not intended to represent any given existential reality. Instead, they are explanatory models that may serve as benchmarks against which to compare empirical actions. To the degree that empirical events can be subsumed by a model's dynamic, the model's particular sociological explanation gains credence. Conversely, if the model's content fails to match up to the empirical data about actions and their patterns, the model may be rejected as a sociological explanation.

Two examples from my study of Peoples Temple may help underscore the meaningful basis of ideal types and show their role in sociological explanation. First, let us take migration. One thing temple members kept doing collectively was to move together. Jones and a small group of followers originally went to rural California from Indianapolis, driven out, Jones claimed, by racism; in California they shifted their locus of operations from rural Redwood Valley to the metropolises of San Francisco and Los Angeles; under investigation by the U.S. Treasury Department, they departed those shores for Guyana, on the northeast coast of South America; there they underwent the final migration, to the hereafter, by the awesome vehicle of mass suicide. Without going into detail, it is possible to describe "religious migration" as an ideal type; the model describes the meaningful structure and developmental dynamics of this type of collective action independently of any specific occurrence, and it applies in varying degrees to the actions of the Puritans, the Huguenots, the Missouri Lutherans, and the Mormons, to mention a few. Applying the model, it is possible to determine how far it goes in explaining the development of Peoples Temple, and what aspects must be subjected to some other explanation (Hall, 1987: 206–9).

Similarly, it is possible to draw on a sociological model of the charlatan in order to consider accusations by Jones's opponents that he was bilking his followers for personal enrichment. Charlatans, it turns out, have a pattern of action very different from that suggested by what evidence we have about Jones, and until new evidence comes to light, the charlatan as an ideal type fails to explain Jones's conduct, and the sociological search for explanation must take other directions (Hall, 1987: 33–35).

Whatever the analytic outcome, use of ideal types as sociohistorical models of meaningfully patterned actions solves the problem of conceptualization of reality by establishing a strategy of analysis that firmly distinguishes between, on the one hand, sociological models of comparison, and on the other, unique empirical actions and events. Empirical typification does much the same thing, but by establishing close analogies between empirical events. In either approach, the empirical models or ideal types do not represent reality; rather, they offer a way of precipitating out the aspects of reality that may be explained by a given meaningful pattern of action, leaving the unexplained to other sociohistorical models, and the residual to historiographic explanation.

HISTORICAL EXPLANATION OF CULTURE

If sociological explanation is directed to understanding the generic features of things, historiographic explanation favors particularistic treatment of factors and events that are held to give rise to unique outcomes. In the case of what I have called an intrinsic historical object, the initial task may be construed as the construction of a narrative that tests a theory of plot against what the analyst knows (Veyne, [1971]1984; Stone, 1979; Danto, 1985). But even with the intrinsic object, and especially when the object transcends the boundaries of a coherent tradition and influence, investigation moves beyond narrative per se to the question of historical explanation—"why?" To answer this question, discourse moves away from narrative's sequenced account and sociology's generic answers, to marshal relevant evidence for and against particularistic, historically unique explanations of a phenomenon.

In an age when deconstructionists are busy assaulting texts as internally ordered assemblages, historical narrative has become suspect as a special kind of storytelling (Cohen, 1986). Rightfully so, I suggested above, when it moves beyond the intrinsic plot. An alternative approach is that of historical explanation, which eschews narrative in favor of identifying necessary and sufficient conditions of events. Yet historical explanation may fare no better than narrative. From the viewpoint of both deconstruction and the interaction perspective, historical explanation moves beyond the interlinked motives of historical actors. It thus would seem to replace intrinsic history with transcendent linkages of the historian's own making, with the unhappy result that abstracted factors such as "the Protestant ethic" or "the culture of narcissism" would substitute for the history of how people understand the world and what they do. How might the interaction perspective help avoid this potential problem and, in turn, clarify the parameters of historical explanation?

We may take it as an article of faith that abstract factors, forces, or variables do not have causal efficacy in their own terms; if things of historical salience happen, they either happen *to* people or through their actions. Thus, the relevance of nonsocial forces (such as weather, accidents) as well as ecological and demographic ones, need not be denied; rather, the problem is to understand such factors as they manifest themselves in direct effects on social actors. The absolutely external and nonhuman cause represents a limiting case of historical explanation. By far the more relevant phenomena, be they external or social, are themselves taken into account in unfolding social interaction (cf. Weber, 1977: 7). "The definition of the situation" thus is an important basis of historical explanation, since the course of actual events frequently is confounded by how historical actors read those events. It is the forte of the interaction perspective to deal with precisely this kind of circumstance.

Briefly, two examples: the tragedy of mass suicide at Jonestown, Guyana, in 1978 most often has been explained as the product of Jim Jones, cast as devil or madman, or both. Yet a close interactionist historical explanation reveals something quite different—a religious conflict between Jones's Peoples Temple and a group called the Concerned Relatives. In terms of an interactionist historical explanation, it matters little in any "objective" terms whether the zealous followers of Jones's Peoples Temple were trapped in a "cult," as its equally zealous opponents charged, just as we do not need to know whether the Concerned Relatives "persecuted" Peoples Temple. What matters is that each side developed such images of its opponents in a way that fueled religious conflict. Jones's staff sometimes misread crucial information by aligning it with the previously established interpretation of conspiratorial persecution. In the same way, opponents misread actions of temple members, and acted to save loved ones who had chosen Jones over their families and had no interest in being "saved." To complicate matters, each side gained "inside" intelligence about the other's true goals in ways that made it possible to discount public performances that contradicted previously framed images. In this interactionist historical explanation of a self-contained or intrinsic historical object, tragedy unfolded not simply on the basis of any objective social conditions, but by the specific interactional dynamic of opponents locked in religious conflict (Hall, 1987).

Even beyond the close sphere of an intrinsic object, the social interaction perspective offers a crucial basis for the historical study of culture, again because it points to the situated and emergent meaningful actions of differently located individuals. Wendy Griswold (1986, 1987) offers as an analytic device "the cultural diamond" that schematically suggests the mutual influence of artists, cultural objects, audiences, and social context. Using the cultural diamond allows the designation of linkages based on social interaction that transcends any intrinsic historical object. In the terms used here, the London theater scene can be considered an arena treated by the historian as a conduit and conjuncture of different series and sequences. Changes in theater architectural plans evoked different heritages of theater, there were transformations of economics and of the way theater audiences incorporated attendance into their daily lives, and particular plays and genres resonated with more or less meaning for the audiences of one era, compared to another. Griswold has been able to offer historical explanations of Renaissance revivals by use of an analytic model that looks to the meaningful ways playwrights, producers, audiences, and state authorities incorporated Elizabethan plays from no longer "living" series and sequences into their spheres of activities decades and centuries later. In this example, interactionist explanation of cultural history moves beyond the intrinsic object.

THE SOCIOHISTORICAL PROBLEM OF CONFIGURATION

By considering series and sequences, the problem of historical objects, and sociological and historical explanation, I have tried to show both the relevance and the potentiality of the interaction perspective for considering the history of culture in relation to social life. Yet it would be a conceit to claim for the perspective a totalistic epistemology for approaching all the problems of social analysis. The crucial problem for the social interaction perspective then becomes one of coming to terms with discourse that exceeds its own limits. One approach would be simply to reject such discourse as violating the assumptions of George Herbert Mead, Max Weber, Georg Simmel, or some other patron saint. Yet paradoxically, the interaction perspective recognizes the socially constructed and relative nature of all knowledge, and it hardly seems fair for relativists to claim their own approach as singularly suited to determine the validity of other forms of knowledge (cf. Becker, [1982]1986). For the interaction perspective, boundaries of analysis come to light with the problem of configurational analysis, where history and sociology meet. Much history "transcends" any intrinsic plot; it is constructed extrinsically as an historical object by the juxtaposition of diverse events in a "narrative" plot of the historian's own making, which gives a thread of reality through imposed "aboutness."

In interactionist terms, even the studies I have so far described within the perspective—of Peoples Temple, Renaissance revivals, and the motel—all go beyond the perspective's limits in certain ways. For Griswold, the tough problem of linking play revival to particular eras is resolved in the end by interpreting quantitative information about revivals in relation to events of each era, proposing archetypal, topical, or social relevance as overlapping processes that might explain actual patterns of revivals. The theory still very much remains interactionist, but its argumentation is forced into a different terrain by the problem of evidence. In studying Jonestown, I was not solely interested in giving a cultural history of Jonestown; to the contrary, I wanted to understand Jonestown *in* American cultural history. The empirical analysis thus offers a mirror and a metaphor for digging beyond the normative perceptions of American culture that give a smooth surface to our everyday experience. If Griswold departs methodologically, my study of Jonestown moves interpretively beyond the strict confines of interactionism insofar as it uses empirical analysis as a springboard for considering broader issues of American culture. These departures extend the interactionist perspective more than they violate it. With Griswold, there may be reasonable ways to engage in quantification without violating the assumptions of the social action perspective (Hall, 1984b). And cultural interpretation, as in *Gone from the Promised Land*, simply marks a different activity that cannot be evaluated in sociological discourse per se.

The more contentious problems have to do with configurational arguments that serve, in Cohen's (1986) terms, as transcendent linking devices. In his study of the motel, for example, Belasco offers a panoramic view of the linked consequences of events; he depicts the invasion of the nouveau riche into the upper-class resort hotels and the emergence of new cultural styles among the elite (Teddy Roosevelt's "strenuous life," for example), the interests of automobile tourists in "making time," and the aversion of travelers with bourgeois sensibilities to associating with the "Okies" in free tourist camps sponsored by small towns hoping to attract business trade from the highways. Much of the power of Belasco's study comes from the convincing way he weaves a story of the motel's emergence out of the conspicuous consumption and social exclusivity and upward mobility aspirations of competing social strata. The argument as a whole is a configurational one that exceeds the strict boundaries of interactionist explanation: a conjunctural set of separate and sometimes totally disconnected processes and events results in an outcome that lies well beyond the intentionalities of any given social actors, well beyond any intrinsic historical object. Unintended consequences in this example are more than results of actions that go beyond their initiators' goals; they represent institutionalized social developments that have no coherent meaningful basis.

The problem becomes more pronounced if we move to a broader scale of historical development, still closely linked to cultural history. While Max Weber is best known for his argument about the Protestant ethic as cultural dimension that fueled the emergence of modern, "rational" capitalism, his overall theory was a configurational one that pointed to diverse changes in accounting procedures, world trade, the emergence of state absolutism, meaningful bases of religious salvation, and so on (Weber, [1927]1981; Collins, [1980]1986). Some of these historical developments occurred in streams of activity isolated from one another, yet they had consequences that are explicable only in terms of their conjuncture, not the intentions of the actors involved. The emergent institutions of modern capitalism certainly may be traced ultimately to meaningful social actions, but the consequences are not reducible to the sum of those actions. At least, so the argument goes. And that is just the point. Studies like Weber's (and more recently, Mukerji's [1983] study of material culture, and Michael Mann's [1986] account of power) move from historical narrative involving culture to the exploration of culture along with other historical factors combined in configurational sociological arguments about history.

By returning to Sande Cohen's (1986) problem of the transcendent staging devices that give history a sense of "aboutness," it is now possible to understand more clearly where history *qua* social interaction tails off, and sociological arguments *about* history begin. So long as historical investigation of culture is confined to the problems of intrinsic historical objects in series and sequences between such objects connected, as Kubler put it, by the "bonds of tradition and influence," we may properly speak of history as a subject of inquiry *within* the interaction perspective. In that domain, it is possible to offer narrative plots about the relations of cultural objects to social action and organization, clarified by sociological and historical explanation.

Yet in practice the study of history does not stop at the boundaries of the interaction perspective, rigorously defined. Configurational (or what used to be called "functional") consequences in the emergence of social institutions are a reasonable subject of historical inquiry, and this applies not only to very broad institutional developments such as modern capitalism, but also to more narrowly construed subjects—the emergence of the asylum as charted by Foucault, bases of modern personal identity, and so forth. But we must be quite clear on two points.

First, while the investigation of events within an intrinsic historical object or sequence can hope to establish an emergent plot that held salience for actors themselves, configurational cultural history can fall back on no such *empirical* narrative claims. As Cohen suggests, transcendent staging devices will not stand on the basis of *historical* argument. But that is not the end of the matter. Instead we need regain Mead's insight and face up to the role of the investigator by understanding that configurational history really amounts to sociological argument *about* history, either by offering a particular theory that weights the importance and interrelations of various factors, or by identifying a particular configuration of interest, and then working back to identify the various, potentially independent developments that gave rise to the configuration. Thus, there is what must be for historians an unsettling conclusion concerning accounts such as Belasco's study described above, on a broader level, Weber's theory of capitalism, and, indeed, many accounts more conventionally historical. Such accounts must legitimate themselves by other claims than those of intrinsic history; they must be accounted either as configurational sociological history or comparative sociology (Hall, 1988b).

Which brings me to a second concluding point. I have just suggested that Cohen's critique can be answered partly by forthrightly acknowledging a realm beyond intrinsic history, for which the claims of "aboutness" in events themselves can no longer be sustained; at the same time I have suggested ways in which that realm may be salvaged as an arena of reasoned discourse. In a way that might seem paradoxical, this same step redeems intrinsic history itself from Cohen's deconstructionist assault by separating it from practices that yield "transcendent" "aboutness." But it only does so to the extent that historical investigation is informed by the interaction perspective, for only within that perspective can we hope to trace the relations between culture and action in intrinsic historical objects and their series and sequences. In the final analysis, even configurational analysis must depend on the more basic task of intrinsic cultural history for the building blocks of its analysis.

In sum, the source of "aboutness" marks a divide within the social interaction perspective itself, between intrinsic history given meaning by its actors and extrinsic or configurational history that obtains its meaning from its analysts. Intrinsic history was given vision by Dilthey, and it has informed diverse histories of culture since, from Weber's treatment of the Protestant ethic to some of the current efforts discussed here. Extrinsic or configurational sociological history was also the object of Weber's efforts, and philosophically, it may be located in the frame of Mead's concept of the historian as social actor. To identify this divide represents one "methodological deconstruction" of historical discourse. Coming to terms with the deconstruction offers a more rigorous basis to practice historiography by clarifying the difference between the sociological and historiographic "moments" of its logic within the social interaction perspective. Yet it must be recognized that, in practice, the best historians combine the various moments as the practice of a craft.

NOTE

1. In that social action has left little of nature untouched, the definition may seem to include too much, and thus become trivial. Still, it does not seem appropriate to exclude as cultural products, for example, domesticated plants and animals (or the landscape, for that matter), insofar as they have been shaped by human agency. But the matter of intention seems important. We may distinguish between the unintentional effects of cultural action (e.g., the ozone layer "greenhouse effect") and the intentional cultural transformation or use of natural objects for social ends. In general, given the complex relations between culture and nature, the analytic distinction is fluid. But if for no other reason, then because the rationalization of nature has been a central feature of social change, it seems crucial to include culturally organized nature as a subject of consideration.

REFERENCES

Aron, Raymond. [1948]1961. *Introduction to the Philosophy of History* (Boston: Beacon).

Atkinson, R. F. 1978. *Knowledge and Explanation in History: An Introduction to the Philosophy of History* (Ithaca, N.Y.: Cornell University Press).

Baxandall, Michael. 1972. *Painting and Experience in Fifteenth Century Italy* (Oxford: Clarendon Press).

Becker, Howard S. 1982. *Art Worlds* (Berkeley: University of California Press).

———. [1982]1986. "Culture: A Sociological View," pp. 11–24 in Becker, *Doing Things Together* (Evanston, Ill.: Northwestern University Press).

Belasco, Warren J. 1979. *Americans on the Road: From Autocamp to Motel, 1910–1945* (Cambridge: MIT Press).

Bendix, Reinhard. 1984. "Objective and Subjective Meaning in History," pp. 27–45 in Bendix, *Force, Fate, and Freedom: On Historical Sociology* (Berkeley: University of California Press).

Berger, Peter, and Thomas Luckmann. 1966. *The Social Construction of Reality* (New York: Doubleday).

Berlin, Edward A. 1980. *Ragtime: A Musical and Cultural History* (Berkeley: University of California Press).

Blumer, Herbert. 1969. *Symbolic Interactionism: Perspective and Method* (Englewood Cliffs, N.J.: Prentice-Hall).

Bourdieu, Pierre. [1972]1977. *Outline of a Theory of Practice* (Cambridge: Cambridge University Press).

Braudel, Fernand. [1966]1972. *The Mediterranean and the Mediterranean World in the Age of Philip the Second*, trans. Sian Reynolds (New York: Harper and Row).

Carroll, David. 1980. "Representation or the End(s) of History: Dialectics and Fiction," *Yale French Studies* 59: 201–29.

Cohen, Sande. 1986. *Historical Culture: On the Recoding of an Academic Discipline* (Berkeley: University of California Press).

Collins, Randall. [1980]1986. "Weber's last theory of capitalism," pp. 19–44 in Collins, *Weberian Sociological Theory* (New York: Cambridge University Press).

Danto, Arthur C. 1985. *Narration and Knowledge* (New York: Columbia University Press).

Denzin, Norman K. 1985. "Towards an Interpretation of Semiotics and History," *Semiotica* 54: 335–50.

Dilthey, Wilhelm. 1976. *Selected Writings*, ed. and trans. by H. P. Rickman (Cambridge: Cambridge University Press).

Gans, Herbert J. 1974. *Popular Culture and High Culture* (New York: Basic).

Geertz, Clifford. 1973. *The Interpretation of Culture* (New York: Basic).

Georgiades, Thrasybulos. [1974]1982. *Music and Language: the Rise of Western Music as Exemplified in Settings of the Mass* (Cambridge: Cambridge University Press).

Griswold, Wendy. 1986. *Renaissance Revivals: City Comedy and Revenge Tragedy in the London Theater,1576–1980* (Chicago: University of Chicago Press).

———. 1987. "A Methodological Framework for the Sociology of Culture," *Sociological Methodology* 14: 1–35.

Hall, John R. 1980. "The Time of History and the History of Times," *History and Theory* 19: 113–31.

———. 1984a. "The Problem of Epistemology in the Social Action Perspective," pp. 253–89 in Randall Collins, ed., *Sociological Theory* (San Francisco, Calif.: Jossey-Bass).

———. 1984b. "Temporality, Social Action, and the Problem of Quantification in Historical Analysis," *Historical Methods* 17: 206–18.

———. 1987. *Gone From the Promised Land: Jonestown in American Cultural History* (New Brunswick, N.J.: Transaction).

———. 1988a. "Social Organization and Pathways of Commitment: Types of Communal Groups, Rational Choice Theory, and the Kanter Thesis," *American Sociological Review* 53: 679–92.

———. 1988b. "Where History and Sociology Meet: Modes of Discourse and Analytic Strategies." Paper presented at the annual meetings of the American Sociological Association, Atlanta, Ga, August.

Hamilton, Gary G. 1987. "The 'New History' in Sociology," *Politics, Culture, and Society* 1: 89–114.

Himmelfarb, Gertrude. 1987. *The New History and the Old* (Cambridge: Harvard University Press).

Hunt, Lynn. 1984. *Politics, Culture, and Class in the French Revolution* (Berkeley: University of California Press).

Jameson, Frederic. 1972. *The Prison House of Language: A Critical Account of Structuralism and Russian Formalism* (Princeton: Princeton University Press).

Johnson, Richard. 1986–87. "What Is Cultural Studies Anyway?" *Social Text* 16 (winter): 38–80.

Kellner, Hans D. 1975. "Time Out: The Discontinuity of Historical Consciousness," *History and Theory* 14: 275–96.

Kracauer, Siegfried. 1966. "Time and History," *History and Theory*, Beiheft 6, *History and the Concept of Time*: 65–78.

Kubler, George. 1962. *The Shape of Time: Remarks on the History of Things* (New Haven: Yale University Press).

Leyden, W. Von. 1962. "History and The Concept of Relative Time," *History and Theory* 2: 263–85.

Lindesmith, Alfred R. 1947. *Opiate Addiction* (Bloomington, IN.: Principia Press).

Maines, David R., Noreen M. Sugrue, and Michael A. Katovich, 1983,

"The Sociological Import of G. H. Mead's Theory of the Past," *American Sociological Review* 48: 161–73.

Mann, Michael. 1986. *The Sources of Social Power,* Vol. I: *A History of Power from the Beginning to A.D. 1760* (New York: Cambridge University Press).

Mead, George Herbert. 1938. *The Philosophy of the Act,* Charles W. Morris, ed. (Chicago: University of Chicago Press).

———. 1956. "Selections from Mind, Self, and Society," in Anselm Strauss, ed., *The Social Psychology of George Herbert Mead* (Chicago: University of Chicago Press).

Meyrowitz, Joshua. 1985. *No Sense of Place: The Impact of Electronic Media on Social Behavior* (New York: Oxford University Press).

Moore, Barrington, Jr. 1984. *Privacy: Studies in Social and Cultural History* (Armonk, N.Y.: M. E. Sharpe).

Mukerji, Chandra. 1983. *From Graven Images: Patterns of Modern Materialism* (New York: Columbia University Press).

Mukerji, Chandra, and Michael Schudson. 1986. "Popular Culture," *Annual Review of Sociology* 12: 47–66.

Oakes, Guy. 1977. "The Verstehen Thesis and the Foundations of Max Weber's Methodology," *History and Theory* 16: 11–29.

Pelikan, Jaroslav. 1985. *Jesus Through the Centuries: His Place in the History of Culture* (New York: Harper and Row).

Peterson, Richard A. 1979. "Revitalizing the Culture Concept," *Annual Review of Sociology* 5: 137–66.

Roth, Guenther. 1976. "History and Sociology in the Work of Max Weber," *British Journal of Sociology* 27: 306–18.

Schutz, Alfred. [1932]1967. *The Phenomenology of the Social World* (Evanston, Il.: Northwestern University Press).

———. 1970. *Reflections on the Problem of Relevance* (New Haven: Yale University Press).

Schwartz, Hillel. 1986. *Never Satisfied: a Cultural History of Diets, Fantasies, and Fat* (New York: Free Press).

Shiner, Larry. 1969. "A Phenomenological Approach to Historical knowledge," *History and Theory* 8: 260–74.

Simmel, Georg. 1950. *The Sociology of Geog Simmel* (New York: Free Press).

———. [1905]1977. *The Problems of the Philosophy of History* (New York: Free Press).

Skocpol, Theda, ed. 1984. *Vision and Method in Historical Sociology* (Cambridge: Cambridge University Press).

Stinchcombe, Arthur L. 1978. *Theoretical Methods in Social History* (New York: Academic Press).

Stone, Lawrence. 1979. "The Revival of Narrative: Reflections on a New Old History," *Past and Present* no. 85 (November): 3–24.

Swidler, Ann. 1986. "Culture in Action: Symbols and Strategies," *American Sociological Review* 51: 273–86.

Thompson, E. P. 1967. "Time, Work-discipline, and Industrial Capitalism," *Past and Present* 38: 56–97.

Veyne, Paul, [1971]1984. *Writing History: Essays on Epistemology* (Middletown, Cn.: Wesleyan University Press).

Weber, Max. 1946. "Science as a Vocation," pp. 129–56 in Hans Gerth and C. Wright Mills, *From Max Weber: Essays in Sociology* (New York: Free Press).

————. 1949. *The Methodology of the Social Sciences* (New York: Free Press of Glencoe).

————. [1905]1958. *The Protestant Ethic and the Spirit of Capitalism* (New York: Scribner's).

————. 1977. *Economy and Society,* ed. Guenther Roth and Claus Wittich, (Berkeley: University of California Press).

————. [1927]1981. *General Economic History* (New Brunswick, N.J.: Transaction).

Wölfflin, Heinrich. [1915]1950. *Principles of Art History: The Problem of the Development of Style in Later Art* (New York: Dover).

Wuthnow, Robert. 1987. *Meaning and Moral Order: Explorations in Cultural Analysis* (Berkeley: University of California Press).

Wuthnow, Robert, James Davison Hunter, Albert Bergesen, and Edith Kurzweil. 1984. *Cultural Analysis: the Work of Peter L. Berger, Mary Douglas, Michel Foucault, and Jurgen Habermas* (Boston: Routledge and Kegan Paul).

Wuthnow, Robert, and Marsha Witten. 1988. "New Directions in the Study of Culture," *Annual Review of Sociology* 14: 49–67.

Zelizer, Viviana A. R. 1979. *Morals and Markets: the Development of Life Insurance in the United States* (New York: Columbia University Press).

3   The Good News about

Life History

Michal M. McCall and

Judith Wittner

The good news is: Life history research is enjoying a revival. Feminist scholars are using life histories to study social life from the vantage point of women. The New Social Historians are using them to rewrite history "from the bottom up"—that is, to write history that includes the daily lives of ordinary people and the experiences of oppressed groups (Gardner and Adams 1983; Zunz 1985; Tyrrell 1986). Anthropologists who recognize that, in writing culture, they structure and interpret the experiences of others, appreciate life histories because "the other" speaks for herself and describes her own experiences in them. Life histories interest scholars engaged in "post-positivist cultural studies" because of their commitment to "lived experience" and to "developing insights and deepening understanding of the complexities and constructedness of culture through participation in forms of life where observer and observed become interlocutors" (Conquergood 1987:2). Because they are stories, life histories also interest narrative theorists and those social scientists who are using the insights of narrative theorists to create postpositivist methodologies and epistemologies (e.g., Denzin 1982; Watson and Watson-Franke 1985).

At one level, the renewed interest in life history research is a product of scholarship that conceptualizes knowledge as inherently ideological. In every field of inquiry where this orientation has taken hold, a basic method for gathering data has been to ask people to talk about their lives. Because they depend less on concepts grounded in the experiences of socially dominant groups and classes, life histories deepen the critique of existing knowledge. They force us to examine our assumptions, incorporate more actors into our models, and generate more inclusive concepts for understanding the actual complexities of social institutions and the processes of social change.

46   To groups who have been ignored, to emergent collectivities who are

just beginning to speak in their own name and to develop their own past and future, life histories are an important, perhaps essential, tool for formulating, publicizing, and pursuing change as well. As new groups emerge into public view and make claims to be heard, life histories become important tools for reconstructing knowledge not only about them, but about the society of which they are part. Stories tell about society from particular vantage points. Who speaks and who is heard are political questions, a fact that is especially apparent when people in positions of low status and power find their voice.

At another level, the renewed interest in life history research represents a loss of faith in positivism (Geertz 1983:19). Critics of the positivist tradition in social science claim that it maintains the subordination of women, workers, and non-European people by excluding their experiential knowledge of social life from our abstract knowledge of society. The experiential knowledge of subordinate people, critics point out, is kept submerged by positivist methodologies which assume social scientists know enough to ask the questions that yield meaningful explanations of society and social life. The life stories of subordinate people, on the contrary, present *their* experiences and meanings; reveal the problematics of *their* social worlds (Denzin 1982); and help subordinate people use their own knowledge to produce lives they want to lead (Armitage 1983; Chesnaux 1978).

At the broadest level, the renewed interest in life history research is a "postmodernist operation," which, like other such operations, is "being staged—not in order to transcend representation, but in order to expose that system of power that authorizes certain representations while blocking, prohibiting or invalidating others" (Owens 1983:59), and which, like the others, owes much to "the presence of an insistent feminist voice" (ibid.:61).

> The key ... is the loosening of the hold over fragmentary scholarly communities of either specific totalizing visions or general paradigmatic styles of organizing research. The authority of "grand theory" seems suspended for the moment in favor of a close consideration of such issues as contextuality, the meaning of social life for those who enact it, and the explanation of exceptions and indeterminants rather than regularities in phenomena observed—all issues that make problematic what were taken for granted as facts or certainties on which the validity of paradigms had rested. (Marcus and Fischer 1986:vii, 8)

More good news: Life history research is no longer an "aimless discipline," used by scholars in various fields without shared methodological and interpretive standards. It is no longer true that "the sad condition of our theoretical knowledge about oral history and the lack of serious efforts to think through exactly what an oral interview is or should be, how it is to be analyzed, or for what purpose, has resulted in a situation of endless activity without goal or meaning" (Grele 1975:132–33). Although interdisciplinary standards for collecting and interpreting life histories never developed, consciously ideological,[1] postpositivist, postmodern standards are being developed now, by feminists, social historians, anthropologists, interpretive social scientists, and critical theorists.

Still more good news: The new life historians are learning from symbolic interactionists[2] and teaching us. We have a tradition that answers some of the questions they are asking and speaks to some of their methodological concerns. They, in turn, question some of our received wisdom and offer us new methods, interpretive standards, textual strategies, and modes of representation, and new ways of thinking about some of our old concepts.

HEADLINES, NEWS, HUMAN INTEREST STORIES, AND OTHER FORMATS

We will report the good news under three headings and in several formats. First, we will assess our own tradition in terms of emerging interdisciplinary, ideological, postpositivist, postmodern standards for life history research. Next, we will show, in the form of imaginary dialogues, some of the questions life historians ask, some of the answers symbolic interactionists give, and some of the questions life historians raise about research methods and rhetorical practices symbolic interactionists take for granted.

From time to time, we will interrupt the news with human interest stories from our own life history research. Judith Wittner used the customary life history method of focused interviewing. She interviewed thirty women who were displaced workers, about their work and family histories. Michal McCall used a different method that its inventor, Jim Spradley, called Cultural Life History but which we call storytelling groups. She met with a dozen groups of adult women and men and with students in four different classes to read and tell autobiographical stories; she kept copies of the stories these people read. We will include excerpts from Wittner's interview transcripts and from the written stories McCall collected.

— ASSESSING OUR TRADITION
Ideological Standards

Does the symbolic interactionist tradition meet the new, ideological standards for collecting and interpreting life histories? The question is usually posed in terms of voice: Whose voices have been heard and whose have been muted, whose have been included and whose left out of codified knowledge, both as knowers and as people whose lives and experiences are known about? For example, a feminist life historian introduced her article on women's life histories this way:

> Refusing to be rendered historically voiceless any longer, women are creating a new history—using our own voices and experiences. We are challenging the traditional concepts of history, of what is "historically important," and we are affirming that our everyday lives *are* history. Using an oral tradition, as old as human memory, we are reconstructing our own past. (Gluck 1977:3)

Our tradition has always included muted voices. Symbolic interactionists have consciously recognized a "hierarchy of credibility" in the creation and dissemination of knowledge and other meanings. For example, interactionists who studied deviance found that, since deviance and deviants are consequences of a process of interaction among people, "some of whom in the service of their interests make and enforce rules which catch others who, in the service of their own interests, have committed acts which are labeled deviant" (Becker 1973: 163), a decision was always necessary: whose viewpoint to take in describing the social organization and social processes involved in the social construction of deviance—those who were treated as deviant or those who labeled others deviant. Interactionists further recognized that the viewpoint of those who represent the State by making and enforcing rules is generally considered more credible because it is the official viewpoint and that the point of view of deviants or innovators is considered less credible because it challenges the official point of view. Therefore, when we take the viewpoint of the deviants, interactionists realized, we are likely to be accused of failure to separate politics and knowledge, of being subjective and failing to maintain value neutrality. As Becker put it,

> When do we accuse ourselves and our fellow sociologists of bias? I think an inspection of representative instances would show that the accusation arises, in one important class of

cases, when the research gives credence, in any serious way, to the perspective of the subordinate group in some hierarchical relationship. In the case of deviants, the hierarchical relationship is a moral one. The superordinate parties in the relationship are those who represent the forces of approved and official morality; the subordinate parties are those who, it is alleged, have violated that morality.

Though deviance is a typical case, it is by no means the only one. . . . We provoke the suspicion that we are biased in favor of . . . subordinate parties when[ever] we tell the story from their point of view . . . when[ever] we assume, for the purposes of our research, that subordinates have as much right to be heard as superordinates, that they are as likely to be telling the truth as they see it as superordinates, that what they say about the institution has a right to be investigated and have its truth or falsity established, even though responsible officials assure us that it is unnecessary because the charges are false.

[In other words] we provoke the charge of bias, in ourselves and others, by refusing to give credence and deference to an established status order, in which knowledge of truth and the right to be heard are not equally distributed. "Everyone knows" that responsible professionals know more about things than laymen, that police are more respectable and their words ought to be taken more seriously than those of the deviants and criminals with whom they deal. By refusing to accept the hierarchy of credibility, we express disrespect for the entire established order. (Becker 1970:125–27)

Post-positivist Standards

How "postpositivist" is our tradition? As Geertz pointed out, the loss of faith in positivism has led many human scientists to "turn away from a laws and explanations approach" to a "cases and interpretations" one.

Interpretive explanation—and it is a form of explanation, not just exalted glossography—trains attention on what institutions, actions, images, utterances, events, customs, all the usual objects of social scientific interest, mean to those whose institutions, actions, customs, and so on they are. As a result, it issues not in laws like Boyle's or forces like Volta's, or mechanisms like Darwin's, but in constructions like Burckhardt's, Weber's, or Freud's: systematic unpackings of the conceptual world in which *condottiere*, Calvinists, or paranoids live.

The manner of these constructions itself varies: Burckhardt

portrays, Weber models, Freud diagnoses. But they all represent attempts to formulate how this people or that, this period or that, this person or that makes sense to itself and, understanding that, what we understand about social order, historical change, or psychic functioning in general. Inquiry is directed toward cases or sets of cases, and toward the particular features that mark them off; but its aims are as far-reaching as those of mechanics or physiology: to distinguish the materials of human existence. (Geertz 1983:22)

From the beginning, symbolic interaction has been associated with the case study tradition in sociology, and we have clung to it, even during the last four decades, when positivist designs—the survey and its template, the experiment—have dominated the field and our work has been out of the methodological mainstream. We have preferred the life history, the case study, and the fieldwork design to either the experiment or the survey, both because these other designs seemed to produce much less humanistic and narrower (although rigorous and precise) knowledge of social life and because their methods seemed "ethnocentric."

> The case study usually has a double purpose. On the one hand, it attempts to arrive at a comprehensive understanding of the group under study: who are its members? what are their stable and recurring modes of activity and interaction? how are they related to one another and how is the group related to the rest of the world? At the same time, the case study also attempts to develop more general theoretical statements about regularities in social structure and process.
>
> Because it aims to understand all of the group's behavior, the case study cannot be designed single-mindedly to test general propositions. In contrast to the laboratory experiment, which is designed to test one or a few closely related propositions as rigorously and precisely as possible, the case study must be prepared to deal with a great variety of descriptive and theoretical problems. The various phenomena uncovered by the investigator's observations must all be incorporated into [the] account of the group and then be given theoretical relevance. (Becker 1970:76)

This . . . study [of life history research] is concerned with depicting and discussing a particular style of investigating and understanding human experience, a style which simply advocates getting close to concrete individual men and women, ac-

curately picking up the way they express their understandings
of the world around them, and, perhaps, providing an analysis
of such expressions. It is a style of research which constitutes
a large underbelly of social science research. . . .

This corrective sociology may be called "humanistic" and
has at least four central criteria. It must pay tribute to *human
subjectivity and creativity*—showing how individuals respond
to social constraints and actively assemble social worlds; it
must deal with concrete human experiences—talk, feelings,
action—through their *social, and especially economic, organisation* (and not just their inner, psychic or biological structuring); it must show a naturalistic *"intimate familiarity"* with
such experiences—abstractions untempered by close involvement are ruled out; and there must be a self-awareness by the
sociologist of the ultimate *moral and political role* in moving
towards a social structure in which there is less exploitation,
oppression, and injustice and more creativity, diversity, and
equality. (Plummer 1983:1–5)

Certainly in the course of studying his own people, the
American sociologist became the most skillful of all sociologists in gathering and analysis of data on current social
behavior. Sociology became very current indeed—a little over-
current. Great ingenuity and money have been put into developing methods and organizations for study of this year's voting
and buying. In addition to being a very diverse people, we are
also probably still that nation which has the largest number of
people who can understand and answer questions—by word or
in writing—in something approaching the same language. We
have the largest number of people with the means to choose
from among the various brands of goods offered in a highly
standardized industry. We combine, in short, a high degree of
likeness in language, taste, exposure to popular arts and news,
with a wide but not unlimited diversity. It is heaven for the
sample-surveyor. But heaven can get to be a dull place. As we
have become the world's best sample-surveyors (using survey
in its present sense rather than that of the earlier survey movement) we have perhaps become a little inclined to believe that
only societies amenable to study by this particular method are
worth studying at all. Even in studying our own country we
are inclined to leave off the ends of the curve. The eccentric are
not our concern. Just as Sears, Roebuck will not stock shirts of
sizes which are not sold by the hundreds of millions (or some

such fantastic number), we sociologists will not count opinions or habits unless they are mass-produced. . . .

We invented ethnocentrism. Now we have fallen into it. We invented sampling and precoding, most excellent devices. But let us not eliminate from the human race, the object of our study, all people who are not precodable; nor those who, embittered by the withholding of freedom and human dignity, refuse to answer our coolly put questions about the future but act with unseemly haste and violence to seize freedom, dignity, food, and land. (Hughes 1971:476–477)

What seems to have changed in recent years is the degree of confidence we have in our own case study tradition and, therefore, the story we tell about it (E. Bruner 1986b). Many of us have stopped talking about our design in the terms established by researchers who use experimental and survey designs: in terms of exploratory, descriptive, and causal research stages or sampling, measurement, and error control decisions. We have stopped telling the story that the fieldwork design is almost as good (rigorous and precise) as the other two. Instead, we have begun talking about things like authenticity, thick description, and verisimilitude (Denzin 1982), negotiation, reciprocity, and empowerment (Lather 1986). We tell a different story: that we were never positivists to begin with; while other sociologists were doing surveys and experiments, we were perfecting a comparative case study design (Chapoulie 1987) and a humanistic style (Plummer 1983) of research.

Maybe we are more confident because mainstream, variable-oriented sociology is being more often and more publicly criticized from within (e.g., Lieberson 1985; Ragin 1987) and because these critiques remind us of the reasons we value case studies. For example:

The essential characteristics of the qualitative/quantitative split in the social sciences are clearly visible in comparative social science. In contrast to other subdisciplines, this field has a long tradition of qualitative work that is stronger and richer than its quantitative counterpart. Not only is this tradition qualitative, but it also tends to be case-oriented (as opposed to variable-oriented) and historical (as opposed to abstractly causal). . . .

The variable-oriented approach . . . is the dominant research strategy of mainstream social science. In this approach cases are disaggregated into variables and distributions. Examination of patterns of covariation among variables is used as a basis

for making general statements about relations among aspects
of cases considered collectively as populations of comparable
observations. These general statements are typically linked to
abstract theoretical ideas about generic properties of macroso-
cial units (such as societies). Because this strategy starts with
simplifying assumptions, it is a powerful data reducer. Thus,
it is an ideal instrument for producing broad statements per-
taining to relatively large bodies of data encompassing diverse
cases. However, the simplifying assumptions that make this
approach possible often violate commonsense notions of causation and sometimes pose serious obstacles to making interpretive statements about specific cases or even about
categories of cases. . . .

Case-oriented methods . . . are holistic—they treat cases as
whole entities and not as collections of parts (or as collections
of scores on variables). Thus, the relations between the parts of
a whole are understood within the context of the whole, not
within the context of general patterns of covariation between
variables characterizing members of a population of comparable units. Second, causation is understood conjuncturally. Outcomes are analyzed in terms of intersections of conditions, and
it is usually assumed that any of several connections might
produce a certain outcome. These and other features of case-
oriented methods make it possible for investigators to interpret
cases historically and make statements about the origins of important qualitative changes in specific settings. (Ragin
1987:viii-x)

Assessing Postmodernity

Finally, how "postmodern" is symbolic interaction? According to
Marcus and Fischer, the most interesting thing about postmodernism
in the human sciences is "what we call a crisis of representation":

This is the intellectual stimulus for the contemporary vitality
of experimental writing in anthropology. The crisis arises from
uncertainty about adequate means of describing social reality.
In the United States, it is an expression of the failure of
post–World War II paradigms, or the unifying ideas of a remarkable number of fields, to account for conditions within
American society, if not within Western societies globally,
which seem to be in a state of profound transition.

Ours is once again a period rich in experimentation and conceptual risktaking. Older dominant frameworks are not so
much denied—there being nothing so grand to replace them—

as suspended. The ideas they embody remain intellectual resources to be used in novel and eclectic ways. The closest such
previous period was the 1920s and 1930s when evolutionary
paradigms, laissez-faire liberalism, and revolutionary social-
ism and marxism all came under energetic critiques. Instead of
grand theories and encyclopedic works, writers devoted themselves to the essay, to documenting diverse social experiences
at close quarters, and to fragmentary illuminations. The atmosphere was one of uncertainty about the nature of major
trends of change and the ability of existing social theories to
grasp it holistically. The essay, experience, documentation, intensive focus on fragments and detail—these were the terms
and vocabulary of the generation of Walter Benjamin, . . . Lud-
wig Wittgenstein, the surrealists, and the American documentary realists of the 1920s and 1930s. (1986:8 and 10)

Our tradition grew out of that period of experimentation, but does it
partake of this one? Is it true in sociology, as anthropologists say it is
in their field, that "sympathetic readerships of experimental ethnographies scrutinize them, not with the hopes of finding a new paradigm, but rather with an eye for picking up ideas, rhetorical moves,
epistemological insights, and analytic strategies generated by different
research situations?" That the "liberating atmosphere of experimentation is in allowing each reader-cum-writer to work out incrementally
new insights?" That "specific works are of general interest as much for
what they are doing textually as for their contents?" (ibid.:41) Can we,
at least, list as many and varied experimental works of life history or
fieldwork done by symbolic interactionists as Clifford and Marcus
(1986) and Marcus and Fischer (1986) can list and discuss? No, we cannot. We will not speculate about the reasons for symbolic interactionists' apparent satisfaction with traditional modes of representation,
leaving that as a question for our readers to discuss. Instead, we turn
to a report of some questions life historians are asking and some answers our tradition provides.

— What They Ask and How We Answer

In this section of our news paper, we have used a dialogic format
to report some of the questions feminist, radical, critical, and experimental life historians are asking and some of the answers symbolic
interactionists can and do give. We found the questions for our dialogue in the published statements of people who work in this genre,
and the answers in the symbolic interactionist literature. We have not

introduced the speakers in the way scholars customarily do, with interpretations of their meaning. We do not wish to privilege our interpretations in that way. We brought the speakers together so our readers
could listen to the voices and arrive at their own interpretations of
what the voices have to say.

The Question of Meaning

The first question is: "What about meaning?" Feminist historians
have recently begun to question the accepted reason for recording oral
histories: to get "eyewitness" accounts of historic events and large-
scale social changes. They have begun to wonder, instead, about the
meanings eyewitnesses give to their own experiences.

> FEMINIST HISTORIAN: Why have not historians, and especially
> historians of women, pursued the subjective experience of
> the past more rigorously? My own interviews and those of
> others show a definite lack of questions about feelings, atti-
> tudes, values and meaning. Traditional historical sources tell
> us more about what happened and how it happened than
> how people felt about it and what it meant to them. As his-
> torians, we are trained to interpret meaning from facts. But
> oral history gives us the unique opportunity to ask people
> directly, How did it feel? What did it mean? (Anderson in
> Anderson et al. 1987:108–9)
>
> FEMINIST FIELDWORKER: In my own discipline of sociology
> there have been significant attempts to overcome the in-
> fluence of dominant ideologies by developing theories and
> methods of research that treat humans as active subjects and
> that consider the part meaning plays in social life. Despite
> the often greater visibility and prestige of abstract theories
> and quantitative analysis, the idea that meaning informs so-
> cial action and is a critical element in its study has been a
> theme running through the history of sociology. . . .
>
> Sociologists in this tradition assume that people's perspec-
> tives and subjective interpretations inform and organize their
> courses of action. They do not treat subjective orientations
> as biases to be eliminated from their studies, as do quantita-
> tively oriented sociologists—quite the opposite. Subjectivity
> is central to their understanding of social action. In their
> lives, people constantly interpret their situations and act in
> terms of the meanings or perspectives they develop within
> particular situations and from specific positions within or-
> ganizations and groups. They view society as a plurality of

interacting and competing groups, each of which develops collective solutions to the problems encountered in their shared situations. In such a society there is no neutral vantage point but only the different viewpoints generated within variously situated collectivities.

Subjective accounts have been useful to symbolic interactionists for many of the same reasons that they are important in women's studies research today. Both oral historians and sociologists often depend upon these to uncover aspects of social life that had been socially invisible and to analyze and interpret social reality from a new vantage point. The very first symbolic interactionists were concerned with socially marginal people and with the theoretical understanding of marginalizing processes such as the production of deviant statuses. Certainly these substantive and theoretical concerns bring them close to the students of women's lives. (Wittner in Anderson et al. 1987:120–21)

Experimental ethnographers and "anthropologists of experience" are also asking questions about meaning, questions that radically alter the meaning of their own concept of culture.

EXPERIMENTALIST: Modernist ethnography is focused primarily on delivering a message by manipulating the form of a text and is radically concerned with what can be learned from another culture from full attention to the enactment of the research process itself. . . .

There is a potential in modernist ethnography for considerable experimentation with textual presentation, some of which has taken its cues from French surrealist, structuralist, and poststructuralist literary theory. Modernist writers seem to be holding the conventional use of the concept of culture itself in question. This is what makes them so potentially radical. Most of the personhood ethnographies [including life histories] still rely firmly on a conventional notion of a shared cultural system on which to build their texts. Experience is thus a direct outcome or reflection of coherent sets of cultural codes and meanings. This is not necessarily the case for those who write with the dialogic motif at the center of their texts. They are at the very least uncertain about the coherence of culture in terms in which anthropology has developed this concept. Starting from such uncertainty, they can do no other than to concentrate upon the immediacy of discourse and the dialogic experience of fieldwork. (Marcus and Fischer 1986:67–68)

EXPERIENTIALIST: The anthropology of experience turns our attention to experience and its expressions as indigenous meanings. The advantage of beginning the study of culture through expressions is that the basic units of analysis are established by the people we study rather than by the anthropologist as alien observer. By focusing on narratives or dramas or carnival or any other expressions, we leave the definition of the unit of investigation up to the people, rather than imposing categories from our own evershifting theoretical frames. . . .

It is in the performances of an expression that we re-experience, re-live, re-create, re-tell, re-construct, and re-fashion our culture. The performance does not release a preexisting meaning that lies dormant in the text. . . . Rather, the performance itself is constitutive. Meaning is always in the present, in the here and now, not in such past manifestations as historical origins or author's intentions. Nor are here silent texts, because once we attend to the text, giving voice or expression to it, it becomes a performed text, active and alive. It is what Victor Turner called "putting experience into circulation." (E. Bruner 1986a:11, 12)

These anthropologists are not necessarily asking symbolic interactionists about meaning, but if they did, we could answer:

SYMBOLIC INTERACTIONIST: Culture [is] a consequence (in this kind of sociological thinking) of the existence of a group of acting people. It has its meaning as one of the resources people draw on in order to coordinate their activities. In this it differs from most anthropological thinking in which the order of importance is reversed, culture leading a kind of independent existence as a system of patterns that make the existence of larger groups possible.

Given new conditions, people invent culture. The way they do it was suggested by William Graham Sumner a century ago in *Folkways*. We can paraphrase him in this way. A group finds itself sharing a common situation and common problems. Various members of the group experiment with possible solutions to those problems and report their experiences to their fellows. In the course of their collective discussion, the members of the group arrive at a definition of the situation, its problems and possibilities, and develop a consensus as to the most appropriate and efficient ways of behaving. This consensus thenceforth constrains the activities of individual members of the group, who will probably act on it, given the opportunity. In other words, new situations provoke new behavior. But people generally find themselves in company when dealing with these new situations, and since they arrive at their solutions collectively, each assumes that the others share them. The beginnings of new shared understandings thus come into play quickly and easily. (Becker 1982:515, 20–521)

Because symbolic interactionists understand the problem of cultural meaning in this way, we have a way of interpreting both the contents of life histories and the act of telling autobiographical stories. We understand that telling stories is one of the ways people "report their experiences to their fellows," or share their experiential solutions to common problems, and thus, create culture: shared understandings of their common situations and agreed-upon ways of acting in them.

"The Significance of Storytelling": A Human Interest Story by Michal M. McCall

Five of my storytelling groups were made up of people born in the 1940s, during and just after World War II. Many of their stories contained reports of individual attempts to solve the problems they had in common by virtue of their shared position in history. For example, the stories they told about the families they grew up in and their stories of everyday life in their households in the present revealed one problem all of them had faced and some of their efforts to solve it: the profound change in the institution of the American family during their lifetime.

When these people were growing up, in the 1940s and 1950s, one family form was paradigmatic: it was modal—nearly everyone lived in one, and if not they knew their families were "deviant"—and it was fully institutionalized, supported by language, law, and custom. It was the family form demographers now call "traditional" to distinguish it from single-parent families, step-families, cohabiting couples, divorced and never-married adults living alone, childless couples, and families in which both parents work.

The most recent traditional family pattern in this country is that of "legal, lifelong, sexually exclusive marriage between one man and one woman, with children, where the male is the sole provider and ultimate authority." (Taubin and Mudd 1983:259).

In the 1980s, there is no modal family form, no single way the majority of people live. "[T]he traditional family—husband, wife, and children from the first marriage of the spouses—accounts for only 45 percent of American families. The next most frequent types are the single-parent family (15 percent) and the nuclear dyad—husband and wife alone without children (15 percent)" (Schorr and Moen 1983:575).

Some new forms, like the remarriages of divorced people with children, are "incompletely institutionalized," in Andrew Cherlin's words (1983). There are no established ways of doing many of the things people in them must do. No one knows the proper way of conversing on the telephone with her ex-husband's new wife, for example. No one knows the proper kinship term for the parents of her child's step-father either. Some new forms are not supported by law or public policy. For example, the single-parent family, the second most common family form in this country, is still considered a "deviant" form (Schorr and Moen 1983).

Without paradigms, people must work out new institutions, to solve the new life problems the old paradigm couldn't solve. Some of the solutions are creative. Always, they require inordinate amounts of time, energy, and goodwill. Jean Richards, for example, was a member of one storytelling group. She was married in 1961 and divorced in 1974, after thirteen years of marriage and four children. As a single parent, she had to devise a new way of life, without benefit of the paradigm she grew up with, or any other paradigm that might have provided her with ready-made solutions to the problems of raising and supporting four children alone. One of her creative solutions was the dressing room she made when she hung a curtain over the laundry-room doorway.

> 1973–4. The years that my life changed the most, personal changes, not global ones, changes caused by changes in interpersonal relationships, not world events. These were the years that "built character," tried my strength, patience and endurance. Ending a marriage and beginning an education, I literally bit off more than I could chew. I lost weight, developed ulcers, became temperamental, angry, sad, depressed, and ultimately BETTER.
>
> I asked all the questions, worried, struggled, and worked, and finally rose to the tasks at hand, successful. How would I make the house payment? Where would I get the money for food and clothes? How could I make the utility payments? What about Christmas? Who can I turn to? How will I ever manage? But then I finally knew that what I had must be worse than what was ahead and I persevered.

Because of all the personal trauma I experienced at this time, world events had little or no effect on me. After all, when you are worried about providing food for four kids, you have little time for self-actualization!

My routine was brutal. I got up early every day and drove to the St. Paul campus for classes (17 miles). I often took buses to the Mpls. campus during the mornings. At noon I ate a bagel and a cup of soup in the student center, often sitting with new acquaintances. I remember what a delight it was to find that there were many women my age in school. I had been encouraged by friends to go get a secretarial job (I was first rate); not attend school. They said I wouldn't fit in, no one in their 30s starts school, and besides, how would I provide for my family in the meantime. I, on the other hand, looked to the long term and knew that an investment in education would pay handsome dividends the rest of my life. This thinking, obviously, represented a major change from my perspective as a twenty-year-old.

Generally, I finished classes by 1:00 pm and drove immediately to my office job in the suburbs. . . . After work I drove 12 miles home and quickly fixed a nutritious dinner. We all ate together almost every night since the kids were 10, 9, 8 and 6—not yet involved in too many independent activities or jobs. I often threw clothes in the washer while we ate and dried them before bedtime. I always hung the clothes on a clothesline as they came out of the dryer. These clothes never made it to closets. The kids would just go into the laundry room, drop the clothes they were wearing right in place, and grab something from the line. Underwear and socks were in four plastic baskets and each kid took his/her own. This system was so handy, convenient, and private after I hung a curtain over the doorway. This was my way of accommodating reality.

After dinner, the kids did homework, watched TV or played outside. I called a friend and talked while I did the dishes. They drained dry. This done, I checked on the action and when possible began my homework. Usually, though, I worked with the kids on one thing or another and began my own homework at midnight. I often worked until 2–3 am, but ran on adrenalin and didn't need much sleep. 7:00 came awful early some days, though. On weekends I religiously cleaned the whole house—every week, whether company was coming or not. Then I did homework, shopped for groceries, or drove the kids to various friends or playgrounds, golf courses, swimming pools, etc. I seldom went out (read that never) until I met Bob. Then he'd

come by or I'd go into the city and we'd take in a movie. By
Saturday night this was a much deserved reward. Before Bob, I
stayed home and felt very lonely and sorry for myself, thinking
the whole world had something to do except me. As I developed a network of women friends these feelings and the emp-
tiness I lived with left.

Now I have way too much to do and am frazzled by it. This
week, for contrast, I have activities 7 nights straight. People
talk about bottoming out—these years of tremendous change,
stress, poverty were my bottom. Physically and mentally, I was
drained, always pushing and being pushed. Struggles then are
taken for granted things now . . . food in the cupboard, clothes
for everyone, a dependable car, gasoline money, bills paid on
time, a solid job, respect and credibility with friends and colleagues, an education, optimism, confidence, a support system,
and hopes and dreams.

Reading their stories aloud and discussing them, members of these storytelling groups also created new shared understandings of their lives
and of the life problems they shared. My life history research shows
how ordinary people create culture when they tell stories: how the
small, insignificant events of daily conversation, modeled somewhat
artificially in the activities of the storytelling groups I created, coalesce
in the broad shifts of cultural understanding we think of as social
change.

For example, the stories they told about daily meals in their households allowed them to show themselves and one another that they had
successfully changed the "cognitive, moral and esthetic premises or
categories" (Berger 1981) they used to interpret situations, construct
action, and identify themselves. In one group, Liz Davis showed that
she did not do all the child-rearing and housework, as her mother did,
and that she and her husband talked to their children, beyond telling
them to "Be quiet" or "Pass the salt." Joe Kamisky told how he "liber-
ated" himself from a traditional marriage and learned, from the woman
he later lived with, that cooking was a way of "sharing and becoming
closer." And Richard Peale showed that he respected the feminist principles of the woman he lived with, by telling about the meals he
cooked every day.

Storytelling with age-mates was also an opportunity to explain lack
of change. People admitted they did not always live up to the cultural
changes expected of them—or so it appeared—and explained why. Liz

Davis, for example, explained why she never finished her Ph.D. in chemistry even though her husband did, and why he had a fulltime academic position and she didn't.

> If you asked either of us whether a woman should give up her career for her husband's, we would say no. It just happened this way and for me, probably wouldn't have been as satisfactory in some other mode, given the parameters imposed by having to move so often. My husband is understanding, supportive, and helpful. On the whole, we have a good relationship, and have enjoyed much of our grand tour.

In another group, Jan Nordstrom explained why the division of household work in her marriage seemed traditional but wasn't.

> My husband has always been very considerate and an equal partner in so many important ways. It's still irritatingly true, however, that he gets lots of "credit" for doing traditionally female chores. As I look at my list of rules and practices in our marriage, I see that ours is quite a traditional division of labor. But I don't feel that the division is unfairly made. We usually operate on the practice that if there's a job to be done neither of us sits until the other can relax, too. We also have a marvelous rule: if you criticize the way something is done, you become the expert and it becomes your job.

Listeners in storytelling groups responded to stories of both change and lack of change with praise or encouragement, reassurance, and commiseration. Sometimes, they disagreed with the storyteller's interpretations or gave advice.

> At tonight's meeting, Joy took exception to Cathy's statement that her husband's hobbies were more important than Cathy's own, on weekends, because her time was more flexible and she could pursue her hobbies during the day, while she stayed home and raised the kids. Cathy thought it was only fair if he spent the day gardening or went off on his boat. Joy said, "My husband tried that one, too," but she didn't accept the idea because "you don't really have any flexibility when the kids are screaming for lunch." (Fieldnotes, October 27, 1982)

In all these ways listeners and storytellers shared information and interpretations. And they learned from one another, new ways of adjusting to change and solving their common problems—as the people in Jan's group, for example, learned her "marvelous rule." (McCall 1989).

"Playskool Plant Closing, Part I": A Human Interest Story by Judith Wittner

Interactionists study social organization as a negotiated order which emerges as people try, collectively and individually, to solve the problems they encounter in concrete situations. I studied women factory workers facing a plant closing in this way. My research began with questions about the role the women workers played in the events surrounding the plant closing; my method of inquiry followed from these questions. I conducted long interviews with thirty women once employed as assemblers, packers, and machine tenders by Playskool Toys, a factory that closed after more than half a century of operations in Chicago. My purpose was to understand the meaning of the plant closing to these workers in order to explain their responses to it.

Over the years, Playskool had grown from a family-owned business to become a subsidiary of a large corporation with headquarters far from Chicago. During its expansion, women—first white women and then Black and Hispanic women—came to fill most of the production jobs in the plant. When the impending closing was announced, community activists, local businessmen, and the city administration attempted to hold the company accountable to its employees through boycotts and legal action. Most of the women workers were not active in these struggles. Their quiescence was not remarkable to observers, because it fit well with the widely held assumption that factory women were politically passive. As I began to interview these workers on the eve of the final shutdown, these were my assumptions as well, and I wanted to know why and how the women maintained this stance.

The interviews revealed a less visible but nonetheless important dimension of workplace activism as women told stories of long years of involvement in shaping and reshaping their jobs and their place in the factory division of labor. Working together, they had developed their own distinctive perspectives on jobs, their own ways of regulating their time and effort, their own understandings of themselves as workers occupying women's places in the factory division of labor. The women helped to define and redefine their tasks, rights, and obligations in the factory and developed standards for evaluating jobs, bosses, and co-workers that reflected their own needs and interests. They calculated the worth of jobs not by pay alone, but also in terms of difficulty and interest. They agreed on norms that limited the profits the company could rightfully claim and criticized the company for violating these norms. They debated the merits and moral standing of various collective and individual strategies for controlling their work. Was it better to work hard for bonus pay or to pace oneself more slowly? Was a strike or a wage demand worth the risk to their jobs? When should workers stand by each other and when pursue their separate interests? How could jobs be redefined to ease the burdens of particular tasks and share them more equitably? Overcoming the internal divisions of age, language, and race that cross-cut the Playskool work force, they began to develop the capacity to speak as a community of workers. As the women's work force grew and as their years of experience accumulated, they more readily and more successfully argued with managers over how to reshape their tasks, control the pace of work, and increase their income.

The women's accounts are filled with descriptions of how they developed this capacity. For example, many recalled the days when women were reluctant to speak up if they disagreed with or felt abused by their bosses. They had trouble voicing their complaints and concerns because they did not feel comfortable speaking out of place, because they feared they would lose their jobs, or because they did not have the language skills or the nerve to stand up to their bosses. Many women had never before worked in a factory or on an assembly line and so were unsure about manufacturing procedures and shop-floor conventions. All operators were dependent on men with experience and technical knowledge to keep their work stations supplied with materials and in repair.

At first, many women endured their situation without comment. Keeping the job, and doing the job, was the important goal.

> I used to say nothing. If they tell me something I'd go ahead and do it and I wouldn't say nothing. And I had one boss, a setup guy. Oh my god, he'd yell at you over nothing, hardly. And you'd break a belt or something, you'd think you committed murder. Or break a drill. Because he had to set the machine, fix the machine. He'd get mad. He had some of them women to crying. He had me to crying a couple of times. That's why one day Jerry, the foreman, he said, "When are you gonna open your mouth to tell him off?" I said, "Oh I don't care. As long as I got a job, I don't care."

As these comments suggest, workers allowed their bosses wide latitude to teach them and direct their work. Yet, over time, they began to set limits, basing these on widely held cultural standards of fairness. For example, the woman quoted above finally spoke up when the set-up man blamed her for the mistakes of another worker.

> He blamed me for something I didn't do. . . . I was so mad I went off and I told (the foreman), "Give me the ticket," and I went back and I throwed it down to him and said, "You better make sure who done it before you blame somebody."

Another woman, an inspector, drew the line when she came under fire from one of the foremen for doing her job.

> One supervisor, he was a lieutenant or something in the army before, he would have the inspectors crying over in his department, because he'd yell at them and it upset them. They started to cry. [Why did he yell at them?] Because they reject something and he didn't want you to reject nothing in his department and we locked horns. He yelled at me. I told him I didn't care. Then he goes to get the supervisor and brings him over, that I was being disrespectful. He wanted me written up. Don't nobody yell at me. I'm not a dog.

Another worker spoke up when she had to relinquish an easy job to one of the foreman's favorites.

> [When did you first use your "big mouth?"] He had me to clamping and unclamping of the jigsaws and he had put me on the glue line. I was on the glue line first. That's an easy job. And one of his little friends that he liked didn't want to do the other, harder job, so he took me off and put her there and that's when I started running my mouth. I wasn't gonna do it and I started cursing. He said, "I'm gonna fire you for insubordination" and I said, "I don't give a fuck about no insubordination. I'm not doing this shit."

Women who were too frightened to speak for themselves found others who would.

> [The women] were always scared to say it to [the bosses]. They would say it to me. Like this one boss would harass the girls. They were scared of him. But I didn't give a damn. I wasn't scared to talk to him.

Because they articulated the anger that others also felt, outspoken women had wide influence. They also served as examples to other workers, making them bolder.

> I would do most of the talking. They would say, "Well Lois,
> you do the talking." And then once I start talking, then the
> other employees would come in and start talking about what
> they didn't like, you know. And usually the company would
> say, "Give us a couple of days and we'll get back to you," and
> in a couple of days they'd get back to me and let me know, and
> usually it'd wind up to our advantage.

Women on the shop floor also identified potential representatives
and pushed them to become active, as this woman's account of how
she became a union steward illustrates.

> Edna [chief steward] was working over that way in puzzles and
> they had no steward downstairs and all the girls would come
> to me and say, "Would you call Elsie and blah, blah, blah, blah."
> I could call her on the phone cause I had a phone close to me.
> So that's how I got involved in the union.

If we narrow the concept of political activism to include only participation in the last-ditch efforts to stop the plant closing, the wom-
en's part in shaping their work and challenging managerial authority
disappears. Knowledge of their everyday activism resides primarily in
women's memories and is retrievable principally through their own accounts. If they do not tell their stories, we cannot know how they
make sense of their experiences. If the women who worked at Playskool had not told their stories, we would not have known how they
made sense of their work, understood the possibilities and limits of the
struggle over the plant, and drew on their years of experience to choose
lines of action that, seen from the outside, only confirmed the stereo-
types we hold.

The Question of Context

A second question currently being asked by various life historians
is "What about context?" They are no longer willing to take life
histories out of their historical, class, and ethnic context or to assume
an individual narrator is typical of some larger group or category.
Feminists no longer assume there are common female experiences and
oppressions; racial, ethnic, and class differences are newly problematic for them. Experimental ethnographers are increasingly aware that
"closely observed cultural worlds are embedded in larger, more impersonal" state systems and in the world political economy (Marcus
1986:165–66). As a result, they, too, have begun to ask how "represen-

tative," of the populations whose experiences interest them, the life histories they collect and interpret are.

One interactionist answer to the question of context—of whether informants or life history narrators are typical of some larger group or category—is the search for negative cases, formalized in Lindesmith's technique of analytic induction (1947). Another is the use of theoretical sampling (Glaser and Strauss 1967) and various other nonprobability sampling procedures. A third is the idea that each case, however unrepresentative, adds a piece to our understanding of the human experience—what Park called the Big News.

> FEMINIST ORAL HISTORIAN: The greatest single criticism of oral
> history projects is that they are simply collections of indi-
> vidual interviews lacking a context. This criticism is com-
> pletely valid. We can greatly strengthen the validity of our
> interviews by paying attention to factors of class, race, age,
> and location when we select our narrators. . . .
>
> There is a considerable body of literature concerning sta-
> tistical sampling, size, randomness, and validity. Most of
> that literature does not fit oral history very well, where by
> definition we are dealing with the survivors, and only the
> willing ones at that. However, statistical measures should
> not just be ignored. Properly understood, statistics focus on
> important questions of representativeness and comparabil-
> ity. You must be aware of these issues. Save yourself some
> time and find a friendly sociologist or political scientist who
> has already struggled with these questions and can translate
> for you. (Armitage 1983:6)
> FRIENDLY SOCIOLOGIST: Field researchers are . . . constantly
> having to select locations, time periods, events, and people
> for study. . . . The basic distinction that is made by [social
> scientists] is between probability and non-probability meth-
> ods of sampling. . . . While both of these forms of sampling
> have been used by field researchers, it is non-probability
> sampling that is more often used and includes: judgment
> and opportunistic sampling [which involves] the selection
> of actions, events and people . . . for study according to a
> number of criteria established by the researcher such as
> their status (age, sex, and occupation) or previous experi-
> ence that endows them with special knowledge, snowball
> sampling, and theoretical sampling . . . [which] Glaser and
> Strauss (1968:45) define as "the process of data collection for
> generating theory whereby the analyst jointly collects, codes
> and analyzes his data and decides what data to collect next

and where to find them, in order to develop his theory as it emerges."... [D]ata collection is controlled by the emerging theory and the researcher has to consider: What groups or subgroups are used in data collection? For what theoretical purpose are the groups or subgroups used? Theoretical sampling therefore involves the researchers in observing groups with a view to extending, modifying, developing and verifying theory.... Glaser and Strauss's term "theoretical sampling" formalizes various activities [fieldworkers] consider ... important ... having enough evidence, having enough data in a particular area, and deciding when to move on to other related problems.... [I]n Smith and Keith's study of Kensington School [for example] this involved focusing on pupils of different age levels or divisions, examining independent study versus tradition versus basic skills and focusing on matters that were internal to the school and external to it." (Burgess 1984:54–56)

SECOND FRIENDLY SOCIOLOGIST: The image of the mosaic is useful in thinking about [the] scientific enterprise. Each piece added to a mosaic adds a little to our understanding of the total picture. When many pieces have been placed we can see, more or less clearly, the objects and the people in the picture and their relation to one another. Different pieces contribute different things to our understanding: some are useful because of their color, others because they make clear the outline of an object. No one piece has any great job to do; if we do not have its contribution, there are still other ways to come to an understanding of the whole....

Criteria have yet to be established for determining how much one piece of a mosaic contributes to the conclusions that are warranted by consideration of the whole, but these are just the kind of criteria that are needed. In their place, we can temporarily install a sympathetic appreciation of some of the functions performed by life history documents, taking *The Jack Roller* as a representative case.

What are those functions? In the first place, *The Jack Roller* can serve as a touchstone to evaluate theories that purport to deal with phenomena like those of Stanley's delinquent career ... any theory of delinquency must, if it is to be considered valid, explain or at least be consistent with the facts of Stanley's case as they are reported here. Thus, even though the life history does not in itself provide definitive proof of a proposition, it can be a negative case that forces us to decide a proposed theory is inadequate.

To say this is to take an approach to scientific generalization that deserves some comment. We may decide to accept
a theory if it explains, let us say, 95 percent of the cases that
fall in its jurisdiction. Many reputable scientists do. In contrast, one can argue that any theory that does not explain all
cases is inadequate, that other factors than those the theory
specifies must be operating to produce the result that we
want to explain. It is primarily a question of strategy. If we
assume that exceptions to any rule are a normal occurrence,
we will perhaps not search as hard for further explanatory
factors as we otherwise might. But if we regard exceptions
as potential negations of our theory, we will be spurred to
search for them. (Becker 1970:65–68)

The Question of Point of View

"From whose point of view is history told?" is a third question life
historians are asking. "Are we treating the people whose life histories
we collect as the subjects of history or as its objects?"

FEMINIST HISTORIAN: It is essential that women become historically visible, but only on terms that they themselves
have fully and consciously accepted. If this principle is ignored, women remain historical objects—just as they have
been in the past. If we do not respect the autonomy and authenticity of the women we interview, how can we then turn
around and use our information to illustrate the historical
validity and importance of those same principles? (Armitage
1983:4–5)

"Playskool Plant Closing, Part II": A Human Interest Story by Judith Wittner

Interactionists seldom see subordinates as victims, but rather look
at how they carve out autonomy despite their lack of formal power.
The women workers I interviewed, for example, successfully changed
the content of their jobs and the distribution of work between women
and men. When it came to ideas about gender differences, many of
them believed men and women were essentially different as workers.
These beliefs legitimated the sexual division of labor at Playskool,
which was typical of many factories. As machine tenders, assembly
workers, and packers, women were the direct producers of toys and
games. Men provided materials to the operators, built and repaired machines, supervised the women, and transported the finished products
to the warehouse and beyond.

The men I interviewed—both managers and hourly employees— believed that women's work was too boring and tedious for men. They gave women credit for the "skill" of managing boredom, and confessed that men were deficient in whatever women had that allowed them to tolerate such activity for long stretches of time. Many women respondents agreed that women workers tolerated boredom more readily and that they were better able than men to remain immobilized in front of a machine for eight hours.

When managers, under pressure from corporate headquarters to increase efficiency, attempted to place women in men's jobs, ideas about gender became weapons in the struggles that arose on the shop floor. Ironically, the managers justified their moves on the basis of equal rights for women, while women countered by refusing to take men's jobs. One woman recalled,

> They got so they started letting the women to do it too. That be like for the last five years or so. . . . If a man didn't come in. Like they were saying, "Well, you know you talking about women's lib, so do it. You women think you just as good as men, so do it." So I did. It make me no difference. I could do it too. Because some women would complain that the work was too hard. "This is too hard, this is a man's job." That's what the girls were saying, so he was saying, "There's no such thing as a man's job. You talking about you're wanting women's lib, so you got it. Do your job." So they would complain and they start crying. They refused to do it. They say it was a man's job. Most of the time they couldn't do it. But if you ask me, they could have did it if they want to, just take their time, just pick a little bit at a time and put it on.

Some women accepted the changes, though grudgingly. Paradoxically, affirmative action laws lent legitimacy to the new practice, though they seemed to make women's lot more difficult.

> Oh, we did all the jobs [then], and when they passed that what you call it, men and women equal, that's when we started doing the men's jobs. I said, "Well, I didn't vote for it." Some jobs you think your arms are gonna fall off.

An observer might interpret Playskool women's self-understanding as a form of false consciousness through which they were led to embrace their particular exploitation. From the vantage point of the women, however, this interpretation misses the important point that the women used the ideology of separateness to build consensus and reorganize their work in the factory. The transformation began with the women's complaints about heavy work, complaints that rested on the common understanding that "heavy work" was men's work. The complaints arose as foremen imposed new quotas and disciplines on the women, changes dictated by company headquarters in Massachusetts. By interpreting equal rights laws as justifying women's "right" to work harder, managers pushed the women to create alternatives to the conflict between the belief in women's natural fitness for certain jobs and the belief in equality and fair play. From the women's point of view, segregating women from men was less of a problem than were new management practices that increased women's work in the name of equality. Beginning from the women's experience, union stewards reworked the meanings of these beliefs and standards into a more far-reaching resolution of the conflict. They argued that the work at issue was too heavy for any worker, man or woman, and that it should be redefined and reorganized. Here is how Elise Burns, the chief steward, described it:

> Now there are some women who could do the job. Now we tried to evolve from that, which we did eventually. We tried to get a job where there were two people with even the men wouldn't get hernias. You're saying this is a man's job and a woman can't do it, so a woman shouldn't be there. But I'm saying that you should not only fight for equal rights. Equal rights also includes men. That they shouldn't be getting hernias. Women's rights are really helping the men and you say, why not have two people lift it, you know. And of course management would always say, "Oh, this is really unpractical." We'd say, "No, it's really practical, cause you get it done faster." It's just a matter of developing a system. On some jobs we got them to agree.

By extending their solution to all workers, the women's strategy changed the terms of the debate with bosses from one that focused on designating individuals for tasks, to one that sought to change the tasks themselves. This was a much more radical approach because it treated the division of labor as a social rather than a natural arrangement and claimed for workers as well as bosses the right to examine, criticize, and change their work to suit themselves. The women, through their union representatives, came to argue not that women were just as good as men, but that men deserved as much as women.

— What They Say That We Can Learn

Symbolic interactionists can also learn from feminists, critical theorists, literary theorists, postmodern anthropologists, and others who have thought about or done life history research. The two of us have learned most about authority, the selves constructed in life stories, and narrative.

Authority

From various disciplines and ideological positions, the new life historians are questioning some of our most sacred methodological and rhetorical principles. For example, they ask why we promise anonymity to the people whose life histories we record. Instead, they say, why not promise to name them? After all, as Chesnaux put it, we academics "set great store by 'name,' as in the phrase 'to make a name for oneself'" (Chesnaux 1978:106). The traditional answer is that people talk more freely, tell us more about themselves and their experience of social life, when they know we will protect their anonymity. Some consciously ideological life historians say, on the contrary, that people tell us something different, not necessarily something less, when they know they will be named, and that we are or should be interested in just that part of their experience they want to publicly own.

> FEMINIST HISTORIAN: I want the woman I interview to be actively responsible for what she says, so at the very beginning I tell her that the interview will be a public document, not a private conversation. I also want her to determine the shape she gives to her life. Within a chronological framework I use interview techniques that give her control over the structure of the interview: I hardly ever interrupt, and I do a great deal of active listening. I handle emotional topics carefully, and I am very respectful and slow moving. I do not confront and I do not probe: I wait for mutual trust. For me, rapport and genuine openness come slowly, as the result of many interviews. Although this technique is slow, it fits my personal style. However, I also insistently teach this technique to my students, regardless of their personal style, because I know that novice interviewers sometimes treat their narrators insensitively and hurt their feelings. I am more concerned about the quality of the interview for the narrator than I am about "getting" every last fact. Sometimes there is a loss of historical information with this technique, but that seems to me acceptable. (Armitage 1983:4)

Again, why do we distance ourselves from the texts we construct
with others' stories? Why privilege our scientific interpretations of
others' experiences? Shouldn't we speak as individuals in our texts?
Shouldn't we find ways to include narrators' interpretations of their
experiences? And why not quote our informants at length instead of
using short quotes? Because when we use short quotes we only include
that part of the others' story that supports our point? Because long
quotes introduce too much of the others' meaning and support different interpretations than our own? Our conventional practices, these
questioners point out, do little more than maintain our authority and,
thereby, the authority of the elite, the official, the educated, the middle
class, and the European, over the other.

> HISTORIAN OF ANTHROPOLOGY: Anthropological fieldwork has
> been represented as both a scientific "laboratory" and a per-
> sonal "rite of passage." The two metaphors capture nicely
> the discipline's impossible attempt to fuse objective and
> subjective practices. Until recently, this impossibility was
> masked by marginalizing the intersubjective foundations
> of fieldwork, by excluding them from serious ethnographic
> texts, relegating them to prefaces, memoirs, anecdotes, con-
> fessions, and so forth. Lately this set of disciplinary rules is
> giving way. The new tendency to name and quote informants
> more fully and to introduce personal elements into the text
> is altering ethnography's discursive strategy and mode of au-
> thority. (Clifford 1986:109)
> FEMINIST HISTORIAN: Surely this is where analysis must begin:
> with awareness of our own motivations, beliefs, and personal
> styles as interviewers. These personal qualities are usually
> the least obvious parts of any published study or article. It is
> rare to read a description of the interaction between inter-
> viewer and narrator, yet everything really depends on it. In
> some fields, such as anthropology, the life history method
> assumes the objectivity of the interviewer as a basic premise.
> I fundamentally do not believe in that idea. It is simply un-
> true to describe oneself as a neutral, anonymous observer,
> when, in fact, one has invested so much emotional effort and
> honesty in achieving rapport in the interview. The bond be-
> tween us and our narrators is close and meaningful, and
> ought to be acknowledged—professionally as well as person-
> ally. (Armitage 1983:4)
> HISTORIAN OF ANTHROPOLOGY: A scientific ethnography nor-
> mally establishes a privileged allegorical register it identifies

as "theory," "interpretation," or "explanation." But once all meaningful levels in a text including theories and interpretations, are recognized as allegorical, it becomes difficult to view one of them as privileged, accounting for the rest. Once this anchor is dislodged, the staging and valuing of multiple alleorical registers, or "voices" becomes an important area of concern for ethnographic writers. Recently this has sometimes meant giving indigenous discourse a semi-independent status in the textual whole, interrupting the privileged monotone of "scientific" representation. Much ethnography, taking its distance from totalizing anthropology, seeks to evoke multiple (not limitless) allegories. (Clifford 1986:103)

Life historians who are conscious of their own ideologies suggest we present ourselves in our texts as we are in our work: interviewers engaged in dialogues with other people who are informants and interpreters engaged in finding the meaning of the stories we hear and retell. At least, we should let our informants speak for themselves. At best, they suggest, we should teach informants to write their own life histories and the histories of their own communities, organizations, and oppressed groups so that they can "participate in setting the historical record straight" (Brecher 1986:6).

EXPERIMENTAL ETHNOGRAPHERS: Dialogue is the fashionable metaphor for modernist concerns. The metaphor can illegitimately be taken too literally or hypostatized into philosophical abstraction. It can, however, also refer to the practical efforts to present multiple voices within a text, and to encourage readings from diverse perspectives. This is the sense in which we use dialogue. . . .

The most interesting aspect of these efforts is their introduction of polyphony: the registering of different points of view in multiple voices. . . . Once this is done, either in terms of the direct inclusion of the material authored by others or in more sociological terms of the description of the idioms of different classes or interest groups—the text becomes more accessible to readerships other than the usually targeted professional one.

Vincent Crapanzano's *Tuhami: Portrait of a Moroccan* (1980) . . . is perhaps the most provocatively modernist of the texts we have considered. It presents a life history as the eliciting of an interview, as a puzzle, asking the reader's help in interpretation. . . . Crapanzano's text breaks the traditional life-history frame, and although it is "realistic" in attempting to represent the actual interview situation, it is one of the first major experiments to use self-consciously modernist techniques. It is fragmentary, almost surrealist in its force; it manipulates form to capture style, mood, and emotional tone; and it effectively engages the willing reader in the work of interpretation. (Marcus and Fischer 1986:68–72)

POSTMODERN ETHNOGRAPHER: A postmodern ethnography is fragmentary because it cannot be otherwise. Life in the field is itself fragmentary, not at all organized around familiar ethnographic categories such as kinship, economy, and religion. . . . At best, we make do with a collection of indexical anecdotes or telling particulars with which to portend that larger unity beyond explicit textualization. . . .

We confirm in our ethnographies our consciousness of the fragmentary nature of the postmodern world, for nothing so well defines our world as the absence of a synthesizing allegory, or perhaps it is only a paralysis of choice brought on by our knowledge of the inexhaustible supply of such allegories that makes us refuse the moment of aesthetic totalization, the story of stories, the hypostatized whole. (Tyler 1986: 131–32)

MARXIST HISTORIAN: In class societies, history is one of the tools the ruling class uses to maintain its power. The state apparatus tries to control the past at the level of both political action and ideology [and] conventional historians, with their pose of objectivity, pretend to be unaware that they are reinforcing the power of an institution or political apparatus by conferring upon it the authority of the past. . . . For peoples engaged in the fight for national and social liberation, the past is a political issue, a theme of struggle [because current political struggles are] nourished by the past. [Therefore, an academic historian must] no longer be satisfied to work . . . *on* peasant struggles or on American utopian communities; what is needed is the ability to work *with* the workers, the peasants, the people. (Chesnaux 1978:16, 22, 26, 107)

CRITICAL ETHNOGRAPHER: Neighborliness is what educational and pastoral workers have been doing in poor villages and neighborhoods in Latin America. It is a kind of praxis, practical activity . . . [with] an intellectual dimension. . . .

Ethnography already threatens "scientism." The notion that cultures are complex and whole and that they can be represented in their mundane density confronts the ten-

dency of scientism to reduce human agency and to decontex-
tualize action. . . .

I think the concept of neighborliness can extend these
qualities by highlighting the fact that research is action with
social and political dimensions. Given the hierarchical positions of universities and schools, relations between university
researchers and school teachers are unequal. Knowledge, pres-
tige, and the power of the profession belong to the researcher,
not the researched. Further, publishing what is learned from
the researched for a disciplinary community is an action that
has the possibility of advancing the career of the researcher
who uses the research as a marketable commodity. This action has the consequent possibility of separating and alienating the researcher more from the "ordinary" teachers. It is
the revulsion against what has been called this "rape model
of research" in which career advancement is built on "alienating and exploitative inquiry methods" that prompts ethnographers to share their findings with their subjects and has
suggested to Patti Lather that research findings should be
jointly negotiated with those who are researched. (Savage
1988 : 8,13–14)

NEW SOCIAL HISTORIAN: The movement for history from below has challenged not only the elitist conception of who
history is about, but also elitist notions of who should do
history and who it should be for. It has emphasized that not
only professional historians but also ordinary people who are
interested in the past of their families, communities, and organizations can contribute to the understanding of history.
And it has shown that history, properly presented, can find a
wide audience when it addresses matters which concern ordinary people.

The result has been an international movement of communities and workers investigating their own neighborhoods
and workplaces. In England, thousands of people have par-
ticipated in local "history workshops" which explore the
history of particular neighborhoods. . . . More dramatically,
when workers in Poland conducted a nationwide general
strike, occupied their own workplaces, and created their own
organization, Solidarity, one of the first things they did was
to try to record and uncover their own history. Through interviews with early participants, published in their local
union newsletters, they made sure that the story of their
own movement was preserved. . . .

This is a guide for people who are not professional historians but who want to explore the history of their own community, workplace, union, or local organization. It will tell you how to design a project you can do with the time and resources you have available; how to collect documents and do interviews; how to put together the material you gather; and how to present it to others in your group and community. (Brecher 1986:1, 2)

Selves

It is a commonplace in our tradition that people perceive themselves, have conceptions of themselves, communicate with themselves, and plan, organize and evaluate their own actions (Blumer 1969; Goffman 1959; McCall and Simmons 1966). We also have a tradition of reading life histories to understand people's conceptions of themselves and their evaluations of their own actions and careers (Becker 1970; Jones 1980; McCall 1985; Denzin 1986). We have considered life history a good way to study people's conceptions of themselves because we know that when we ask people to write life history we are eliciting autobiography and autobiography, as literary critics tell us, is "the activity of explaining oneself by telling one's story" (Stone 1982:10). The autobiographer "discovers who he is—*that?* he is—through inspection of what he has done. He deduces a self and accounts for it" (Spacks 1976:17–18). We know that the self explained in autobiography, like the self presented in interaction, is an image of social life; explaining themselves, autobiographers explain what they understand about society and social change.

Recently, life history researchers from other traditions have begun to talk this way about stories and selves:

[In some of the best recent work] the life history ... is no longer simply a narrative frame for stringing together life-cycle rituals, socialization patterns, and a generational history as experienced by one individual; nor is it left to unique individuals. Indeed, life history deconstructs in the fullest sense: not making the subject disappear, but rather illuminating the social and constructive elements of an individual that make him or her potent in social context. Insofar as life history is the locus of experience it is important to specify the cultural meanings that figure and compose it. (Marcus and Fischer 1986:182–83)

Some of them have gone beyond our recognition that we can read selves in the life histories we elicit. They point out that everyday sto-

rytelling is as important as everyday interaction to the construction
and maintenance of self.

> FIRST ANTHROPOLOGIST: [The] people [I studied], like so many
> of the elderly, were very fond of reminiscing and storytelling,
> eager to be heard from, eager to relate parts of their life his-
> tory. More afraid of oblivion than pain or death, they always
> sought opportunities to become visible. Narrative activity
> among them was intense and relentless. . . . In their stories,
> as in their cultural dramas, they witnessed themselves, and
> thus knew who they were, serving as subject and object at
> once. They narrated themselves perpetually, in the form of
> keeping notes, journals, writing poems and reflections spon-
> taneously, and also telling their stories to whoever would
> listen. Their histories were not devoted to marking their
> successes or unusual merits. Rather they were efforts at or-
> dering, sorting, explaining—rendering consistent their long
> life, finding integrating ideas and characteristics that helped
> them know themselves as the same person over time, despite
> great ruptures and shifts. (Myerhoff 1978:33–34)
>
> SECOND ANTHROPOLOGIST: By considering two current notions
> of ethnographic description, ethnoscientific models of emic
> analysis and detailed monographs as versions of realism, we
> can ask how anthropologists should represent other people's
> lives. Despite their proven strengths, I shall argue in what
> follows that ethnoscience and ethnographic realism share a
> specific limitation. Neither approach makes central the sto-
> ries people tell themselves about themselves and this crucial
> omission robs a certain human significance from anthropo-
> logical accounts. Ethnographers can learn much about mean-
> ingful action by listening to storytellers as they depict their
> own lives. . . .
>
> Rather than seeing human activities unfold through such
> programmed sequences as the daily round, the annual cycle,
> or the life cycle . . . I will attempt to show how narrative can
> provide a particularly rich source of knowledge about the sig-
> nificance people find in their workaday lives. Such narratives
> often reveal more about what can make life worth living
> than about how it is routinely lived. (Rosaldo 1986:97–98)
>
> PSYCHOLOGISTS: In developing a self-narrative the individual
> attempts to establish coherent connections among life
> events. . . . Rather than seeing one's life as simply "one
> damned thing after another," the individual attempts to

understand life events as systematically related. They are
rendered intelligible by locating them in a sequence or "unfolding process." One's present identity is thus not a sudden
and mysterious event, but a sensible result of a life story. As
Bettelheim has argued, such recreations of narrative order
may be essential in giving one's life a sense of meaning and
direction. (Gergen and Gergen 1983:252).

Another recent development is the recognition, by experimental anthropologists, that autobiographical selves may be a culture-bound
phenomenon. Clifford, for example, has argued that "the exemplary,
coherent self (or rather, the self pulling itself together in autobiography)" is "a potent and pervasive mechanism for the production of
meaning in the West," but that there is "nothing universal or natural
about the fictional processes of biography and autobiography" (Clifford 1986b:106). Marcus and Fischer have added,

The Samoan language has no terms corresponding to "personality, self, character"; instead of our Socratic "know thyself,"
Samoans say "take care of the relationships"; instead of the
European image of a rounded, integrated personality, like a
sphere with no sides, Samoans are like gems cut with many
distinct sides. The greater the number of sides, or parts, defined
by relationships, the more brilliant the form, the greater the
craft and skill of the person. Personal qualities are relative to
context rather than descriptive of a persistent and consistent
quality or essence. Samoans comment upon these differences
in concepts of personhood between Euro-Americans and Samoans as much as do Westerners themselves. The Samoan
sense of shifting, flexible personhood explains the difficulty
traditional anthropological theory has had in accommodating
Samoans within its constructs of kinship systems as static
frameworks of roles associated with well-defined rights and obligations. (1986:65)

Narrative

The renewed interest in life history research we have been discussing is, in part, a result of recent changes in the scholarly reputation of
narrative representations. Proponents of narrative deny that all stories
and, among modes of representation, *only* stories are fictions and
myths. According to Geertz, for example, "anthropological writings
are themselves interpretations [and] thus, fictions: fictions in the sense
that they are 'something made,' something fashioned'—the original

meaning of *fictio*—not that they are false, unfactual, or merely 'as if' thought experiments" (1973:15).

Proponents of narrative also deny that stories are cognitively inferior to scientific modes of representation, "belonging to a different mentality: savage, primitive, underdeveloped, backward," and, therefore, "fit only for women and children" (Lyotard 1984:27). According to this view, the tendency "to depreciate narrative as a form of knowledge, and the personal narrative particularly, in contrast to other forms of discourse considered scholarly, scientific, technical or the like ... [is merely] part of a general predisposition in [Western] culture to dichotomize forms and functions of language use, and to treat one side of the dichotomy as superior, the other side as something to be disdained, discouraged, diagnosed as evidence or cause of subordinate status" (Hymes 1980:129).

Conversely, symbolic interactionists who talk about and do life history research have benefited from the narrative theories that brought about this change. In a series of frequently cited articles, the humanist Louis O. Mink has argued that narrative is "not just a technical problem for writers and critics but a fundamental mode of comprehension ... irreducible to other [modes] or to any more general mode" (quoted in White 1981:252). Similarly, the literary critic Barbara Hardy (1975) has argued that narrative is a "common human possession," a "primary act of mind transferred to art from life" and not an "aesthetic invention" of literary artists. More recently, Jerome Bruner, the cognitive psychologist, has argued that stories and arguments are "two modes of cognitive functioning, two modes of thought, each providing distinctive ways of ordering experience, of constructing reality" and that each has its own "criteria of well-formedness" and "procedures for verification":

> A good story and a well-formed argument are different natural kinds. Both can be used as means for convincing another. Yet what they convince of is fundamentally different: arguments convince one of their truth, stories of their lifelikeness. The one verifies by eventual appeal to procedures for establishing formal and empirical proof. The other establishes not truth but verisimilitude. It has been claimed that one is a refinement of or an abstraction from the other. But this must be either false or true only in the most unenlightening way. (J. Bruner 1986:11)

Building on the insights of various narrative theorists, Norman Denzin has proposed that we use authenticity, thick description, and verisimilitude as standards for interpreting life histories and other qualitative (anecdotal, case study) data:

> Elsewhere . . . I have reviewed the matters of reliability, external and internal validity, sampling representativeness, generalizability, causal adequacy, and causal analysis and suggested strategies for confronting these traditional quantitative questions. In this chapter, I will address the questions of authenticity, thick description, and verisimilitude. Traditional, positivistic, quantitative criteria of evaluation are not relevant when the investigator is committed to the qualitative study of everyday life.
>
> Authenticity raises the criterion of lived relevance. Are the researcher's observations and records grounded in the natural, everyday language, behaviors, meanings, and interactions of those studied? If they are authentically real, the world of the subject speaks through the researcher's document. . . . An authentic document discloses the hiddenness of the world and reveals its underlying problematic and the structures that are taken for granted. . . .
>
> An authentic document rests on thick description. . . . A thick description goes beyond fact to detail, context, emotion, and webs of relationship. In a thick description, the voices, feelings, and meanings of persons are heard. In the social sciences, thin descriptions abound and find their expression in correlation coefficients, path diagrams, F-ratios, dummy variables, structural equations, tests of significance, and social indicators. Thick descriptions are exceedingly rare, yet they are the stuff of interpretation and qualitative evaluation in the social sciences.
>
> Verisimilitude derives from authentic, thick descriptions. It is achieved when the author of a document brings the life world alive in the mind of the reader. The intent of verisimilitude is to convey that the experiences recorded and experienced by the observer would have been sensed by the reader, had he been present during the actual moments of interaction that are reflected in the document.
>
> If one's goal is the understanding and interpretation of the world as it is lived, experienced, and practiced, then the methodological strategies discussed in this chapter seem warranted. (Denzin 1982:20–21, 25)

Recently, some interpretive anthropologists have suggested that narrative theories are also culture-bound. Because most theorists work with texts and ignore storytelling as a social act, they often commit the errors of presentism and ethnocentrism.

> Although they find certain tales to be better told than others, Ilongots claim that listing the place-names where somebody walked is just as much a story (and indeed cannot be omitted from any true story) as a more fully elaborated narrative. Perhaps this indigenous viewpoint can be placed in sharper relief by juxtaposing minimal Ilongot narratives and history's conventional threefold division into the annals, the chronicle, and history proper. Ordered only by chronological sequence rather than narrative logic, Ilongot hunting stories resemble the lowest order of historical texts: that is, they resemble annals, not chronicles, and certainly not history proper. Yet precisely where historical studies see differences of this kind, Ilongots perceive only differences in degree. Indeed, I shall argue that [the] ethnographic evidence suggests that history's threefold division, particularly insofar as it is hierarchical and evolutionary, derives more from parochial modern canons of narrative excellence than from the realities of other times and places. In this respect, we can lump together the errors of presentism and ethnocentrism.
>
> Even the most astute historical thinkers could learn from what Ilongots tell in their minimal story form. Hayden White (1980:12), for example, claims that in the annals, "social events are apparently as incomprehensible as natural events. . . . In fact, it seems that their importance consists of nothing other than the fact that they were recorded." In other words, the events recorded read like a random list that neither elaborates linkages between events nor tells readers about the greater and lesser significance of specific recorded items. Thus, according to White, events matter only because they are written down, and once recorded they assume equal import. White ignores the fact that people whose biographies significantly overlap can communicate rich understandings in telegraphic form. People who share a complex knowledge about their worlds can assume a common background and speak through allusion, whereas writers in the modern world of print must spell things out for their relatively unknown readers. (Rosaldo 1986:106–8)

One exception is Barbara Herrnstein Smith, a literary critic who has proposed an alternative to the "current narratological model." In Smith's alternative model, narratives are "regarded not only as structures but also as acts, the features of which—like the features of all other social acts—are functions of the variable sets of conditions in response to which they are performed" (Smith 1981:182).

> [We] might conceive of narrative discourse most minimally and most generally as verbal acts consisting of *someone telling someone else that something happened*. Among the advantages of such a conception is that it makes explicit the relation of narrative discourse to other forms of discourse and, thereby, to verbal, symbolic, and social behavior generally. . . .
>
> A second, related advantage of conceiving of narrative this way—which is to say, as part of a *social transaction*—is that it encourages us to notice and explore certain aspects of narrative that tend to remain obscure or elusive when we conceive of it primarily as a kind of text or structure or any other form of detached and decontextualized entity. For it suggests not only that every telling is produced and experienced under certain social conditions and constraints and that it always involves two parties, an audience as well as a narrator, but also that, as in any other social transaction, each party must be individually motivated to participate in it: in other words, that each party must have some interest in telling or listening to that narrative.
>
> The significance of this emphasis for narrative theory is that it suggests why, in seeking to account for either the forms and features of individual narratives or the similarities and differences among sets of narratives, we might profitably direct our attention to the major variables involved in those transactions: that is to the particular motives and interests of narrators and audiences and to the particular social and circumstantial conditions that elicit and constrain the behavior of each of them. (ibid.:182–84)

The significance of Smith's model for symbolic interaction theory is that it directs us to consider storytelling as a collective activity, whether in life history interviews, in storytelling groups, or in everyday life, and to use our tradition to study all kinds of storytelling. That is, we can see stories and other modes of representing knowledge about society as "ways some people tell what they think they know to other people who want to know it, as organized activities shaped by the joint efforts of everyone involved":

> The form and content of representations vary because social organzation shapes not only what is made, but also what people want their representation to do, what job they think they need done (like finding their way or knowing what the

latest findings in their field are), and what standards they will use to judge it. Because the jobs users call on representations to do depend so heavily on organizational definitions, we [need not be] concerned with . . . what is the best way [to represent knowledge of social life]. . . . It seems more useful, more likely to lead to new understanding, to think of every way of representing social reality as perfect—for something. The question is what it is good for. The answer to that is organizational. (Becker 1986:123–125)

CONCLUSION

Symbolic interaction's theoretical and methodological tradition could help the new life historians understand the stories they hear in terms of meaning, context, and perspective. It could help them to approach the task of describing and analyzing social groups as concrete, complex, dense, and dynamic wholes. But symbolic interactionists have at least as much to learn from the greater willingness of life historians in anthropology and literature to take their project to its logical conclusion by trying to develop new forms of analysis and presentation that support rather than undermine their own meanings and intentions. What does it mean for our work to speak of subjects and agency if our analysis functions as the authoritative voice, controlling subjects' speech and interpreting it for the audience? In sociology, symbolic interactionists have challenged conventional ways of studying society. Can we continue that challenge without a critical look at how standards of presentation and forms of authority support each other? This paper has experimented with new ways of presenting and representing knowledge of social life. We see storytelling as the foundation of what we know and how we know it, as sociologists and as members of society. We ought to join our colleagues in other disciplines and begin to build this insight into the form as well as the content of our work.

And that's the news.

NOTES

1. Patti Lather has written, "While in my earlier work I used the term 'openly ideological', I find 'praxis-oriented' better describes the emergent paradigm I have been tracking over the last few years. 'Openly ideological' invites comparisons with fundamentalist and conservative movements, whereas 'praxis-oriented' clarifies the critical and empowering roots of a research paradigm openly committed to critiquing the status quo and building a more just society" (1986:258). Although we agree with Lather, we have used the terms

"consciously ideological" and "openly ideological" in this paper because we think their meaning is more obvious.

2. In deference to the title of this symposium, we have used the terms symbolic interaction and symbolic interactionist in this paper, although, following Chapoulie (1987), we prefer to call ourselves fieldworkers and our life history research fieldwork.

REFERENCES

Anderson, Kathryn, Susan Armitage, Dana Jack, and Judith Wittner. 1987. "Beginning Where We Are: Feminist Methodology in Oral History." *Oral History Review* 15 (Spring):103–27.

Armitage, Susan. 1983. "The Next Step." *Frontiers* 8 (no. 1):3–8.

Becker, Howard S. 1970. *Sociological Work*. Chicago: Aldine.

———. 1973. *Outsiders: Studies in the Sociology of Deviance*. New York: Free Press.

———. 1982. "Culture: A Sociological View." *Yale Review* (Summer):513–27.

———. 1986. "Telling About Society." Pp. 121–36 in *Doing Things Together*. Evanston: Northwestern University Press.

Berger, Bennett M. 1981. *The Survival of a Counterculture*. Berkeley: University of California Press.

Blumer, Herbert. 1969. *Symbolic Interactionism: Perspective and Method*. Englewood Cliffs, NJ: Prentice Hall.

Brecher, Jeremy. 1986. *History from Below: How to Uncover and Tell the Story of Your Community, Association, or Union*. New Haven: Commonwealth Pamphlets/Advocate Press.

Bruner, Edward. 1986a. "Introduction: Experience and Its Expressions." Pp. 3–30 in *The Anthropology of Experience*, edited by Victor Turner and Edward Bruner. Chicago: University of Chicago Press.

———. 1986b. "Ethnography as Narrative." Pp. 139–155 in *The Anthropology of Experience*, edited by Victor Turner and Edward Bruner. Chicago: University of Chicago Press.

Bruner, Jerome. 1986. *Actual Minds, Possible Worlds*. Cambridge, MA: Harvard University Press.

Burgess, Robert G. 1984. *In the Field: An Introduction to Field Research*. London: George Allen and Unwin.

Chapoulie, Jean-Michel. 1987. "Everett C. Hughes and the Development of Fieldwork in Sociology." *Urban Life* 15 (January):259–97.

Cherlin, Andrew. 1983. "Remarriage as an Incomplete Institution." Pp. 388–402 in *Family in Transition*, edited by Arlene S. Skolnick and Jerome H. Skolnick. Boston: Little, Brown.

Chesnaux, Jean. 1978. *Pasts And Futures or What Is History For?* London: Thames and Hudson.

Clifford, James. 1986b. "On Ethnographic Allegory." Pp. 98–121 in *Writing Culture: The Poetics and Politics of Ethnography,* edited by James Clifford and George E. Marcus. Berkeley, CA: The University of California Press.

———, and George E. Marcus (eds). 1986. Writing Culture: The Poetics and Politics of Ethnography. Berkeley: University of California Press.

Conquergood, Dwight. 1987. "Performance Paradigms and Cultural Studies: Conceptual Boundaries and Research Agendas." Unpublished paper presented at the Speech Communication Association Convention, Boston, November.

Crapanzano, Vincent. 1980. *Tuhami: Portrait of a Moroccan.* Chicago: University of Chicago Press.

Denzin, Norman K. 1982. "Contributions of Anthropology and Sociology to Qualitative Research Methods." Pp. 17–26 in *New Directions for Institutional Research: Qualitative Method for Institutional Research,* edited by E. Kuhns and S. V. Martorana. San Francisco: Jossey-Bass.

———. 1986. *The Alcoholic Self.* Beverly Hills, CA: Sage Publications.

Gardner, James B., and George Rollie Adams. 1983. *Ordinary People and Everyday Life: Perspectives on the New Social History.* Nashville, TN: American Association for State and Local History.

Geertz, Clifford. 1973. *The Interpretation of Cultures.* New York: Basic Books.

———. 1983. *Local Knowledge.* New York: Basic Books.

Gergen, Kenneth J., and Mary M. Gergen. 1983. "Narratives of the Self." Pp. 251–273 in *Studies in Social Identity,* edited by T.R. Sarbin and K.E. Scheibe. New York: Praeger.

Glaser, Barney G. and Anselm L. Strauss. 1967. *The Discovery of Grounded Theory.* Chicago: Aldine.

Gluck, Sherna. 1977. "What So Special about Women? Women's Oral History." *Frontiers* 7 (No. 2): 3–14.

Goffman, Erving. 1959. *The Presentation of Self in Everday Life.* Garden City, NY: Doubleday Anchor.

Grele, Ronald J. 1975. "Movement without Aim." Pp. 126–54 in *Envelopes of Sound,* edited by Ronald J. Grele. Chicago: Precedent Publishing

Hardy, Barbara. 1975. *Tellers and Listeners: The Narrative Imagination.* London: Athlone Press.

Hughes, Everett C. 1971. *The Sociological Eye.* Chicago: Aldine.

Hymes, Dell, with Courtney Cazden. 1980. "Narrative Thinking and

Story-Telling Rights: A Folklorist's Critique of Education." Pp. 126–38 in *Language in Education: Essays in Ethnolinguistics.* Washington, DC: Center for Applied Linguistics.

Jones, Wendy L. 1980. "Newcomers' Biographical Explanations: The Self as Adjustment Process." *Symbolic Interaction* 3:83–94.

Lather, Patti. 1986. "Research as Praxis." *Harvard Educational Review* 56 (August):257–77.

Lieberson, Stanley. 1985. *Making It Count: The Improvement of Social Research and Theory.* Berkeley: University of California Press.

Lindesmith, Alfred R. 1947. *Opiate Addiction.* Bloomington, IN: Principia Press.

Lyotard, Jean-François. 1984. *The Postmodern Condition: A Report on Knowledge.* Translated from the French by Geoff Bennington and Brian Massumi. Minneapolis: University of Minnesota Press.

Marcus, George E., and Michael M. J. Fischer. 1986. *Anthropology as Cultural Critique: An Experimental Moment in the Human Sciences.* Chicago: University of Chicago Press.

Marcus, George E. 1986. "Contemporary Problems of Ethnography in the Modern World System" Pp. 165–93 in *Writing Culture: The Poetics and Politics of Ethnography,* edited by James Clifford and George E. Marcus. Berkeley: University of California Press.

McCall, George J., and J. L. Simmons. 1966. *Identities and Interactions.* New York: The Free Press.

McCall, Michal M. 1989. "The Significance of Storytelling." *Life Stories/Récits de vie.* 5. Forthcoming.

———. 1985. "Life History and Social Change." *Studies in Symbolic Interaction* 6: 169–82.

Myerhoff, Barbara. 1978. *Number Our Days.* New York: Simon and Schuster.

Owens, Craig. 1983. "The Discourse of Others: Feminists and Postmodernism." Pp. 57–81 in *The Anti-Aesthetic: Essays on Postmodern Culture,* edited by Hal Foster. Port Townsend, WA: Bay Press.

Plummer, Ken. 1983. *Documents of Life: An Introduction to the Problems and Literature of a Humanistic Method.* London: George Allen and Unwin.

Ragin, Charles. 1987. *The Comparative Method: Moving Beyond Qualitative and Quantitative Strategies.* Berkeley: University of California Press.

Rosaldo, Renato. 1986. "Ilongot Hunting as Story and Experience." Pp. 97–138 in *The Anthropology of Experience,* edited by Victor Turner and Edward Bruner. Chicago: University of Chicago Press.

Savage, Mary C. 1988. "Can Ethnographic Narrative Be a Neighborly Act?" *Anthropology and Education Quarterly* 19 (March): 3–19.

Schorr, Alvin L. and Phyllis Moen. 1983. "The Single Parent and Public Policy." Pp. 575–86 in *Family in Transition,* edited by Arlene S. Skolnick and Jerome H. Skolnick. Boston: Little, Brown.

Smith, Barbara Herrnstein. 1981. "Narrative Versions, Narrative Theories." Pp. 162–86 in *American Criticism In the Post-Structuralist Age,* edited by Ira Konigsberg. Ann Arbor, MI: Michigan Studies in the Humanities.

Spacks, Patricia Meyer. 1976. *Imagining a Self: Autobiography and the Novel in Eighteenth Century England.* Cambridge, MA: Harvard University Press.

Stone, Albert E. 1982. *Autobiographical Occasions and Original Acts.* Philadelphia: University of Pennsylvania Press.

Taubin, Sara B., and Emily H. Mudd. 1983. "Contemporary Traditional Families: The Undefined Majority." Pp. 256–68 in *Contemporary Familes and Alternative Lifestyles,* edited by Eleanor D. Macklin and Roger H. Rubin. Beverly Hills, CA: Sage Publications.

Tyler, Stephen A. 1986. "Post-Modern Ethnography: From Document of the Occult to Occult Document." Pp. 122–41 in *Writing Culture: The Poetics and Politics of Ethnography,* edited by James Clifford and George E. Marcus. Berkeley: University of California Press.

Tyrrell, Ian. 1986. *The Absent Marx: Class Analysis and Liberal History in Twentieth Century America.* Westport, CT: Greenwood Press.

Watson, Lawrence C., and Maria-Barbara Watson-Franke. 1985. *Interpreting Life Histories: An Anthropological Inquiry.* New Brunswick, NJ: Rutgers University Press.

White, Hayden. 1980. "The Value of Narrativity in the Representation of Reality." *Critical Inquiry* 7:5–27.

———. 1981. "The Narrativization of Real Events." Pp. 249–51 in *On Narrative,* edited by W.J.T. Mitchell. Chicago: University of Chicago Press.

Zunz, Oliver, ed. 1985 *Reliving the Past: The Worlds of Social History.* Chapel Hill: University of North Carolina Press.

Studying Religion
in the Eighties
Mary Jo Neitz

At one time sociologists pretty much assumed that if one knew a person's ethnicity, class, and region, one could predict his or her religious preference. If one knew religious preference one could predict religious beliefs and attitudes on a score of questions ranging from abortion to nuclear disarmament. Everyone knew that Irish and Italian residents of old industrial cities were Catholics, prayed to Mary, believed that sex was sinful, and voted for liberal Democratic candidates. Everyone knew that Pentecostals lived in the South (or had recently relocated in northern cities where they felt far from home); white or black, they had little education and made little money, spoke in tongues, believed that drinking and dancing were sinful, and were politically conservative and/or outside the political process. These correspondences no longer adequately describe religion in American society (if they ever did), and, in attempting to understand recent changes in religious phenomena, sociology of religion has adopted approaches that bring it very close to the traditional concerns of symbolic interactionists. I suggest that symbolic interaction is well suited to helping us understand the fluid relationships that today often obtain between religions and social structures and between religions and cultural change, as well as the personal transformations experienced by individuals moving between religious systems of meaning.

CHANGES IN AMERICAN RELIGION

The last twenty-five years have seen the appearance of Charismatics and Neo-Pentecostals in the mainline denominations, the growth of fundamentalism, the appearance of "new religions," and an increasing involvement of religion in politics, left and right, throughout the world. My own observation of religion began in this dynamic period. In 1977 I was teaching at a Catholic college in northern Indiana, and I encountered among my students—who were preparing for careers in social work and counselling—enthusiastic participants in Catholic Pentecostalism. These upwardly mobile, college-educated young people were speaking in tongues and practicing faith healing within the Catholic church. I made an appointment to see Andrew Greeley at the National Opinion Research Center, and I asked him whether we had any survey data on whether or not Catholics before this had believed that accepting Jesus into their hearts meant they were saved. Greeley told me that this was not a Catholic question and that nobody had asked it.[1] When I accompanied my students to their prayer group in a prosperous suburb, I met lawyers and business executives, hardly the dispossessed individuals deprivation theory led me to expect in such a religious setting. My sociological training had not prepared me very well for neo-Pentecostalism.

R. Stephen Warner has argued that sociologists could not see what was happening in evangelical religion because of their biases. He claims that sociologists believed that evangelicals were lower class, politically conservative, and historically regressive:

> Each of these preconceptions is based on a perfectly respectable empirical correlation: the correlation between denomination and social class; the correlation between religious orthodoxy and political conservatism; and the observation that disenchantment or secularization advanced over a century long period, especially from the mid-nineteenth to the mid-twentieth century. However, these empirical generalizations have been hypostatized to the status of theoretical constructs so that the correlations have come to take the appearances of identities (1979:4).

These theoretical constructs, as well as many other received notions about religion, were not useful in understanding what was happening in the 1970s and 1980s. In fact, they got in the way of understanding religion.

We can no longer assume that class, religious orthodoxy, and attitudes on social issues would fall into neat ideological packages. An example from my research is that the middle-class Catholics I studied who became Charismatics were actively against abortion. Their "pro-family" stance, however, differed from that observed among middle-class, born-again Protestants for whom being "pro-family" meant being actively against the ratification of the ERA and against homosexuality as well. For Protestants tradition held that only married men could be elders of the church, but a history of unmarried clerics and religious workers in the Catholic church contributed to a culture in the Charismatic Renewal quite different from that of their Protestant allies in the anti-abortion fight (Neitz 1981).

In other ways our received wisdom based on theory and previous research no longer fits the empirical reality. Denomination now does not predict religious beliefs as we once thought it did (Roof and McKinney 1987). In the seventies, in "liberal" denominations like the Episcopalians and Presbyterians members divided over questions of fundamentalism (Warner 1983, 1988). Fundamentalists and moderates are now fighting for the soul of the Southern Baptist Convention (Ammerman 1987).[2] Furthermore individuals' commitments to their denominations seem less likely to survive a geographic move than we might have thought. Studies of interstate migration in the United States suggest that individuals who move adapt to the religious patterns of the new region: they are more likely to attend church in regions where church attendance is high, less likely to attend church in regions where it is low (Stump 1984:292–303), and they may even change denominations to accommodate to prevailing regional patterns (Newman and Halvorson 1984:313).

In addition to changes in the relations between religious affiliation and other variables, in the late sixties and seventies new sects and cults spread through American culture.[3] Converts, at first part of the sixties counterculture but enduring into the eighties, sought moral and ethical alternatives to liberal Protestant culture. In many cases participants took on a vision of sacred power within themselves, not outside and above. The new religions emphasized the emotional and experiential; as Robbins, Anthony, and Richardson described it, "authentic values are being generated by intense experience rather than by rational thought and analysis" (1979:113; see also Westley 1978; Tipton 1982).

The arrival of the new religions had a significant impact on the sociology of religion. Church-sect typologies came under attack, and social movement theory was brought in to analyze these religious movements.[4] Participant observation studies, often by relatively sympathetic researchers (see Richardson 1985a:176), not only offered new views of conversion and power, but raised questions about secularization itself.

INTERPRETIVE FRAMEWORKS

Inspired both by what was going on in the world and by developments in sociology, sociologists of religion turned to interpretive modes of analysis, especially to the anthropologists Clifford Geertz and Victor Turner, but also to Mary Douglas and A. F. C. Wallace. The work of these anthropologists was of interest to sociologists studying other cultural forms as well (see Mukerji and Schudson 1986). But it was particularly important for those sociologists who wished to study religious phenomena that did not fit into established categories. The anthropologists took for granted that religion was worth studying and offered models for looking at it that were similar to those that others in cultural studies generally were developing.

Geertz focuses on the human capacity for making symbols. In his discussion of symbols as "models of and models for" he argued that symbols were not just expressive. Symbols reflect social arrangements, but they also affect social arrangements. The essay "Religion as a Cultural System" offered more than a definition of religion: it presented a research agenda for investigating religion as a "system of meanings" and relating them to social structural and psychological processes (1973:87–125).

Turner also suggested ways that cultural forms reflected social structures but could potentially change it. He focused on rituals, ceremonies, and performances, describing these as possible moments of contrast with daily life. He used the term "anti-structure" to talk about how these "sustained public actions" stand in relation to the social order. His early work described in detail Ndembu ritual; later work extended his early insights to monks, hippies, and pilgrims, among others (1967, 1969). He believed that in modern societies religion was often a repository of countercultural values which could be exhibited in a ritual or a way of life.

For Douglas culture is "a medium of exchange for people giving accounts to one another." Often drawing comparisons across societies, she has written of the meaning in food and goods (1966; with Isherwood, 1979). Her conceptual scheme generalizes relations between cosmologies and social structures (1970). Wallace's model of revitalization movements has been used by those who want to understand religious social movements as forces for change (1956). Again, one of the attractions in Wallace's work is that he knits together social structure, cultural change, and personality.

These anthropologists were important for sociologists of religion for the same reasons that they were important to so many other students of culture. They saw understanding culture and meaning as central to social science. All saw symbols and rituals as reflecting social structure but also holding the possibility of transforming it. All were concerned with the relationship between the cultural and social levels. Finally, each has produced exciting empirical exemplars along with programmatic theoretical statements.

Equally important, these anthropologists did not share biases of the sociologists who believed secularization theory. In fact, given the grimness of much work in the sociology of religion, it was almost refreshing when one occasionally ran into the opposite bias, as for example, when, on the basis of her theory, Mary Douglas condemns the Second Vatican Council for trying to purge the magic from the Catholic church (1970).

This is not to say that no one in the sociology of religion had any part in the turning toward meaning, ritual, and symbolic systems. Peter Berger and Thomas Luckmann (e.g., 1966), writing together and each on his own, have had a tremendous influence. However, their phenomenological understanding of religion was deeply embedded in classical theories of secularization. Berger himself was profoundly unsympathetic to many of the religious movements of the seventies and eighties, and his ideas about religion and modernization have been challenged by many of those who studied the new religions (see Beckford 1983; Neitz 1987; Richardson 1985b).

NEW APPROACHES IN THE SOCIOLOGY OF RELIGION

In this necessarily abbreviated review I hope to show how recent research in the sociology of religion is using approaches similar to those traditionally used by symbolic interactionists. I will start with conversion. Although I only touch the surface of the voluminous literature on this topic, I devote a significant portion of the paper to it because here we can clearly see emerging a new paradigm that views conversion as an interactive process in which the convert interprets alternative social realities, including that offered by the proselytizers. Attention to the process by which individuals undergo self-transformation brings to the fore other issues, two of which I will discuss briefly. One concerns the nature of religious experience—what it is and how it gets interpreted. Participants' claims about experiences of empowerment in particular raise many issues for how we conceptualize power, religious and otherwise. The other issue is methodological as well as conceptual. Although new converts to religious groups may find themselves encapsulated by the sect, in many cases the kinds of cultural transformations achieved by religious movements flow across group boundaries. Sociologists of religion are only starting to figure out how to study these kinds of cultural movements.

Conversion

Early approaches to conversion saw Paul's experience on the Damascus road as paradigmatic: conversion was instantaneous, irrational, and determined. Lofland and Stark's influential study broke with this by showing conversion to be a process occurring over time, but their model still depicted conversion as something that happened (or did not happen) to a passive actor (1965). Through the seventies sociologists elaborated on this model, studying the fit between potential converts and the ideologies of groups, and converts' patterns of affiliation. In a further break with the original model, some analysts began to examine conversion as an interactive process with the potential convert having a part in producing a conversion.

Early explanations of conversion to sects and cults saw religion as compensating for deprivation experienced in other aspects of life: individuals who converted to sects or cults did so because their deprivations predisposed them in that direction. Sociologists defined deprivation broadly to include relative deprivation: "ways that an individual or group may be or feel disadvantaged in comparison to other individuals or groups or to an internalized set of standards" (Glock 1964: 27). Glock's five types of deprivation—economic, social, organismic (deprivation of health), ethical, and psychical—also extended the earlier theories. The current controversy over cults can be understood as a controversy between those who continue to adhere to brainwashing theory and adherents of theories that look at individuals as agents in their own conversion (see Richardson 1985a). These differences in theoretical perspective are often accompanied by differences in methods: psychologists who see cults as engaging in brainwashing use case studies of often troubled clients, as opposed to sociologists who are more likely to use participant observation methods.

Sociologists attempted to match the deprivations of individuals with the ideology of a particular group. But recent researchers have criticized this approach. As conceptions of deprivation expanded, it became clear that the relationship between deprivations and compensations is not direct. To postulate that people join social movements because the ideology matches their deprivations tells us little if they may join because it justifies the deprivations (see Davis 1980: 130), or because it actually alleviates them (Stark and Bainbridge 1980: 1394).

Many people feel deprived, either absolutely or in relation to others; only some of them will join social movements. Furthermore researchers have become more aware of the enormous difficulties introduced by using converts' accounts of their own conversion to tell us about their previous lives and the changes wrought by conversion (Beckford 1978). This does not mean that we cannot use converts' accounts as evidence, but the question is, how should the evidence be interpreted? Snow and Machalek have suggested that evidence of biographical reconstruction in conversion accounts should be considered one of four distinguishing properties of conversion (1983:266–69). The story that a convert tells is an important indicator of her or his conversion, but it tells us less about who the person used to be and more about who he or she is now.

Lofland's and Stark's (1965) study of "The Divine Precepts" in the early sixties brought to our collective attention the way that new people were drawn into cults through ties to their friends. Potential converts came to accept the ideology after having had considerable contact with members of the cult and forming personal attachments to them. Bainbridge's (1978) study of a satanic cult demonstrated that interpersonal bonds were crucial not only in recruiting new members, but also in the initial formation of the sect. Richardson and Stewart (1977) found social networks played an important role in conversion within the Jesus movement, as well. Stark and Bainbridge (1980) attribute the rapid growth of the contemporary Mormon church to an aggressive recruiting policy that emphasizes the development of social networks. In Snow's and Phillips's test of the Lofland and Stark model only affiliation factors—cult affective bonds and intense social interaction—came out as important. Snow and Phillips conclude that "the salience of intense interaction to conversion cannot be overemphasized" (1980:443).

Taken together the factors of deprivation and social networks have been used to develop a model explaining the situations under which conversions are most likely to occur. Stark and Bainbridge (1980) present a more cautious and economical revision of the Lofland and Stark model. They argue that first, people do not convert unless they have acutely felt tensions; second, they must be ideologically predisposed to accept, at the very least, the plausibility of the supernatural; third, they must have some dissatisfaction with the ways that beliefs about the supernatural are presented in the established churches; and fourth, they must be placed in a situation where they will develop social bonds with members. They qualify this basic model by suggesting that the importance of deprivation will be less if there are few costs to converting: if the established faiths are weak and the society shows little disapproval of novel religious movements (see Stark and Bainbridge 1980:1381–82).

Snow, Zurcher, and Ekland-Olson refine the analysis of the relationship between social networks and recruitment to social movements. Starting from the familiar proposition that those who have contact with members through preexisting networks have a greater probability of being recruited than those who do not, the authors go on to specify that people who have fewer and weaker ties to other networks will be more available to recruiters and more likely to accept (1980:782–94). In addition, Snow et al. propose that recruitment is likely to vary with the type of social movement. Movements that require exclusive commitments (their example is the Hare Krishna) will attract a larger proportion of their members from recruitment in public places such as streets or airports, and will grow at a slower rate than those movements that do not require exclusive commitments (796–97).

The notion that individuals vary in their availability—not merely in individual predispositions—to a social movement was confirmed in my study of Charismatics. Membership in the group I studied included a high proportion of individuals at transition points in their lives: adolescents undergoing identity crises, middle-aged women whose children were leaving home, men and women recently retired from their jobs, and new widows or widowers. Although not all members fit into these categories, it does seem that many were, while not clearly deprived, at least structurally available due to relative absence of conflicting commitments (see also Downton 1980:394).

The factors considered in this growing literature obviously have some relevance in understanding conversion. In an important test of dominant explanations of conversion Heirich found that these factors explain a portion of the variance. Yet Heirich called for a new approach that would examine the circumstances under which a person would develop a different grounding, destroying what had been before (1977). Affinity and affiliation ignore the role of the actor in the conversion process. They present the convert being drawn to the social movement or group on the basis of something within him/herself or as encapsulated by a social network and therefore becoming a part of the social movement. In neither case is the individual's decision process examined.

By the end of the seventies the emphasis on recruitment began to be supplemented by analyses of the how transformation takes place. Concern turned to how the self makes choices over time to commit or fail to commit to a new identity (Neitz 1987). Attendance at a meeting, in the company of a friend or a relative, may mean that an individual is open to considering the group, but it may not. Certainly it does not, in itself, mean that conversion has taken place. Once at a meeting the potential convert is given an interpretation of the world, including a new view of his or her own affinities. Rewards of attending may begin to accrue even before full identification is made. For the potential convert, and for the researcher as well, the process of conversion provides the context for making sense of the various affinities and affiliations that may act as factors in the individual's becoming converted. Alone, however, these factors provide little insight into how a new view of human experience develops.

In line with these concerns those studying conversion suggested a more interactionist, processual view of conversion. Out of the new religious movements came a new type, the religious seekers: "the individual human being acting creatively within a natural life setting to construct a meaningful life" (Straus 1976:252, see also Straus 1979). Religious seekers were clearly active and, far from being manipulated by cults, might pass from one religious movement to another in the course of a "conversion career" (see Richardson and Stewart 1977). In a study of a flying saucer cult Balch found participants could not be viewed as individuals manipulated by the cult. In this group the leaders supplied little direction, and participants' self-identification as seekers came before their identification with the cult. Those who joined engaged in a kind of role playing within the group, participating in activities at times when their commitments were uncertain (Balch and Taylor 1977, Balch 1980). In examining the Divine Light Mission, a group with more structure and direction than the flying saucer cult, Downton (1980) also posited an active subject.

With this approach conversion becomes less a subject exclusively for sociologists of religion and more a concern with general issues of socialization.[5] Once we abandon the notion that converts experience a particular kind of stress or strain, then we can apply (and advance) more general understandings of how people come to make sense of their worlds. In fact, one of the things that is appealing about studying conversion is that it provides a window on the usually taken-for-granted process of making sense of the world.

In my work on Catholic Charismatics, I described conversion as a practical and even rational (in a limited sense) process of assessing the claims of belief systems in the light of daily experience, with an eye toward particular goals. At the same time, individuals may report cathartic experiences which they describe as moments of personal knowledge of an ultimate reality. The rational process, then, is accompanied by transformative moments which are quite outside it, but which become incorporated into the understandings that will then be used to assess future claims (Neitz 1987).

This leads to a tentative answer to Heirich's question of what circumstances destroy root reality and how an alternative sense of grounding is built. To talk of the "destruction of the root reality" does not quite describe what happens; rather, root realities, when they exist prior to conversion, get replaced. I suggest that the appropriate analogy here is the molting process. The old carapace falls away in a cathartic experience, but when it does so the new one is already substantially in place. The notion that the old reality must be destroyed comes, in part, from the tendency to think of conversion as only the momentary, irrational process like that of Paul on the road to Damascus. In fact, realities are "destroyed" in the same, often gradual, process through which new ones are built up.

Looking at conversion as a problem in the social construction of reality suggests new research possibilities. One is to examine the process by which individuals leave sects and cults. We know that attrition rates are high. Studies of deconversion examine how individuals become disillusioned with participation in the group, how they leave, and how they feel about their experience as members (Jacobs 1984, 1987; Wright 1984, 1987). One can compare the construction of religious meaning systems with one another, or with other meaning systems such as science or common sense. David Matza (1969) and Diane Vaughan (1986) have analyzed deviance and divorce in similar terms.

However, some (practitioners and researchers) would argue that, although religious conversion can be profitably studied by applying general theories of how people learn things and make sense of their worlds, religion is different because what is being learned is some kind of fundamental grounding. For example, Heirich (1977:674–77) assumes that individuals possess a dominant root reality in which identity is grounded, and that conversion must replace one reality with another. Yet it may be the case that there is no dominating reality.

In an early statement of this perspective, Simmel argued that the proliferation of social roles in modern society meant that the whole person could no longer be comprehended within any one relationship. Rather a person interacted with others on the basis of one or another social role, sacrificing the security of traditional society, but gaining new freedom possible only in modern society. Most modern interpreters who discuss this aspect of modernization take a more dismal view of it than did Simmel. Peter Berger, for example, thinks the possibility of dominating root reality no longer exists for modern individuals. In his terms modern society is characterized by a "plurality of life-worlds," which renders individuals psychologically "homeless" (Berger, Berger, and Kellner 1973:63–82).

Such a view of the modern condition requires a different notion of conversion: perhaps it is possible for an individual to convert from "nothing"—from nihilism—to a religious reality. Or, perhaps, one could convert from being a Catholic to being a Charismatic Catholic, involving only a change inside a particular sphere affecting one of many "multiple realities" that a person inhabits and not a "root reality." Another possibility is that, in spite of the claim "it changed my life," conversion is a matter of degree: while not quite providing a new, pervasive, integrating reality, conversion may effect a shift in perspective that has repercussions for various "realities."

What makes the issue of conversion particularly difficult is that there are at least two dimensions with which one needs to be concerned. The obvious dimension is the time dimension: conversion involves a change from one reality in one time period to another reality in a different time period. But conversion can also be a change in the salience of the reality. Theoretical discussions of conversion have often been confused because these two dimensions have not been analytically separated.

Formulations of conversion that talk about changes in "root reality" (such as Heirich's) assume that the changes are between realities that are highly salient to the individual. The concept of alternation (proposed by Berger 1963:54–55), which assumes changes within one of many multiple realities or compartments of the individual's life, assumes that no one reality (including the one in which the change occurs) is more salient than others to the individual's sense of self.

If we combine the two dimensions there are four possible types of change: (1) one trades one root reality for another (ardent communist becomes a Hare Krishna); (2) one's dominant root reality loses meaning (ardent communist becomes Episcopalian businessman who votes the Democratic party ticket); (3) one gains a dominant reality where before one had none (Episcopalian businessman becomes a Hare Krishna), (4) one experiences change within one of the multiple realities or compartments (Methodist businessman becomes Episcopalian businessman). Berger's claim is that what we call conversion in modern society is most often the fourth type, which he labels "alternation"(1963:48–52). Travisano (1970) agrees that alternation is common, but he contends that one can still find instances of the first type of conversion where there is a real change in the informing aspect of identity. Many Catholic Charismatics I studied came closest to fitting the third type: they described themselves as "searching" for meaning in life, and they claimed that prior to their conversion they were without the sense of wholeness which they felt as a result of their new understanding of the world and their place in it. My informants converted from the condition of "homelessness" as described by Berger, and in the process, created a grounding.[6] In effect, they converted from nothing.[7]

The Experience of Power

The process of conversion within these religious movements is not a cognitive process alone. Participants in the movements emphasize the primacy of experience over doctrine.[8] The Catholic Charismatics I spoke with saw things, felt things, heard things that I did not. These "experiences of God," as the Charismatics referred to them, were taken to be critical information in the rational process of assessing the claims being made about the new religious reality. Indeed, the testimony of religious converts is replete with references to such experiences.

The analysis of religious movements and conversion, however, rarely looks systematically at religious experience. This may be in part because we lack conceptual tools for looking at experience sociologically (see Neitz and Spickard 1989). In part it is because of an old link between emotional experiences and deprivation theories: when sociology of religion had talked about experience it did so to claim that cathartic experiences in "the religions of the poor" offered compensation for deprivation in other parts of their lives. As conversion models moved away from deprivation theory, sociologists of religion stressed cognitive and organizational factors in their analyses and avoided emotion and experience. Wilson and Clow (1981) and Lefever (1977) attempt to move away from this tendency to explaining away cathartic religious experience by considering it "compensatory."

Researchers not working primarily among the "disinherited," but among middle-class seekers, have been struck by religious participants' claims about power being at the core of their religious practice.

With the revival of esoteric, mystical, and shamanic traditions among religious practitioners we hear talk about "power" in terms of the ability to achieve personal and spiritual goals. McGuire encountered themes of empowerment in her work on faith healing in both Christian and non-Christian traditions. Beckford interprets the new religions as drawing members because they see the religions as "sources of power." Yet McGuire and Beckford are closer to a new analysis of experience and emotion than to the traditional ways that sociologists (including sociologists of religion) have talked about power. Beckford, for example, speaks of "the power to cultivate" as critical to the new religions, and goes on to define it as "the chance to cultivate various spiritual qualities, personal goals, or social arrangements is the attraction" (1983:26).

I am currently engaged in fieldwork among urban and rural neopagan and feminist witches. The neopagan witches base their practices (albeit sometimes loosely) on the modern wiccan tradition formulated by Gerald Gardner in England during the Second World War. Although some feminist witches have contact with the neopagans, many "created" feminist witchcraft as they looked in the mythologies of the past for a woman-affirming goddess religion (Neitz 1989). As the head of the Reformed Congregation of the Goddess told me about the process that many of the members of her church went through, when they discovered witchcraft as the religion of the goddess, "they were amazed to find out that someone else had gotten there first, and that it was a man [Gardner]." The neopagan and feminist witches tell me that their religious practices "are about power." Witches define themselves as those who have the power to "bend and shape reality."

There have always been a few sociologists of religion who have been concerned with the power of religion vis-à-vis the state, and even the world system.[9] However, as the secularization thesis combined with ideas about the "end of ideology" gained acceptance in the sixties, many sociologists of religion began to feel that there was less and less to say on this topic. Beckford suggests that during this period those who studied religious power came to describe it as derived from its "functional capacity" to provide meaning and identity consonant with an overarching social structure (1983). Although the exemplars he chooses to discuss—Berger, Luckmann, Mol—are phenomenologists, he argues that they present religious power as limited to a kind of latent pattern maintenance.

Beckford argues that, contrary to the assumptions of this literature, there is no guarantee that coherent meaning systems integrate individuals into the social order.[10] Beckford suggests that this should be an empirical question:

> What I have proposed is that, in focusing on the capacity or function of religion to supply meaning, integration and identity, the theoretical cart has been put before the empirical horse. The sociologists' interpretations of religious phenomena have been mistaken for their subjects' motives and intentions. In short, I agree that meaning and identity are important aspects of religion: but at the same time I dispute whether actors act out of consideration for them directly. Rather I believe that actors respond to perceived sources of power, and their responses may or may not supply the meaning and identity of which we have heard so much.(1983:29)

The notion of "perceived sources of power" is consonant with the rhetoric of empowerment and self-actualization commonly spoken by adherents of new religions. Yet their usage departs significantly from received sociological definitions. Like Janice Radway (1985), who had to think about what it meant when readers of romance novels claimed that reading the novels made them stronger, more independent women, we must think about what people mean when they talk about empowerment in these religious contexts.

In the neopagan literature there is a conscious repudiation of what is often termed "power over," meaning overpowering an individual's will, coercion of one kind or another. The code of ethics requires that one's magic not interfere with the will of another. The power that is cultivated in this setting is something akin to control over one's own life. (See Weinstein 1981; Starhawk 1982.) A task for sociologists is to understand what believers mean when they use this rhetoric of power, and to establish links between feelings of empowerment and the sociological concept of power.

Meredith McGuire, first in her research on Catholic Charismatics and then on spiritual healing practices, has explored the connections between religion and the experience of empowerment (1982, 1983b). Although a student of Peter Berger's, McGuire is not guilty of the sins that concern Beckford: looking at meaning led her to investigate the experience of power. McGuire (1983a) reminds us of three ways of looking at religion and power: first, the power and influence of religious groups; second, the religious legitimation of positions and privileges of those in power; and, third, the individuals' experiences of power. McGuire's work has taken the third, the least explored of these, and worked toward the other two. McGuire's respondents experienced spiritual power as out of the ordinary, as "having real consequences for the physical (as well as emotional or spiritual) conditions of human beings" (1983a:4). Healing groups developed rituals that created feelings of empowerment, bestowing on individuals symbols of the transmission of spiritual power. McGuire uses this empirical material on individuals' experiences of power to ask questions about religious groups, including the following: How does religion per se contribute to the group's perceived power? To its power vis-à-vis others? Does religion expand or diminish members' sense of a group's internal power through ritual or symbols? How are nonmaterial and material rewards used to enhance the power of leaders? of the whole groups? (1983a:5).

McGuire sees religious legitimation as an interactional process, charismatic authority as the successful "result of negotiation between a would be leader and followers" (1983a:7). McGuire advocates an observational approach with emphasis on the collection of experiential data: she suggests analyzing personal accounts and working with traditional forms of religious discourse such as witnessing. (See Harding 1987 for an example of this.) She advocates comparative work in order to "isolate those specific components of the religion and power nexus which are important" (1983a:8).[11]

In her explorations McGuire is moving toward an analysis of power and religion that is quite different from previous works. It reframes long-standing sociological questions about how charisma develops and is maintained, and how symbolic resources are used in struggles for power between advocates of different positions on moral issues. Christian's (1987) study of the process of negotiating whether or not church officials would accept individual's claims to have received visions, for example, shows the visions being shaped as visionaries and leaders developed ways of speaking to their audiences.

The experience of power is not the same as power in the social world, yet these religious practices raise questions about where they overlap. Advocates of faith healing implicitly oppose the medical establishment: to say that faith healing is an experience of power is part of a critique of this powerful institution. In my work I am exploring what it means when women, members of a historically subordinate group, reclaim the witchcraft tradition as a means of empowering themselves in order to "save the earth." The potential overlap between the experience of power and social power nudges sociologists of religion to look in new ways at the expressive aspects of religion and at questions of legitimacy, and questions of the powers of groups.

CULTURAL MOVEMENTS AND CULTURAL ANALYSIS

If writers since the sixties have studied the new religions in terms of how they solve problems of meaning and identity, it is partly because the new religions have in common a focus on the therapeutic transformation of the self. They are distinguished from new therapies, which have proliferated in the same period, by the fact that the former "provide a reliable community of fellow adherents who are bound by a common regimen, including a common moral code" (Johnson 1981: 61). Yet defining the boundaries of such communities can be quite problematic. The community boundaries separating off those who share a common regimen and moral code often are not coterminous with the boundaries of recognized groups. While the new religions focus attention—both for their adherents and for the sociologist—on meaning, organizational features show a considerable range. The degree of commitment required and the degree to which adherents constitute a closed group are highly variable. When I moved from studying Charismatic Catholics to studying neopagan and feminist witches I encountered a tremendous difference in boundedness. The witches seemed elusive in part because formal groups tend to be unstable, but in part because the identifiable group is not the meaningful unit.

Sociologists, even when studying religious meaning, have tended to do so within identifiable organizations—religious movement organizations. Sociologists of religion here followed the tactic of the resource mobilization theorists who made progress when they delimited the field by moving social movement theory from the study of "social movements" to the study of "social movement organizations." (For a formal treatment see Lofland and Richardson 1984). That meant that less "organized" religious traditions, such as the neopagans and witches, tended to get left out.[12]

Because of this organizational bias researchers usually evaluate a movement in terms of organizational success. Yet clearly part of what we are looking at is *cultural* movements and *cultural* change. This often does not fit with our usual frameworks for studying social movements and for evaluating their success. Organizations, even when we can locate them, may not be the only or most appropriate sites to study cultural movements.

Beckford has suggested that the study of new religions might benefit from a more "fluid" perspective on religious movements (1987). In contrast with a "linear perspective," a fluid perspective would not limit itself to organizations and associations; rather it might examine diffuse movements and collections of movements for the transformations of values. Borrowing from Gusfield (1981), he suggests that a fluid perspective might be more useful for analyzing both social and cultural change. We also might usefully look at ties between movements and how individuals move from movement to movement both "carrying on and carrying over," in Gusfield's terms (1981:324). When feminists and ecologists become witches, they appear to "carry over" their previous political commitments and value orientations. A woman who was active in a pro-abortion organization as a college student may not continue the activity when she graduates and moves to a new place, but she may "carry on" by making financial contributions to a national organization and deciding whether or not to vote for political candidates on the basis of their stand on abortion.

The fact that individuals carry with them the ideas and values of a social movement, sometimes even when they are not active in an organization, has implications for cultural transformation at both the public and private level. The nature of public discourse shifts; what had been unthinkable becomes thinkable, and individuals reflect on the movement and monitor society in new ways (Gusfield 1981: 325–26). It is this process that Gusfield is referring to when he says that social movements are reflexive. He states, "I might even say that a social movement occurs when people are conscious that a movement is occurring. . . . The awareness of change is itself a second step in the production of change" (1981:326).

A fluid conception of social movements is particularly appropriate for looking at many current religious movements. When individuals identify as witches, they do so in a specific context and bring with them important parts of their pasts. Many of the striking differences between neopagan and feminist witches, for example, can be explained by their differing relationships to local communities. Neopagan covens are likely to have a hierarchical structure and to have elaborate procedures for initiation. A prominent feminist writing in the early seventies proclaimed that "if you say you are a witch three times, you are a witch." While feminist witches who repeat that today may be making a joke about their movement, feminists tend to have neither hierarchy nor initiatory processes. The feminists carried "structure-lessness" with them, and their part of the movement approaches anarchy if examined on the level of organizations. Yet there are important anchors in the feminist and lesbian communities that serve to define and bound the movement.

Our ways of evaluating movements also shifts when the movements we study are cultural movements. In terms of organizational growth, the Charismatic Renewal hit a high point around 1978. Some analysts evaluate the subsequent failure of the movement to sustain growth as evidence for the failure of the movement (e.g., Bord and Faulkner 1983). Yet a better measure of success may be the degree to which symbols and behaviors first found in Charismatic groups have now diffused into parishes.

Treating religious movements as cultural movements will also mean paying more attention to symbols and rituals at several levels, starting with the process of culture creation among the smallest units, what Fine (1979) has called "ideoculture." Symbols and rituals also need to be examined within movements, and as they are carried outside of movements. As we begin to do these analyses it is clear that symbols and rituals are not just expressions of emotional catharsis or cultural objects created with the intent of manipulating potential audiences. In religious movements symbols and rituals can be the mediums through which groups negotiate an understanding of who they are, and work out their public and private faces.

CONCLUSION

Thus far, I have tried to show some of the recent developments in American religion and to suggest ways that the sociology of religion, in attempting to understand those developments, is producing analyses of religion and programmatic stands that look very much like symbolic interactionist positions. The new research looks at how meanings are socially constructed through interaction: it sees conversion as a process, power as a product of negotiation, movements as fluid. At this point I return to the impact of cultural studies.

I will present two problems of using the anthropologists discussed above as models for studying religion in American society. Then I will sketch how symbolic interactionists' approaches to social organization could be applied in helpful ways to these problems. Finally, I will suggest that it would be fruitful for cultural studies if the subdisciplinary barriers between symbolic interactionists and sociologists of religion were breached.

One problem with the interpretive approach, especially as advocated by Geertz in his recent works (1983, 1988), is that it is not clear how this kind of research adds up or what standards of evidence can be used to evaluate it. Geertz himself argues that generalization is not desirable: there are enough laws, he says. Backing away from the influence of the phenomenological and hermeneutic interpretive approach, Robert Wuthnow has advocated that we abandon attempts to understand "meaning," and stick with "structural approaches" to studying cultural phenomena (1981, 1987).[13] Wuthnow claims that, rather than describing in detail the meaning of cultural objects of various kinds, the appropriate task of the sociologist is to identify the rules that make a symbol meaningful (1981:30).[14]

In an important response to Wuthnow, Griswold (1987) has argued that one need not trade away richly detailed accounts of cultural objects in order to achieve reliability, validity, and predictability.[15] Here symbolic interactionists have something to contribute to the discussion. They have a long history of building a nonpositivistic sociology through studying meaning in rigorous ways. The current interest in generic principles reflects concern with developing our understanding of basic processes (Lofland 1976; Couch 1984). Symbolic interactionists have been concerned with developing both "substantive theory" in specific subareas, (e.g., delinquency) and "formal theory" reaching across the substantive subareas. Comparisons of various kinds—within groups and between groups—offer one strategy for qualitative researchers who want to escape the interpretive dilemma. The methodology of grounded theory uses "constant comparisons" and "theoretical sampling" to build theory that cumulates (Glaser and Strauss 1967; Charmaz 1983).

There is a second problem with the application of the work of the anthropologists in cultural studies. It is that the approaches of Geertz, Douglas, Turner, Wallace and others were developed in very different kinds of societies than the modern heterogenous societies to which they are now being applied. For the most part the former were *societies* where social norms could be enforced in the context in face-to-face interaction. Douglas has defined culture as "the medium of exchange for people giving accounts to one another" (1970:185). For example, Wallace's theory of revitalization movements comes out of a study of a society of approximately 4000 people (1969:196). When we try to apply the theory to a movement in the United States today it is not clear what the units of analysis should be. Is it American society that would be revitalized by the evangelical movement? Protestantism? Evangelicals themselves?[16] Reading Geertz's analysis of the cockfight we learn something about one set of "emotional tendencies" in Balinese society (1973). A detailed description of a Ndembu ritual is more satisfying if we can assume it exists in a small, relatively cohesive society where the symbols are shared. A similar description of a ritual in this country needs to be understood in terms not only of the set of meanings directly incorporated into the ritual and its local setting, but we also want to know how the local setting is connected to other local settings and to American culture and society in general.

Sociologists of religion have attempted to talk about the relation between religious culture and American society without properly recognizing diversity in American culture and how "American" values are mediated by local contexts. In *Habits of the Heart,* Bellah and his co-authors describe American culture as without a language for discussing moral issues (1985). Yet this indictment only appears to be true for a segment of Protestant culture. The Catholics I interviewed continued to use the language of sin to talk about moral issues. In fact, they had extended the notion of sin to address "social evils" such as discrimination or war (Neitz 1983). Benton Johnson has commented that "[i]t has been a long time since educated Protestants could believe that national sins require national punishments" (1984:82). Contrast his observations with James Kelly's discussion of the American bishops' pastoral letter, "The Challenge of Peace," in which Kelly suggests that Catholicism has come to define itself as the locus of moral memory (1984).

The questions raised by Bellah et al. are important ones, but we need better ways of understanding "local culture" and the relationships between various local cultures and the national culture and society. I am intrigued by recent attempts of symbolic interactionists to work out the linkages between detailed studies of "situated activities" and larger structural contexts and historical forces.[17] For my work, looking at religious subcultures in American society, Fine and Kleinman's work on networks and subcultures is suggestive. Fine and Kleinman note that although symbolic interaction appears to suggest an "open approach," that interactionists have tended to study groups—"empirically closed systems." They argue that "by putting the assumption of 'openness' into practice, symbolic interactionists can address 'macro'-sociological concerns, such as the constraining features of organizations, while still grounding constraints in interaction" (1983:105). They suggest that the advantage of a network approach is that it allows one to study "groups with their interconnections—multiple group memberships, weak ties, structural roles, and mass media connections" (1983:104).

Looking at religious social movements we see cultures that are relatively bounded, yet they are defined in relation to American culture. Although the concept of subculture has fallen into relative disuse, it seems appropriate for some of these movements. It is more constraining to be a moonie than it is to belong to an occupational group: other doctors do not usually try to dictate whom one will marry and when. Religious movements such as the Unification Church or the Charismatic Renewal create separate societies with separate cultures. Yet what is created will reflect the larger context: the Unification Church in Korea differs from the Unification Church in Japan, which differs from the Unification Church in the United States.[18]

In Fine and Kleinman's treatment, the concept of subculture offers a way to locate culture in an interacting group without assuming that the interacting group is closed. In a subculture, individuals share "information" (including values, norms, behaviors, and artifacts) and identify as members of the subculture. They also communicate directly and indirectly with others outside the subculture. Fine and Kleinman suggest that communication across networks is facilitated by "communication interlocks," such as multiple group memberships, weak ties between individuals, structural roles,[19] and media diffusion (1979: 9–12). In their view "research should focus on uncovering linkages among groups, looking at what kinds of information are transmitted, and the type and extent of identification with the larger segment" (1979:17). For their work on Little League baseball and preadolescent subculture they are especially concerned that research not presume that an individual who is a member of an age category will also identify with a subculture; thus they are careful to distinguish empirically between subculture, subsociety, and population segment. Their emphasis on looking at both interaction within a group and communications with outsiders, including mass media communications, suggests a level of analysis that goes beyond the case study without forsaking meaning.

Symbolic interactionists have long identified themselves as studying meaning. A significant portion of sociologists studying culture (and religion as a part of culture) share this concern. Symbolic interactionists have worked out methods and concepts that address concerns now being voiced by sociologists of culture. Concepts such as "network" pull symbolic interactionists away from the frequent preoccupation with case studies of a single group.

The questions of meaning raised by sociologists of religion include "meaning" in small groups, but they are not limited to that. We all need to be working at linking face-to-face interaction and local culture to the broader culture, social structures, and history. For those of us studying religious movements—new in their current manifestations but often connected to historical institutions and other cultural movements—questions about such linkages clamor for our attention.

NOTES

1. Survey research in the 1970s began to collect information about religious beliefs so that the data base has been significantly extended. (See Roof 1985.)

2. One of the reasons why the squabble over Jim and Tammy Bakker's empire was so intense is that the Bakkers are Charismatics, and others on the religious right, such as the Baptist Jerry Falwell, disapprove of their religious beliefs.

3. Any generalization about the new religions is hazardous, but see review articles by Barker 1985, Robbins and Anthony 1981, and Robbins, Anthony, and Richardson, 1978.

4. See Robbins, Anthony, and Richardson 1979:110. Gerlach and Hine's pioneering work looked at both Pentecostalism and the Black Power Movement (1970). See also Lofland and Richardson's reformulation of resource mobilization theory for the study of religious movements (1984), and Stark and Bainbridge's attempt to reformulate church-sect-cult theory in light of the new research on religious social movements (1985).

5. Long and Hadden (1983) suggest one way of aligning socialization and conversion literatures.

6. The exception to this pattern among my respondents was a subgroup of individuals who were devoutly religious Catholics before becoming Charismatics. For these people religion was already the dominating reality and the new beliefs were easily assimilated into that reality. (In fact, for at least two, the Charismatic Renewal served to validate previous mystical experiences.) The change in the content of the reality was so slight as to require no major adjustments, and there was no change in the salience of the reality. Therefore, I would hesitate to call the experiences of these people conversion. Yet, their experiences are also quite different from those described by Travisano and Berger, since the religious reality is extremely salient for them.

7. Using Canadian survey data Bibby (1983) finds traditional religion as a dominant meaning system, but also large numbers of people who do not have lives that are tightly integrated by identifiable meaning systems. He suggests that the proposition that all people have identifiable meaning systems is erroneous. But consider the arguments of Bainbridge and Stark (1981) and Wuthnow (1981) concerning the conceptual and methodological underpinnings of attempts by survey researchers to study meaning.

8. Lofland and Skonovd (1981) offer a typology of conversions and suggest that particular sorts of conversions may be more likely at particular times in history.

9. See, for example, Hammond 1985, essays by Johnson, Carroll, Neal, and Robertson.

10. The issue that Beckford raises is related to the concern above, what individuals convert from. There the issue was a social psychological question, whether or not individuals have coherent meaning systems. There is also a cultural question about who shares the meaning system. I will suggest below that in modern heterogeneous societies coherent meaning systems are most likely to be subcultural.

11. Her program no doubt sounds familiar to symbolic interactionists. Yet she does not cite them, and symbolic interactionists for the most part are not aware of her work.

12. Eileen Barker notes that "[n]umerous occult, pagan, and Witchcraft movements are known to exist . . . but, like the tribal and folk based religions that have emerged around the world . . . , these have received comparatively little attention as new religious movements from the sociologists of religion" (1985:41).

13. While Wuthnow attacks theories that "conceptualize culture in radically subjectivist terms," he does not see himself as a positivist: "To say that culture must be approached interpretively certainly should not preclude a call to conceive of it in ways that make it more observable or to ask that investigators be more candid about disclosing their methods and assumptions. Cultural analysis remains a matter of interpretation whether we conceive of culture as subjective beliefs or as symbolic acts. But there may be strategic advantages to thinking of it one way rather than another" (1987:17).

14. Of the anthropologists who influenced cultural studies, Mary Douglas is an exception in that she has moved toward creating generalizations and predictions. See Wuthnow's discussion of her (e.g., 1987:53–54).

15. Griswold renews questions of validity for cultural studies. She argues that we need to move away from vague notions that an analysis should be convincing to asking whether an analysis is "correct." She argues for developing standards for cultural analysis. Such standards would include "parsimony (if two connecting hypotheses are equally supported by the evidence, the simpler one should be favored); plenitude (if two connecting hypotheses are equally supported by the evidence but one illuminates more characteristics of the cultural object than another, that one should be favored); and amplitude (if two connecting hypotheses are equally supported by the evidence and the criteria of parsimony and plenitude, the one that seems to illuminate the greatest range of cultural objects should be preferred)"(1987:27).

16. For an example of the problem see McLoughlin 1978.

17. Hall (1987:1) presents a set of six analytic categories that he sees as constituting a paradigm for "making linkages between situated activity and the broader and larger social environment." In addition to network they are collective activity, conventions-practices, resources, processuality-temporality, and grounding.

18. Fine and Kleinman's (1979) example of this is the textbook salesman who, in the process of trying to get faculty members to adopt his company's textbooks, conveys information about what is going on in other places. Religious cultures develop "star" healers and preachers who travel around the country giving lectures and workshops. As they travel they convey information about practices in other related groups in other places.

19. I discuss at some length how the Catholic Charismatic Renewal as it came to be in the U.S. was a response by the American Catholic Church to influences here (Neitz 1987:187–248). Looking at a very different religious subculture, I have seen bumper stickers proclaiming "I [heart] Allah," certainly an Americanization of Islamic fundamentalism.

REFERENCES

Ammerman, Nancy. 1987. "Southern Baptist Fundamentalists and the New Christian Right." Paper delivered at the annual meeting of the Society for the Scientific Study of Religion, Louisville, KY.

Bainbridge, William. 1978. *Satan's Power* (Berkeley: University of California Press).

Bainbridge, William, and Rodney Stark. 1981. "The Consciousness Reformation Reconsidered," *Journal for the Scientific Study of Religion* 20:1–16.

Balch, Robert. 1980. "Looking behind the Scenes in a Religious Cult: Implications for the Study of Conversion," *Sociological Analysis* 41:137–43.

Balch, Robert, and David Taylor. 1977. "Seekers and Saucers," *American Behavioral Scientist* 20:43–64.

Barker, Eileen. 1985. "New Religious Movements: Yet Another Great Awakening?" pp. 36–57 in Phillip Hammond, ed., *The Sacred in a Secular Age* (Berkeley: The University of California Press).

Beckford, James. 1978. "Accounting for Conversion," *British Journal of Sociology* 29:249–62.

———. 1983. "The Restoration of 'Power' to the Sociology of Religion," *Sociological Analysis* 44:11–32.

———. 1987. "Assessing the New Religions," Panel presentation at the meetings of the Association for the Sociology of Religion, Chicago.

Bellah, Robert, et al. 1985. *Habits of the Heart*, (Berkeley: University of California Press).

Berger, Peter. 1963. *Invitation to Sociology*, (New York: Doubleday).

———. 1967. *The Sacred Canopy*, (Garden City: Anchor Books).

Berger, Peter, Brigitte Berger, and Hansfried Kellner. 1973. *The Homeless Mind*, (New York: Vintage Books).

Berger, Peter, and Thomas Luckmann. 1966. *The Social Construction of Reality* (Garden City , N.Y.: Doubleday).

Bibby, Reginald. 1983. "Searching for Invisible Thread," *Journal for the Scientific Study of Religion* 22:101–19.

Bord, Richard J. and Joseph Faulkner. 1983. *The Catholic Charismatics: The Anatomy of a Modern Religious Movement* (University Park: Pennsylvania State University Press).

Charmaz, Kathy. 1983. "The Grounded Theory Method: An Explication and Interpretation," pp. 109–26 in Robert Emerson, ed., *Contemporary Field Research* (Boston: Little, Brown).

Christian, William. 1987. "Tapping and Defining New Power: The First Month of Visions at Ezquioga, July 1931," *American Ethnologist* 14:140–66.

Couch, Carl. 1984. "Symbolic Interaction and Generic Sociological Principles," *Symbolic Interaction* 7 : 1–13.

Davis, Winston. 1980. *DOJO: Magic and Exorcism in Modern Japan* (Stanford: Stanford University Press).

Douglas, Mary. 1966. *Purity and Danger* (London:Penguin).

———. 1970, *Natural Symbols* (New York: Vintage).

Douglas, Mary, with Baron Isherwood. 1979. *The World of Goods* (New York: Basic Books).

Downton, James V. 1980. "An Evolutionary Theory of Spiritual Conversion and Commitment: The Case of the Divine Light Mission,"*Journal for the Scientific Study of Religion* 19 : 381–96.

Fine, Gary Alan. 1979. "Small Groups and Culture Creation," *American Sociological Review* 44 : 733–45.

———, and Sherryl Kleinman. 1979. "Subculture: An Interactionist Analysis," *American Journal of Sociology* 85 : 1–20.

———. 1983. "Network and Meaning: An Interactionist Approach to Structure," *Symbolic Interaction* 6 : 97–110.

Geertz, Clifford. 1973. *Interpretations of Culture* (New York: Basic Books).

———. 1983. *Local Knowledge: Further Essays in Interpretive Anthropology* (New York: Basic Books).

———. 1988. *The Anthropologist as Author* (Stanford: Stanford University Press).

Gerlach, Luther, and Virginia Hine. 1970. *People, Power,and Change: Movements of Social Transformation* (Indianapolis: Bobbs-Merill).

Glaser, Barney, and Anselm L. Strauss. 1967. *The Discovery of Grounded Theory* (Chicago: Aldine).

Glock, Charles. 1964. "The Role of Deprivation in the Origin and Evolution of Religious Groups," pp. 24–36, in Robert Lee and Martin Marty, eds., *Religion and Social Conflict* (New York: Oxford University Press).

Griswold, Wendy. 1987. "A Methodological Framework for the Study of Culture," *Sociological Methodology* 17 : 1–35.

Gusfield, Joseph R. 1981. "Social Movements and Social Change: Perspectives of Linearity and Fluidity," pp. 317–39 in L. Kreisberg, ed., *Social Movements, Conflict, and Change*, Vol. 4 (Greenwich, Conn.: JAI Press).

Hall, Peter. 1987. "Interactionism and the Study of Social Organization," *Sociological Quarterly* 28 : 1–22.

Hammond, Phillip, ed. 1985. *The Sacred in a Secular Age* (Berkeley: University of California Press).

Harding, Susan. 1982. "Convicted by the Holy Spirit: The Rhetoric of Fundamental Baptist Conversion," *American Ethnologist* 14 : 167–80.

Heirich, Max. 1977. "A Change of Heart," *American Journal of Sociology* 83:653–80.

Jacobs, Janet. 1984. "The Economy of Love in Religious Commitment: The Deconversion of Women from Nontraditional Religious Movements" *Journal for the Scientific Study of Religion,* 23:155–71.

———. 1987. "Deconversion from Religious Movements: An Analysis of Charismatic Bonding and Spiritual Commitment," *Journal for the Scientific Study of Religion* 26:294–308.

Johnson, Benton. 1981. "A Sociological Perspective on the New Religions," pp. 51–66 in Thomas Robbins and Dick Anthony, eds., *In Gods We Trust* (New Brunswick, N.J.: Transaction Books).

———. 1984. "Continuity and Quest in the Work of Harvey Cox," *Sociological Analysis* 45:79–84

Kelly, James R. 1984. "Catholicism and Modern Memory," *Sociological Analysis* 45:131–44.

Lefever, Harry, 1977, "The Religion of the Poor: Escape or Creative Force?" *Journal of the Scientific Study of Religion* 16:225–36.

Lofland, John. 1976. *Doing Social Life* (New York: Wiley).

Lofland, John, and James T. Richardson. 1984. "Religious Movement Organizations," pp. in L. Kreisberg, ed. *Social Movements, Conflict, and Change* (Greenwich, Conn: JAI Publishers).

Lofland, John, and L. N. Skonovd. 1981. "Conversion Motifs," *Journal of the Scientific Study of Religion* 20:373–85.

Lofland, John, and Rodney Stark, 1965, "Becoming a World Saver: A Theory of Conversion to a Deviant Perspective," *American Sociological Review* 30:863–74.

Long, Theodore and Jeffery Haddon. 1983. "Religious Conversion and Socialization," *Journal for the ScientificStudy of Religion* 22:1–14.

Luckmann, Thomas. 1967. *The Invisible Religion* (London: Macmillan).

McGuire, Meredith. 1982. *Pentecostal Catholics: Power, Charisma, and Order in a Religious Movement* (Philadelphia: Temple University Press).

———. 1983a. "Discovering Religious Power," *Sociological Analysis* 44:1–9

———. 1983b, "Words of Power: Personal Empowerment and Healing." *Culture, Medicine, and Psychiatry* 7:1–20.

McLoughlin, William G. 1978. *Revivals, Awakenings and Reform* (Chicago: University of Chicago Press).

Matza, David, 1969, *Becoming Deviant* (Englewood Cliffs, N.J.: Prentice Hall.)

Mol, J. J. 1977. *Identity and the Sacred* (New York: Free Press).

Mukerji, Chandra, and Michael Schudson. 1986. "Popular Culture," *Annual Review of Sociology* 12:47–66.

Neitz, Mary Jo. 1981. "Family, State, and God: Ideologies of the Right to Life Movement," *Sociological Analysis* 42:265–76.

———. 1983. "Church Authority and the Changing Definition of Sin," Paper presented at the meeting of the Midwest Sociological Society, Chicago.

———. 1987. *Charisma and Community: A Study of Religious Commitment within the Charismatic Renewal* (New Brunswick, N. J.: Transaction Press).

———. 1989. "In Goddess We Trust," in Thomas Robbins and Dick Anthony, eds., *In Gods We Trust*, revised edition (New Brunswick: N. J.: Transaction Press.)

Neitz, Mary Jo, and James Spickard. 1989. "Steps toward a Sociology of Religious Experience," *Sociological Analysis* 50, forthcoming.

Newman, William M,, and Peter L, Halvorson. 1984. "Religion and Regional Culture," *Journal for the Scientific Study of Religion* 23:304–14.

Radway, Janice. 1985. *Reading the Romance* (Chapel Hill: University of North Carolina Press).

Richardson, James T. 1985a. "Paradigm Conflict in Conversion Research," *Journal for the Scientific Study of Religion* 24:163–79.

———. 1985b. "Studies of Conversion: Secularization or Re-enchantment?" pp. 104–121 in Phillip Hammond, ed., *The Sacred in a Secular Age* (Berkeley: University of California Press).

Richardson, James T., and Mary Stewart. 1977. "Conversion Process Models and the Jesus Movement," *American Behavioral Scientist* 20:819–38.

Robbins, Thomas and Dick Anthony. 1981. *In Gods We Trust* (New Brunswick, N. J.: Transaction Press).

Robbins, Thomas, Dick Anthony and James Richardson. 1978. "Theory and Research on Today's 'New Religions'," *Sociological Analysis* 39:95–122.

Roof, Wade Clark. 1985. "The Study of Social Change in Religion," pp. 75–89 in Phillip Hammond, ed., *The Sacred in a Secular Age* (Berkeley: The University of California Press).

Roof, Wade Clark, and William McKinney. 1987. *American Mainline Religion* (New Brunswick, N.J.: Rutgers University Press).

Snow, David, and Richard Machalek. 1983. "The Convert as a Social Type," pp. 259–89 in Randall Collins, ed., *Sociological Theory* (San Francisco: Jossey-Bass).

Snow, David, and C.L. Phillips. 1980. "The Lofland-Stark Conversion Model: A Critical Reassessment," *SocialProblems* 27:430–37.

Snow, David, Louis Zurcher, and Sheldon Ekland-Olson. 1980. "Social Networks and Social Movements: A Microstructural Approach to Differential Recruitment," *American Sociological Review* 45: 782–801.

Starhawk, 1982, *Dreaming the Dark* (Boston: Beacon Press).

Stark, Rodney, and William Bainbridge. 1980. "Networks of Faith: Interpersonal Bonds and Recruitment to Cults and Sects," *American Journal of Sociology* 85:1376–95.

———. 1985. *The Future of Religion* (Berkeley: University of California Press.

Straus, Roger. 1976. "Changing Oneself: Seekers and the Creative Transformation of Life Experience," pp. 251–73 in John Lofland, ed., *Doing Social Life* (New York: Wiley).

———. 1979. "Religious Conversion as a Personal and Collective Accomplishment," *Sociological Analysis* 40:158–65.

Stump, Roger. 1984. "Regional Migration and Religious Commitment," *Journal for the Scientific Study of Religion* 23:292–303.

Tipton, Stephen. 1982. *Getting Saved from the Sixties* (Berkeley: University of California Press).

Travisano, Richard. 1970. "Alternation and Conversion as Qualitatively Different Transformations," pp.594–606 in Gregory Stone and Harvey Farberman, eds., *Social Psychology through Symbolic Interaction* (Waltham, Mass.: Xerox College Publishing).

Turner, Victor. 1967. *The Forest of Symbols* (Ithaca: Cornell University Press).

———. 1969. *The Ritual Process* (Chicago, Aldine).

Vaughan, Diane. 1986. *Uncoupling* (New York: Oxford University Press).

Wallace, A. F. C. 1956. "Revitalization Movements," *The American Anthropologist* 58:264–81.

———. 1969. *The Death and Rebirth of the Seneca* (New York: Vintage).

Warner, R. Stephen. 1979. "Theoretical Barriers to the Understanding of Evangelical Christianity," *Sociological Analysis* 40:1–24.

———. 1983. "Research Note: Visits to a Growing Evangelical Church and a Declining Liberal Church in 1978," *Sociological Analysis* 44:243–53.

———. 1988. *New Wine in Old Wineskins* (Berkeley: University of California Press).

Weinstein, Marion. 1981. *Positive Magic* (Custer, Wash.: Phoenix Publishing).

Westley, Frances. 1978. "The Cult of Man: Durkheim's Predictions and the New Religious Movements," *Sociological Analysis* 39:135–45.

Wilson, John and Harvey Clow. 1981. "Themes of Power and Control in a Pentecostal Assembly," *Journal for the Scientific Study of Religion* 20:241–50.

Wright, Stuart. 1984. "Post Involvement Attitudes of Voluntary Defectors from New Religious Movements," *Journal for the Scientific Study of Religion* 23:172–82.

———. 1987. *Leaving the Cults: The Dynamics of Defection*, Monograph Series, No 7.)(Washington, D.C.: Society for the Scientific Study of Religion).

Wuthnow, Robert. 1981. "Two Traditions of Religious Studies," *Journal for the Scientific Study of Religion* 20:16–32.

———. 1987. *Meaning and Moral Order: Explorations in Cultural Analysis* (Berkeley: University of California Press).

5   # Why Philosophers Should Become Sociologists (and Vice Versa)

Kathryn Pyne Addelson

Today, philosophy and sociology are in a ferment—new concepts and theories, new methods, even newly opened fields of research. This volume attests to it. The ferment is the consequence of many historical changes, but intellectually, within the disciplines, it owes a great deal to the collapse of what has been dubbed "the enlightenment orientation." That orientation came to dominance in sociology and philosophy departments in the United States after World War II, though it has often been read back into history, particularly to the origins of modern science and liberal democratic theory (see MacIntyre, 1984).[1]

Under the enlightenment orientation, objective knowledge is the goal of sociology and philosophy—one world, one truth, a unity of science and a unity of morality for all mankind.[2] It is the foundation of a liberal, secular humanism. This metaphysics and epistemology justified the methods philosophers and sociologists used within their disciplines, and it justified their authority as educators and policy advisors. The justification is familiar to sociologists.

> An enlightenment orientation toward social science has been a major presupposition of conventional sociology. The hope has been that public policy could be made to rest on a body of politically neutral theory and fact, validated by scientific method and beyond the disputes of moral and political sides. . . . (Gusfield, 1984:48)

Philosophers rely on conceptual or linguistic methods to provide theories and analyses which are also supposed to be neutral among moral and political sides. The enlightenment orientation justifies scholars' authority as researchers and as educators and policy advisors.

It sets philosophers and sociologists as professional experts, not as partisans.

Even in its heyday, the enlightenment orientation was never without its serious critics. By the mid-1960s, the criticisms were widespread and widely known in the United States—in history, sociology, philosophy, and even some of the natural sciences. Thomas Kuhn described scientific progress in terms that had more to do with science training and politics than enlightenment rationality.[3]

In philosophy W. V. Quine made seemingly parochial arguments against the analytic-synthetic distinction. But one consequence of the arguments is that there are no neutral, theory-independent, observable facts. Observation (Quine said) is polluted by scientific language and theory, and by the language and conceptual scheme of the society at large (Quine 1963, 1969). These arguments have generally been accepted about natural and social science. They affect the philosopher's use of conceptual analysis as well. If observation is inseparable from concept, then concept is inseparable from observation. Scientists have no neutral observational data, and philosophers have no neutral conceptual data—both methods fail when the analytic-synthetic distinction collapses.

In the philosophy of the social sciences, Peter Winch (1972) pressed his earlier distinction between scientist's rules and native's rules. Cultural relativism was extended to fact and science, not simply value and morality. The question became, How are we to study a human world in which meaning and morality, science and truth are all in the process of construction?

In philosophy, there is ferment as scholars work out methods and metaphysics for studying such worlds, but so far, the efforts amount to work of the "transition," as Richard Rorty (1979) calls it, not the new philosophy itself. In contrast, in sociology the collapse of the enlightenment orientation can be seen as a triumph of symbolic interactionism.[4] In this paper, I'll argue that in their research, philosophers should move out of the "transition" by adopting the methods and metaphysics of the symbolic interactionists. That move would resolve the internal problems that philosophers are struggling with within their discipline. That is why (and how) philosophers should become sociologists. It doesn't solve the "external" problems that philosophers and sociologists alike face as educators and policy advisors—Gusfield's worry. That requires some philosophical work—and so the phrase "(and vice versa)" in the title of this essay.

Because of our social locations as researchers, educators, and policy advisors, we have, as a matter of fact, institutional warrant for making and dispersing knowledge. The enlightenment orientation, with its ideal of objectivity and the unity of mankind, gives a metaphysical and epistemological basis for that warrant, not a political and institutional one: if we develop our methods properly, we will discover neutral fact and make neutral theory. On the enlightenment approach, the methods and metaphysics that we develop internally justify the authority that we exercise externally.[5] The social, political, and moral questions about our cognitive authority in the society become moot.

Some of the critics of the enlightenment orientation have taken our authority seriously. Feminist Dorothy Smith speaks of the ruling apparatus—"that familiar complex of management, government administration, professions, and intelligentsia, as well as the textually mediated discourses that coordinate and interpenetrate it"(1987:109). Smith says that sociology is part of the ruling apparatus, and of course, philosophy is as well. That is another way of talking about our authority as scholars. But we shouldn't understand Smith as saying that as part of the ruling apparatus, we mechanically and ineluctably manufacture oppression. As a feminist scholar, Smith works at producing a sociology for women, presumably as a work of liberation. In this anthology addressed to professional scholars, the question is what a sociology for sociologists ought to be, scientifically and morally, given that sociology is part of what Smith calls the ruling apparatus. And a similar question must be asked about a philosophy for philosophers. These are social, political, and moral questions about our cognitive authority in society, questions that become moot under the enlightenment orientation.[6]

As scholarly authorities, symbolic interactionists have been in a curious position. Internally, they use a metaphysics and method that is contrary to the enlightenment orientation, and they have often criticized sociologists using that orientation.[7] But externally, it is the dominant enlightenment orientation that justifies their authority as educators and policy advisors—as part of the ruling apparatus. In its popular (rather than scholarly) form, the orientation justified developing the academic professions and disciplines. If we are explicit about changing our methods and metaphysics to those of symbolic interactionism, then we have to be explicit about the social, political, and moral questions about our authority.

The postenlightenment question is, how are we to study a human world in which meaning and morality, science and truth are all in the process of construction? We must give a double answer, one that takes account of method and metaphysics within the disciplines and our authority outside them. Both philosophers and sociologists have to make the double answer together. Here is my own beginning on the answer.

On the enlightenment orientation, the world is a world of facts and objects in which truth is discovered. My own understanding of the metaphysics of symbolic interactionism is this. Truth is not discovered, it is enacted. Enacting truth requires authority of one sort or another. The folk, whose activities both philosophers and sociologists are concerned with, enact truth in various ways, and both philosophers and sociologists must be able to explain how. Symbolic interactionists have ways of explaining how. But in doing research on those folk, scholars also enact truth. The question of how they do so is in part a question internal to their disciplines, as a question of method and evidence. But it is also, in part, a question of the social organization of knowledge in the United States today. In both cases, it concerns our scholarly authority and our moral responsibility. It concerns our authority as scholars living in the folk society. The question of a sociology for sociologists (or a philosophy for philosophers) is a question of how to be morally, politically, and scientifically responsible in our place within the "ruling apparatus."

I'll proceed to expand my remarks by making links between philosophy and sociology. I'll draw my cases from ethics and the study of morality, in part because morality is central to sociological work—even as philosophers benefit from knowing the empirical work, sociologists benefit from a more precise understanding of moral theories. And, of course, morality is also central to solving our own scholarly problem of passing beyond the enlightenment orientation.

But first, a look at the state of philosophy today.

SOME PROBLEMS OF PHILOSOPHY

The profession of philosophy has been in a state of flux for the past fifteen years. The *New York Times* playfully represents the flux as a dispute between analytic philosophers and "philosophers for pluralism" and has fun talking about philosophers doing battle (see, for example, December 20, 1987, front page). The internecine squabble is an outward sign of transformations within analytic philosophy that have already taken place—transformations that came out of a crisis in analytic philosophy. The crisis shows in the titles of books of the recent past—*Beyond Objectivism and Relativism* (Bernstein, 1983); *Revisions* (Hauerwas and MacIntyre, 1983); *Post Analytic Philosophy*

(Rajchman and West,1985); *After Philosophy* (Baynes, Bohman, and McCarthy, 1987); and *After Virtue* (MacIntyre, 1984). Some of the best sellers are books dismantling the analytic tradition, books of the transition—as Richard Rorty (1979) says of *Philosophy and the Mirror of Nature*. Rorty has remarked, "The notion of 'logical analysis' turned upon itself and committed slow suicide" (1982:227).[8]

Analytic philosophy came to dominance in the United States after World War II. In its more technical quarters, it was rooted in the scientific revolutions of the earlier twentieth century—not only in physics, but the great advances in logic, formal languages, and metamathematics based on work by Gottlob Frege, Bertrand Russell, Alfred Tarski, Kurt Gödel and others. In its less technical quarters, including ethics, it relied on the premise that the conceptual (or linguistic) is separable from the empirical (or factual).[9] This is a version of the analytic-synthetic distinction, and it relies on analyses within the enlightenment orientation. The philosophical method is conceptual or linguistic analysis.

Use of the analytic method is widespread, and it dominates the understanding of philosophical research and teaching. In sheer numbers, most analytic philosophers continue with their old methods of conceptual analysis. In "basic research" they construct moral theories or new moral vocabularies. In applied philosophy (a counterpart of policy work in sociology), they analyze moral concepts and arguments that they feel are relevant to social problems (abortion, animal rights, environmental issues are examples), or institutional settings (informed consent, issues in professional ethics), or to everyday life (promising, sex, drugs, love, racism, pornography). The grand effort in the discipline is still on reasoning, and one of the expanding areas for jobs in philosophy is that of "critical thinking." One quite typical introductory text published in 1988 tells students that philosophy trains us in "the critical and rational examination of the most fundamental assumptions that underlie our lives" (Velasquez and Barry, 1988:4) An introductory text in applied ethics defines four goals of the philosophical study of morality: clarification of moral ideas and issues, comprehensive vision of ideas and insights, critical assessment of moral claims, and moral guidance. (Martin, 1989).

In her 1985 paper reviewing current, workaday, philosophical research, "Standards in Philosophy," analytic philosopher Ruth Macklin cited some "paradigmatic characteristics of the Philosophical enterprise."[10]

A. Defining terms and analyzing concepts.

B. Attending to the logic of arguments, detecting fallacies, and uncovering assumptions.

C. Analyzing and interpreting other writings—within or without philosophy.

D. Constructing hypothetical arguments for or against positions (whether or not one accepts the underlying assumptions or the conclusions of the arguments).

E. Offering sustained normative arguments in favor of a substantive position held by thinkers outside philosophy. (Macklin, 1985:276) This is a succinct statement of the traditional conceptual method.

No one would argue that muddy thinking is preferable to clear thinking. But these definitions of philosophical work preserve the separation of concept and fact as well as the image of human society as an aggregate of individuals doing mental gymnastics on the way to separate value choices and decisions. That is the enlightenment orientation in ethics, as it shows in a liberal, secular humanism.

What of the "postanalytic philosophers" (as we might call them) who are making a new philosophy out of the collapse of the enlightenment orientation?[11] In ethics, there is a focus on character, community, narrative, care, trust, and the like. However, the main emphasis is still on language and ideas.. At times, "conversation" is a term that substitutes for method. Richard Rorty says that philosophy becomes "a voice in the conversation of mankind" (1979).[12] In the source reader for the television series, "Ethics in America" Lisa Newton speaks of "the conversation about ethics" which "intensifies and dies out as the civilizations around it provide or deny" what is needed for systematic, extended thought (1988:3). The prime difficulty here is that "conversation of mankind" is a metaphor when we need to know literally who is making the meaning of ethics, how they do it, what authority they exercise in doing it, and what are the outcomes of their doing it. In Dorothy Smith's language, what does this "conversation" amount to in the work of the ruling apparatus? These are not questions extrinsic to the doing of philosophy, they are questions that are constitutive of the philosophical task.

The conversational method hasn't been the only one proposed, of course. And, of course, other critics have argued that philosophy should be given up in favor of some science or other. W. V. Quine came to that conclusion from his own criticism of the analytic tradition. His point was that we cannot separate meaning of terms from their references in the world. We cannot peel the concepts off the facts. The consequence is that we cannot distinguish the task of philosophy from that of science. Quine concluded that epistemology (the study of our knowledge of the world) should be done not by philosophers but by neurophysiologists. The neurophysiologists, of course, cannot get outside our conceptual scheme to give us neutral theories about the objective facts. There are no neutral facts, says Quine, only a world conceptualized; the best we can do is go with the best science of the day (Quine, 1963, 1969).

Neurophysiology won't do as the best science of the day because the human world is a world of meaning, and for scientific and moral reasons, we must respect that. Symbolic interactionism offers appropriate methods for studying a world of meaning. Symbolic interactionism offers an appropriate metaphysics of human nature and human group life (which neurophysiology does not and cannot).

A criticism of the enlightenment orientation must give us a way to move beyond the transition to a new philosophy and sociology. In the next section, I'll discuss the "rules and norms" view of morality that attends the enlightenment orientation in order to give an interactionist criticism that leads to a new understanding of human nature and society. In the following section, I'll discuss postanalytic ethics of narrative and character to show how interactionist sociologists can work with philosophers in making a more adequate ethics. In the last section, I'll return to the fundamental question of how our method and metaphysics can allow us to do responsible sociology and philosophy, even within the ruling apparatus.

MORAL THEORY: PRINCIPLES AND RULES

In *The Idea of a Social Science*, Peter Winch claimed that "the analysis of meaningful behaviour must allot a central role to the notion of a rule; that all behavior which is meaningful (therefore all specifically human behaviour) is ipso facto rule governed" (1963:51–52). Not everyone agrees with Winch—Quine talked about neurophysiology replacing epistemology; behavioral psychologists and population geneticists formulate their own theories. Not everyone who agrees with Winch's remark means the same thing by it. But the view that meaningful behavior involves rules has been compelling for many people. The ethics of principles and rules is one important mainstream interpretation of it.

The Encyclopedia of Philosophy was published in 1968. The philosopher writing the entry "Rules" gave a general statement of the approach in ethics. He describes rules as "prescribed guides for conduct" which are essential to any practice or institution "such as a game"—and he gives the standard philosophic examples of baseball, bridge, and informal children's games. He goes on,

> morality is a rule-governed activity that guides conduct and molds and alters actions and attitudes. . . .
>
> Moral rules are precepts that ought to be followed, whether they are in fact followed or not. Moral rules, in this sense, are very different from rules which define customs and practices: one can find out empirically what rules people advocate or observe, but, as Hume and G. E. Moore insisted, one cannot determine by such empirical study whether these rules really ought to be followed—that is, whether they are moral rules. (*Encyclopedia of Philosophy*: s.v. "rules," 232)

These remarks presuppose that morality has to do with rules (or principles) and that there is some criterion for distinguishing moral rules from rules of custom. The encyclopedia sets a division of labor between philosophers and social scientists: philosophers set out the criterion, social scientists empirically investigate the customs. The remarks presuppose a metaphysics of human nature and group life and a philosophic method.

In the enlightenment orientation, there are two aspects to the distinction between moral and customary rules that are important for sociologists to understand. The first is set in terms of the distinction between autonomy and heteronomy, and it concerns the way in which the moral rules affect an individual's decisions and actions. An individual acts autonomously when he or she freely and rationally choses the rule that governs his or her behavior. In contrast, a person acts heteronomously when his or her behavior is conditioned by custom or arises out of socialization. In this aspect, genuine moral decision and action is contrasted with mere customary behavior. Both involve rules. Both take the individual as the source of decision and action. But the way the rules enter is different. Philosophers analyze rules and reasoning allegedly involved in autonomous moral action; sociologists describe rules and behavior allegedly involved in heteronomous moral action.

The second aspect concerns the nature of the rules: the form of moral rules is different from that of customary rules. In one of its phrasings, Kant's categorical imperative gives a criterion for distinguishing genuine moral rules from other rules: Act always so that you could consistently will your maxim to be a universal law. As a criterion, the imperative is a second order principle that we are to use to criticize our rules of practice. Philosophers have put this by saying that genuine moral rules or principles must be universalizable. Although Kant believed that the imperative defined one morality for all rational beings, most analytic philosophers wouldn't require that all human groups have the same rules. But though the rules might have different content, to be moral rules, they would have to satisfy the universalizability criterion. And to be morally rational, group members would have to give reasons in terms of the moral rules and principles, accept reasons in those terms, and criticize the rules they use by some version of the categorical imperative. This argument acknowledges the fact of cultural difference while preserving the moral unity of mankind.

Contemporary philosophers working in principle ethics downplay or ignore the claim that philosophers are supposed to analyze the a priori framework for human morality. However, they keep the definition of moral rationality and they keep the a priori, conceptual method. Faced with the moral diversity of the United States, many of them have retreated to analyzing the principles and rules of "public morality" in the United States. Public morality is the morality of obligations and rights that we are said to share in the United States (or perhaps in the West), in contrast to various religious or ethnic or communal or individual moralities. For the most part, it is what Lawrence Kohlberg (1971) called "the official morality of the United States" (level three, stage five of his developmental scheme). Ruth Macklin's remarks (quoted above) describe this sort of work in applied ethics. The "official morality" shares the liberal, secular humanist metaphysics of individuals as the source of decisions in a society that is an aggregate of ideally free, rational atoms.

There has been sustained criticism of this approach. In fact, when Winch wrote that "all specifically human behavior is ipso facto rule governed," he did not mean that the governing rules exist in some reified conceptual or linguistic form that is open to "objective" analysis by sociologists and philosophers. Quite the contrary. His point, following Wittgenstein, is that the meaning of the rules is made by group members in action together, as they apply the rules in living their personal and group lives. In some ways, this is close to symbolic interactionism.[13]

In his statement of the metaphysics of interactionist sociology, Herbert Blumer says,

> A gratuitous acceptance of the concepts of norms, values, social rules, and the like should not blind the social scientist to the fact that any one of them is subtended by a process of social interaction—a process that is necessary not only for their change but equally well for their retention in a fixed form. It is the social process in group life that creates and upholds the rules, not the rules that create and uphold group life. (1969:19)

This statement puts the focus not on the rules and principles but on their creation and retention. More than that, it offers a metaphysics of the human world in which the creation of moral theories and vocabularies is shown to be a political act, not simply a conceptual one. With such a metaphysics, we need an empirical method, not a conceptual one.

Howard Becker writes in more general terms of ways in which rules and definitions of all sorts operate in the process of creating and maintaining social structure.

> Interactionist theories of deviance, like interactionist theories generally, pay attention to how social actors define each other and their environments. They pay particular attention to differentials in the power to define; in the way one group achieves and uses the power to define how other groups will be regarded, understood, and treated. Elites, ruling classes, bosses, adults, men, Caucasians—superordinate groups generally—maintain their power as much by controlling how people define the world, its components, and its possibilities, as by the use of more primitive forms of control. They may use more primitive means to establish hegemony. But control based on the manipulation of definitions and labels works more smoothly and costs less; superordinates prefer it. (1973:204)

Rather than rules and principles defining the morality of a group, the proper group members are "morally bound to accept the definition imposed on reality by a superordinate group in preference to the definitions espoused by subordinates" (Becker, 1970:126).

Here we see the question of scholars' authority and our place in the ruling apparatus. In the United States, scholars are members of a superordinate group. Philosophers (and other academics of course) have significant "power to define," as Becker puts it.

The political consequences of an unexamined "power to define" are blatant in applied ethics. For example, analytic philosophers regularly define the moral problem of abortion as a conflict of rights: the right of the woman to determine what happens in and to her body versus the right to life of the fetus. Despite much criticism, that definition is still the one that dominates introductory texts and classroom discussion. It formulates the central moral issue of the social problem of abortion in a way that limits debate. It leaves in limbo those who oppose or support public policies on abortion on moral grounds of love, sexuality, or the good of mankind, rather than on the basis of rights. In "clarifying the moral issue," the analytic philosophers silence others.[14] To the degree that they do so, they define public morality, not analyze it—a problem that is analogous to the much discussed issue of sociologists defining social problems. But philosophic method and metaphysics obscure this fact, making it difficult to face the responsibilities of an elite defining the public morality.

The scholarly error can basically be seen as a false understanding of human nature and human group life. These philosophers analyze the products of group life—rules and individuals are both products. In doing so, they ignore the process by which the products come to be constructed as products. They study group life as if it consisted of objects not actions, rules and individuals, not collective making of meaning. These mistakes lead to their faulty method. They also, of course, lead to moral failure. Although the analytic philosophers have always been outstanding at criticizing their intellectual work within their disciplines ("the notion of logical analysis turned upon itself and committed slow suicide"), they have traditionally ignored the social organization of knowledge and their place in it.[15] With their expertise justified by the enlightenment orientation, analytic philosophers have refused to discuss their actual places in the ruling apparatus. For them, the large questions of scholarly authority and responsibility are moot.

Today, many of the vanguard workers in philosophical ethics have rejected the old rules and principles view and are devising new approaches to moral theory. Because I'm seriously recommending that philosophers become sociologists (and vice versa), I'll describe some of the new work on narrative, to make links between philosophy and sociology.

NARRATIVE, CHARACTER, AND THE SELF

The premises on the rational and moral unity of mankind collapsed along with the enlightenment orientation. The new premises include the thesis that the human world is structured by language in ways that vary with convention and forms of life: There is no way to get at the world outside of language, either to compare language with the world or to compare different forms of life (or even scientific paradigms) with each other. There is no neutral, outside vantage point for an observer to take. One way the premises are interpreted in the new ethics is by emphasizing narrative language.

Over the past generation, narrative has become increasingly important as a scholarly method in history, women's studies, psychology, political science, and even in some quarters of sociology (see Polkinghorne, 1987). Jerome Bruner has elevated narrative to one of the two basic modes of human cognition, the other being the logico-scientific mode that is used in the morality of principles and rules, the mode presupposed in the enlightenment orientation (Bruner, 1986). In contrast, narrative is said to be historical and contextual. Alasdair MacIntyre is a major proponent of the narrative approach.

MacIntyre uses narrative as his own philosophical method, telling a story of intellectual arguments from the Middle Ages to the present as a way of defining and criticizing the enlightenment orientation.[16] He also claims that narrative is the way human beings explain the moral doings in life: man is a storytelling animal. MacIntyre prefers to talk about intelligibility rather than rationality, and he claims that we make things intelligible through narrative. Our human nature differs from the beasts' natures because we converse and tell stories, and because we have histories and biographies. He says,

> [E]very moral philosophy offers explicitly or implicitly at least a partial conceptual analysis of the relationship of an agent to his or her reasons, motives, intentions and actions, and in so doing generally presupposes some claim that these concepts are embodied in or at least can be in the real social world. (1984:23)[17]

His analysis is that narrative (in history and biography) relates agent to motive, intention, and action.

Richard Bondi states a principle of the narrative approach when he says, "[H]uman beings are creatures formed in communities marked by allegiance to a normative story [or narrative]. This formation can best be discussed in the language of character" (1984:201). Human nature is said to be essentially historical, and character and community necessarily linked. Human beings require "a narrative to give our life coherence" (Hauerwas 1977:27).[18]

This approach in ethics seems compatible with C. Wright Mills's well known discussion of vocabularies of motive. Motives, Mills says, are explanations given in answer to questions about a person's activity. The search for "real" motives is mistaken.

> Rather than fixed elements "in" an individual, motives are the terms with which interpretation of conduct by social actors proceeds. This imputation and avowal of motives by actors are social phenomena to be explained. The differing reasons men give for their actions are not themselves without reasons. (1963:439–40)

Using narrative as the mode of explanation in moral theory makes philosophical sense of Mills's remarks. We may need a conceptual analysis of the relationship of an agent to his or her reasons and motives (as MacIntyre says), but we must proceed by seeing how the relationship is socially constructed in the making of the narrative. We need empirically adequate concepts, theories, methods, and a stock of good empirical studies.[19]

If we insist on empirical adequacy, we begin to see how "narrative" operates in creating and maintaining the social order. In interactionist field studies, we find that some people have the authority or power to define the terms in which their own and other people's stories are to be officially narrated. This authority must be taken account of.[20] There are as many errors in speaking of the narrative of a community as there are in speaking of the rules or principles of a community, and Blumer's advice is as good here as there: the processes of human group life must be known, and scholars should not take the products as self-evident. This is true whether we call the products rules or narratives.

If we say the moral world consists in action interpreted through narrative, then we need scholarly methods, concepts, and theories suited to studying such a world of action. We need to find out what the narratives are and how they are constructed in specific cases. This requires methods, concepts, and theories of an empirical science. But the science cannot be empirical in the enlightenment sense that either narrative or constructions exist as neutral data. In the rest of this section, I'll mention some of the interactionist concepts and theories that I find useful to moral theory.

It is in theory guided by field studies that the symbolic interactionist tradition is most valuable—including its accounts of the self, character, and virtue and vice. Studies of deviance are prime examples, particularly because they give us concepts to guide the study. For example, Lemert's notion of secondary deviance shows how a self and human character are formed in the labeling process, i.e., in the course of acquiring the biography of a deviant (Lemert, 1951).

The notion of a career has been useful in a multitude of field studies. Erving Goffman was only sometimes a symbolic interactionist. But his widely quoted remark from "The Moral Career of the Mental Patient" states how the dual nature of the self is captured by the concept.

> One value of the concept of career is its two-sidedness. One side is linked to internal matters held dearly and closely, such as the image of self and felt identity; the other side concerns official position, jural relations, and style of life, and is part of a publicly accessible institutional complex. The concept of career, then, allows one to move back and forth between the personal and the public, between the self and its significant society, without having to rely overly for data upon what the person says he thinks he imagines himself to be. (1961:127)

Goffman calls his paper "an exercise in the institutional approach to the self."

In my paper "Moral Passages" (1987), I used research by Prudence Rains to talk about a network of careers that may chart social options available to different people within a group. Rains did several field studies in the late 1960s, which she reported and discussed in her book *Becoming an Unwed Mother*. They included studies of mainly white and middle-class young women at a home for unwed mothers and of black, mainly poor teenagers at a day school for unwed mothers.

Rains's studies make it clear that narratives and biographies were indeed constructed as accounts of the young women's behavior. They show that the social workers involved had tremendous influence in "coauthoring" the narratives of the mostly white, middle-class women, and very little influence in coauthoring the black teenagers' personal biographies. In the case of the black teenagers, certain narratives were recorded in official places—with the police, the schools, the social service agencies, and the registry of births. One of the teens said of officials, "They keep records."[21] The black teens had, in effect, at least two biographies—the one they lived in the home neighborhood and the one in the official records. And, of course, all of them had many more "narratives" than that. Unitary life histories are for public figures, and for them only as they appear in school history books.

There are other new approaches in ethics that stress narrative and the historical nature of the self. Under the rules and principles ethics, the moral notions of responsibility and care were neglected in favor of obligations and rights. Carol Gilligan's work (1982) is probably the best known of the efforts to make notions of responsibility and care central.[22] Gilligan developed the responsibility-care orientation by criticizing Lawrence Kohlberg's principle morality of obligation and rights. The latter imposed male gender dominance. Gilligan saw that moral reasoning was being socially constructed in the Kohlberg "laboratory" and classroom. But in spite of that criticism, she herself ignored the processes by which narratives are made. It is within these processes that systematic relations of gender, and of age, race, class, ethnicity, and so on, are constructed.[23]

On the other hand, with the help of moral theorists, it may be possible to answer some of the criticisms perennially aimed at interactionist work. One common complaint has been that the tradition emphasizes the social at the cost of the personal—the public at the cost of the internal self and its creativity. An analogous criticism is that the tradition emphasizes the cognitive at the cost of the emotional. Some moral theorists and some feminist theorists offer help here.

Richard Bondi criticizes some of the "narrative" moral theories because they do not give a way of speaking about the self as we experience it, which is at the same time the self in relation to the world. As a first step toward correcting the defects, he sets out "the elements of character" that must be analyzed and accounted for. They include the human capacity for intentional action; the involvement that affections and passions have with moral action and character; the subjection to the accidents of history; and what he calls "the capacity of the heart," "that intimate mix of memory, imagination and the desire for union we experience as marking the center of ourselves" (1984: 204–5). Bondi is setting out a program rather than giving a finished analysis, but it is a program that is important for both sociologists and philosophers.

Other philosophers have other offerings. For example, Annette Baier has written on the importance of trust as a moral concept that is essential to understanding community (1986). It is also important for interactionists to understand the moral notion of responsibility. The old "principle morality" and the old "rules and norms" sociology dealt with obligations and sanctions. Responsibility is receiving renewed attention in philosophy, and it is a moral notion that fits better with an ethics of narrative and character (Ladd, 1970; Whitbeck, 1982).

At this point, we need to turn more directly to interactionist metaphysics and method and its relation to scholarly authority.[24]

METHODS AND MORALS

The enlightenment world was one of objects and concepts that could be objectively observed and neutrally reported. In contrast, the postanalytic philosophers and the symbolic interactionists agree that the human world is a world not of objects but of action and interpretation. Our question here is, What is a morally and scientifically responsible way to study such a world, given our social positions as scholarly authorities within the ruling apparatus? This is the double question that concerns responsible methods and metaphysics to serve as a basis for responsible work by members of our disciplines for members of the society as a whole. On the one hand, it is a question of honesty in our vocations; on the other, it is a question of responsible service—I hope we are serving the people as members of the ruling apparatus, rather than serving the ruling apparatus (or our own little disciplinary segments of it).

The methods and metaphysics of symbolic interactionism are those of an empirical science—but not an empirical science as defined within the enlightenment orientation. Our first movement toward meeting the double question is to see what sort of empirical science symbolic interactionism is.

Herbert Blumer's statement of the basic premises of interactionism characterize the empirical world that social scientists and philosophers study as scholars. Blumer says,

> Let me begin by identifying the empirical social world in the case of human beings. This world is the actual group life of human beings. . . . The life of a human society, or of any segment of it, or of any organization in it, or of its participants consists of the action and experience of people as they meet the situations that arise in their respective worlds.
>
> . . . [T]he empirical social world consists of ongoing group life and one has to get close to this life to know what is going on in it. If one is going to respect the social world, one's problems, guiding conceptions, data, schemes of relationship, and ideas of interpretation have to be faithful to that empirical world. (Blumer, 1969:35, 38)

Blumer talks about respecting the social world and having concepts and methods that are faithful to it. The methods Blumer names include direct observation, field study, participant observation, case study, interviewing, use of life histories, use of letters and diaries, public documents, and conversation (Blumer, 1969:50). These are methods that are learned, used, criticized, changed, and developed, i.e., they are scientific methods, not procedures carved in stone. Among these sociologists, the methods are continually examined to see whether they allow researchers to remain faithful to the empirical world. They are also examined to see whether they allow researchers to be respectful of the subjects and cognizant of their own authority in the research situation.[25] The methods are the basis of gathering data, even for dissident sociologists like Dorothy Smith. Criticism comes from "traditionals" and feminists alike. But we must be careful about what "data" means.

Within the enlightenment orientation, the problem of data is an ontological and epistemological one: there must be neutral, observable facts and distinct language and concepts if science is to find out the truth about the objects of the world.[26] This is because the enlightenment truth is one to be discovered. In contrast, as I said at the beginning of the paper, the interactionist truth is enacted. Under interactionist ontology, facts are enacted through political and social processes.

To a limited degree, the enlightenment notion of truth has been overcome in philosophy and sociology. For example, when Thomas Kuhn discusses revolutionary science, he describes processes by which the facts and truths of a new paradigm come to be enacted within a scientific discipline. Kuhn clung to the enlightenment approach by assuming that scientists had authority to enact truth for the larger society. He did not explicitly analyze scientific authority in *The Structure of Scientific Revolutions*.[27] Enacting facts and truth requires authority of one sort or another. It requires authority to define the world and authority to have the definitions officially accepted. These are startling claims only if we cling to an enlightenment view of facts and truth.

Much interactionist work concerns how truth is enacted among the folk—studies on deviance and social problems fall into this category. Take, as an example, Prudence Rains' study on unwed mothers mentioned above. In the late 1960s in the Midwest, the truth that unwed motherhood was deviant was enacted among her white middle-class subjects by the efforts of families to conceal these pregnancies, by the existence of maternity homes that guarded the secrets, and by the social and economic systems that made it very difficult for the families to raise an "illegitimate" child while preserving the young mother's future options. In the black Chicago neighborhoods, the truth of a girl's having a deviant (or incorrigible) character was constructed by social workers, police reports, and a whole coordinated edifice of action and recordkeeping.

Today, unwed motherhood is deviant in some communities but not others. Teen pregnancy has emerged out of secrecy and become a social problem. The social problem has been enacted as a fact by thousands of political and scholarly efforts. This does not mean that "if we believe it true, then it is true." Enacting truth isn't a matter of mere belief and attitude. Enacting truth means living together so that our worlds, our lives and our characters are made in certain ways.

The emphasis on enacting truth is connected with knowing how to get along in our collective life rather than knowing that some proposition is true or some fact exists. The enlightenment tradition was obsessed with "knowing that." The analysis of scientific theories and concepts and scientific truth was slave to that obsession. In contrast, the interactionist tradition requires that "knowing how" be taken seriously. Consider Howard Becker's notion of a folk concept.

Folk concepts give meaning to our activities in the sense that they help us know how to do those activities together. Becker says, in fact, that folk concepts are shorthand terms people use to organize the way they do things together (see Becker, 1970:92). They convey a conception of a distinctive way of organizing what we do, including characteristic activities, typical settings, cast of characters, typical careers and problems. The folk term suggests that all these things hang together in a neat pattern. In some interesting cases, like "profession" or "discipline," the term carries with it a justification that rationalizes the social and political place of the work and those who do it. In others, like "lesbian," "drug dealer," or "pregnant teen," the term carries a justification for treating such people and activities as deviant.

Folk concepts are used by us folk to point to what we do, and to coordinate what we do together (in the sense that even a war requires coordinating both sides). Folk terms point out activities that "the folk" take to be the same, in the sense that they know how to do the same thing again. The shorthand folk term may suggest certain neat patterns, but that suggestion is persuasive and used in explanations and arguments that ultimately involve authority, not criteria. Through folk terms, we enact truth and make our communities and our characters.[28]

In discussing how the folk enact truth, I have implicitly made a distinction between the folk ways of enacting the truth that are being described by sociologists, and the ways of enacting truth that sociologists use in doing the describing. In the enlightenment orientation, this is usually set as a normative distinction between the value-laden ways of the folk and the objective, rational ways of the scientist or philosopher. In philosophy, it has sometimes been set as a distinction between unruly ordinary language and precise scientific or philosophical language.

It is obvious that scientists and philosophers are members of the folk, and their ways can be studied. Studying ourselves as members of the folk is essential to our methods and morals. But here I am making a distinction between the ways of the folk that we are describing and the ways that we are using in doing the describing. This can't be reduced to a distinction between the language the folk use versus the language we use in describing them. It is a question of authority and modes of action. To act responsibly, we have to take on the double task of criticizing our methods as well as understanding our authority as professionals, i.e., as enactors of truth within the folk society.

If we accept the premise that truth is enacted, then our understanding of concepts and theories must change accordingly. In the enlightenment view, truth is discovered about a world of objects open to neutral observation. Truth is embodied in language, not in action. Scientific concepts must be defined so as to clearly distinguish their instances, ultimately in terms of observation. The definitions have to give necessary or sufficient conditions for the term's application—the movement for operational definitions was one extreme manifestation of this approach.[29] If terms do not give us criteria for telling when an event happens or fails to happen, we will be unable to confirm or falsify our propositions.

The enlightenment account of scientific concepts won't do for a world in which truth is enacted. In contrast, Herbert Blumer calls the sociologists' concepts "sensitizing concepts," or "sensitizing instruments." They are not the sort of concepts that define necessary or sufficient conditions for their instances. With sensitizing concepts, Blumer says, "we seem forced to reach what is common by accepting and using what is distinctive to the given empirical instance." This, he said, is due not to the immaturity of sociology but to the nature of the empirical world which is its object of study (1969:148).

In his 1987 book, *Qualitative Analysis for Social Scientists*, Anselm Strauss lays out some methods appropriate to developing adequate concepts. In contrast to the abstract conceptual analysis of the philosophers, Strauss insists that analysis is synonymous with interpretation of data (1987:4). The interpretation, and the progressive data collection, must pass through stages of evolution structured according to an ongoing process of coding and memo writing. "Coding" is his general term for conceptualizing the data.

Developing rich and complex concepts with which to discuss a field study, through coding and memo writing, is the focus of Strauss's idea of grounded theory (1987:26). That is, "theory" in this sense is not an abstract set of universal laws to be tied to observation by definitions of its terms. But it is genuine theory in the sense of giving a general picture of human group life and social structure—as general as the data allow. Theory in a particular field study may use concepts or categories developed in other studies. For example, the concept of a career (and its associated theory) is used in many studies. But the concept must be developed and tested within the present study just as if it were new and derived from the coding of present material. Strauss himself warns against assuming the "analytic relevance of any face sheet or traditional variable such as age, sex, social class, or race until it emerges as relevant" (1987:32). They too must earn a way into the grounded theory. By using these methods, the community of fieldworkers continually test theory and develop a system of concepts useful for showing patterns across cases.

At this point, enter the sceptical chorus: To whom are those patterns useful? To whom are they the same—according to whose concepts, rules, theories, practices, language, conversation, or narrative? [30] The answer is that, initially at least, they are patterns according to the researchers' concepts, theories, practices, and so on. Given the researchers' places of authority in the social organization of knowledge, the concepts may be extended to the rest of the folk through the educational system, the media, and other institutional means. This is how folk understanding changes according to the scholarly way of enacting truth. Initially, the patterns are useful to the researchers, but if the research is successful, they must ultimately be useful to the folk as well, and the folk ways of enacting truth and doing things together. And at this point, we meet the other side of the double question—the question of responsible service to the people as members of the ruling apparatus.

According to the enlightenment orientation, we do responsible work by sticking to the facts and concepts and leaving the values and policy decisions to the appropriate officeholders. Rejecting the enlightenment orientation leaves us face to face with our moral and political tasks. If the enlightenment approach allowed us to be blindly partisan as a group, we now run the danger of being self-consciously partisan as individuals.

The individualistic metaphysics of the enlightenment orientation has collapsed within the disciplines. But its individualistic, secular humanism remains behind as the folk ethics of most of us scholars. I say folk ethics here because it is an ethics most of us use even when we criticize it. Robert Bellah and Richard Rorty (and many others) individualistically choose to become patriots, then use their authority in advising us to polish up the old stories of the American tradition to serve up to school children. Other scholars individualistically chose to become feminists or Marxists or minority advocates, then use their authority in espousing whatever cause they feel is appropriate. In their research, these scholars may raise issues and give criticisms that are essential to our work—I am not questioning that. I am saying that we should not reject the old, enlightenment orientation in our methods and metaphysics, then unself-consciously presuppose it in an ethics that has us "choosing" liberalism, Marxism, feminism, or whatever as basic "values" to direct our individual work. This is self-deception, because truth is not enacted by individuals choosing basic values. Values are not ideas on which we individually act—even though our folk concepts may explain them in that way.

Philosophers and other scholars have, of course, influenced the folk explanations and, perhaps, the course of history. In commenting on an earlier version of this essay, Jerry Schneewind argued that inventing moral theory and vocabulary has been, socially and politically, an important philosophical task. He wrote to me concerning Kant's contribution,

> Imagine a society where people weren't well educated and didn't have time to think about politics but are coming to be in that position. Suppose their sole vocabulary was one that stressed individual subordination to the law: to the king, to the pastor, to God. And suppose someone said, "Think of yourselves as making your own laws. All our moral terms can be explained that way. And you then can see that you can't be ruled by just anyone, because you rule yourself first."
>
> There's a political and social point to the Kantian vocabulary; people could use it for definite situated purposes. (personal correspondence, Fall, 1988)

I agree that what Schneewind says is important. Philosophers have filled and will continue to fill political and social roles. And so will sociologists and all the other varieties of humanists and scientists. My point in this paper is that when we are exercising our authority as members of academic disciplines, we must be morally and intellectually honest about what we are doing. We must consistently extend our sound scholarly methods and judgments into our action as authorities enacting truth in the social world.

Kant devised a moral vocabulary that contributed to social and political changes in the making of the modern world. His moral theory (and its successors) has been a cornerstone of the enlightenment orientation. The most difficult task we scholars face now is overcoming the enlightenment orientation in our work lives, leaving behind the Kantian moral theory and its relativistic, modern successors that I discussed above. To serve others, we have to begin by serving ourselves. We need a moral theory that is useful to us, given our positions of authority, and one that is consistent with our new metaphysics and method. None of the philosophical theories I have mentioned in this paper will do. They do not take into account the processes by which moral and empirical truth are enacted. The new theory must be one that makes scholarly sense and that can be enacted as we try to do responsible service as scholars and teachers and policy advisers. Making the moral theory requires changing ourselves and our work.

I have argued that, for reasons of good scholarship, sociologists and philosophers should work together. Symbolic interactionism (broadly understood) offers an appropriate metaphysics and method for studying society and making philosophical moral theory. But in the end, I believe that symbolic interactionism requires that we change ourselves and our world. Enacting a new moral theory is the real reason that philosophers should become sociologists (and vice versa).

NOTES

1. I was trained as an analytic philosopher, and I started becoming a sociologist in 1974 when I attended Howard Becker's class in field methods. After that, my sociological training was a kind of informal apprenticeship. I pursued it with the intelligent, patient, and generous help of Howie Becker, Arlene Daniels, Judy Wittner, and Joseph Schneider. In this paper, I have been helped by comments from the audience and my commentators at the 1988 Stone Symposium of the Society for Symbolic Interaction; I was also helped by the philosophers of the Propositional Attitudes Task Force at Smith College. I owe special thanks to Jerry Schneewind for his comments on the penultimate draft.

2. This last, at least, is the way it appears in Karl Popper's presentations. See Jarvie, 1984 for a discussion in these terms.

3. Thomas Kuhn's criticism addresses the internal question of authority in scientific revolution, and he reduces it to disciplinary politics and careerism(Kuhn, 1970). He never deals with the question of scientific authority in the society at large, and, in that sense, he doesn't escape the enlightenment orientation. I say more about this in Addelson, 1983.

4. I am using "symbolic interactionism" in a broad sense here, one that covers the essays in this volume. In my use (and the use in the title of this volume), the term includes work by some of the ethnomethodologists and by some sociologists who can't really be classified by school. More strictly, symbolic interactionism has philosophical roots in the American pragmatism of the early twentieth century. It should be attractive to philosophers because an important segment of the philosophical vanguard looks back to the pragmatist philosophers Peirce, James, Dewey, and Mead in search of a new foundation for philosophy. But to settle questions of authority and method, we must follow the pragmatist philosophical tradition forward to one of its natural outcomes in a sociological tradition of today. In this normative sense, becoming a sociologist requires working within a research tradition that has corrected and extended the original, philosophical ideas of its founders by making them empirical. It requires working within a tradition whose members create new ideas out of the tradition and correct and extend them in the course of empirical research. What I have just given is, of course, a normative as well as a descriptive characterization of symbolic interactionism—a gesture in the direction of a disciplinary tradition.

5. The distinction between internal and external, once used in history, philosophy, and sociology of science, relies on an enlightenment orientation. I'm using it for pedagogical reasons here, not because I believe it constitutes a valid distinction—quite the contrary.

6. My discussion of Dorothy Smith's work in this context comes out of correspondence with Joseph Schneider. Smith's work raises issues that are crucially important to all sociologists and philosophers, not just feminist ones. On the other hand, there may be questions of warrant that Smith needs to address. For example, the institutional possibility of making a sociology for women seems to rely on conventions of autonomy in the scholarly disciplines which are entangled with individualist, voluntarist notions of science. For feminists, the questions of warrant include the warrants given by a feminist political movement or by "women." See Addelson and Potter, forthcoming for some discussion of these issues.

7. For criticisms arising out of the study of social problems, see Spector and Kitsuse, 1977 for a review. Gusfield's discussion of Merton and Nisbet in Gusfield, 1984 is of this sort. The labeling theory of deviance was developed in criticism of the enlightenment orientation—that is the implicit basis of Becker's *Outsiders*, for example. There is conflict in these writings because the enlightenment orientation justifies our authority (as I say in the text) but also because as intellectuals, we tend unconsciously to accept a secular humanist morality that is in fact closely tied to the enlightenment orientation. We need a morality based on interactionist sorts of principles (see the last section of the paper).

8. For a very good, brief overview of the transformation see the introduction to Baynes, Bohman, and McCarthy, 1987, written by Thomas McCarthy.

9. From the logical positivists, the legacy was precision in the philosophy of language and philosophy of science. In other quarters, and particularly in ethics, the influence came from Great Britain, and it included the British "ordinary language philosophers."

10. The paper contains outstanding examples of workaday philosophical work in its various gradations. In her own work, Macklin pays attention to cultural and legal data, however.

11. The term "postanalytic" is inadequate and even misleading, but no single term will do the job. The introduction to Baynes, Bohman, and McCarthy, 1987) contains a taxonomy of philosophic positions that is exact and enlightening but much too complex to use in this paper.

12. Rorty borrows the phrase from Michael Oakshott.

13. In *The Idea of a Social Science,* the point is less clear than it ought to be because Winch uses simple, hypothetical examples and he pays little attention to the political nature of the interpretation and application of the rules. To make sense of Winch's (and Wittgenstein's) recommendations about rules, we need a way to understand the process of applying rules, and that requires an empirical method, not hypothetical examples. In a nutshell, that is why I believe philosophers must become sociologists. I argue this at greater length in the text.

14. Philosophical critics have long made a point of saying this. See, for example, Hauerwas (1981) for a philosophical criticism by a theologian, Whitbeck (1982) for a criticism by a feminist philosopher, and MacIntyre (1984) for a widely read effort. See my criticism of the approach (Addelson, 1979). Meyers and Kittay, 1987, contains papers that offer criticisms from a variety of standpoints. As we shall see, some of the critics run into difficulties that resemble those the analytic philosophers face.

15. In this they have been supported by distinctions made within the enlightenment orientation—the distinction between justification and discovery and the distinction between internal and external studies of science.

16. His way of judging one position (or conceptual scheme) to be rationally superior to another is to appeal to the history of arguments within a tradition—the rationally superior is the best so far. This line of thought sounds dangerously like the self-congratulatory stories of scientific progress in the West, with the latest being the best so far. Much turns on the empirical adequacy of the way the narrative is constructed and the way the authority of the narrator is taken account of. MacIntyre published *After Virtue* in an effort to meet criticisms that he didn't pay enough attention to social history. (See his remarks on Abraham Edel's criticisms in the Afterword to the second edition of MacIntyre, 1984). I believe he doesn't succeed.

17. MacIntyre's is one of the most widely discussed "new" answers to the question, "What is morality?" He pursues many of the questions that Elizabeth Anscombe raised in, "Modern Moral Philosophy," though from his own more "sociological" angle (Anscombe 1957).

18. Danto (1985) has an interesting discussion of narrative. He still seems to believe in objective facts that can be found out, however. Polkinghorne (1987) gives an overview on the growing importance of narrative in a variety of disciplines. Addelson (1987) discusses problems with a model that assumes agents' motives, intentions, and the like are given in the moment of acting or deciding.

19. Consider MacIntyre's remarks on accountability and the interlocking nature of narratives: "[N]arrative selfhood is correlative. I am not only ac-

countable, I am one who can always ask others for an account, who can put others to the question. I am part of their story, as they are part of mine. The narrative of any one life is part of an interlocking set of narratives. Moreover, this asking for and giving of accounts itself plays an important part in constituting narratives" (1984:218). There are empirical questions that concern the moral and scientific acceptability of his new theory. Who may ask whom for accounts, and in what terms are the accounts given? Can deviants ask for an account of the respectable (or of the police)? Deviants might ask, but they would certainly not receive answers in their terms. That, after all, is why Becker's book is ambiguously called *Outsiders* (1973). See also my discussion below, on Prudence Rains.

20. Feminist historians (and others) have called this "the periodization problem," the double claim that historians have periodized history in terms of men's experience (a methodological claim) and that history and the narratives of group life have been defined in terms of (higher class) men's experience. See Dye, 1979. This is, of course, relevant to Dorothy Smith's discussion of the ruling apparatus and a sociology for women.

21. Rains's studies also show that in the case of the middle-class teenagers in a maternity home, the narratives were not recorded in official places. A conspiracy among family, schools, maternity home, and officials kept these nice, middle-class girls' records clear. MacIntyre speaks of life narratives as being "coauthored" and he says the self inhabits a character whose unity is given as the unity of a character (1984:217). Maybe so, but we need empirical study to see who does the coauthoring, and to see whether there really is unity of character. Without empirical study, the philosophical theory quickly goes astray.

22. But see also Noddings (1984) and a multitude of other feminist writings.

23. This paragraph is an edited version of a portion of Addelson, 1987.

24. Joseph Schneider and Jerry Schneewind made comments on an earlier draft that I used in the revision of the next section.

25. Dorothy Smith and other feminist sociologists are particularly sensitive to these questions, but the issues arise in one form or another among many sociologists. See, for example, Stacey and Thorne, 1985; Stacey, 1988; Clifford and Marcus, 1986; and Clifford, 1988.

26. The data problem is faced fairly directly in the interactionist tradition in a number of discussions of social problems. See Spector and Kitsuse, 1977; Rains, 1975; Woolgar and Pawluch, 1985; and Schneider, 1985.

27. Quite a lot is implicit in Kuhn, 1970, however, and his discussion of textbooks is particularly important. See my discussion in Addelson, 1983. Interactionists offer case studies in science that serve as a basis for analyzing the place of scientists and other scholars in the ruling apparatus (see references in Clarke and Gerson, this volume).

28. This is as good a place as any to express my wariness about Smith's term, "the ruling apparatus." Smith is making a sociology for women in a political sense, as a feminist much influenced by Marxist themes and politics, and so she selects out elements of social organization that are integrated into a centralized authority, albeit of a many-faceted sort. As professional scholars, we are part of that ruling apparatus. As an interactionist sociologist, however, I

see authority operating systematically in all sorts of situations, not all of them linked in interesting ways to centralized authority. I think Smith would agree, of course, and her focus on the ruling apparatus is a mark of her feminist politics. I have my own feminist politics, but in this essay, I'm trying to speak to issues that directly concern sociologists and philosophers in their work, whether they take themselves to be feminists or not.

29. Philosophers have struggled with this problem in philosophy of science and philosophy of language. In the "transitional years" of 1965–75, it often emerged as a problem of meaning change, the point being that if the necessary or sufficient conditions for application of a term change when the scientific theory changes, how can we say that a later theory falsifies an earlier one? Paul Feyerabend was famous for his arguments here, but W. V. Quine's arguments against reference have similar import. Rescue efforts were made by Saul Kripke (with his notion of rigid designators), Hillary Putnam, and many others. Rorty, 1979, reviews some of the efforts and gives a bibliography.

30. Enlightenment relativists are part of the chorus, but so are numberless post-analytic philosophers. For an argument directed explicitly against interactionist social problems research see Woolgar, 1985, which reveals how difficult it is for interactionists to leave behind an enlightenment orientation. These questions of sameness are crucial to philosophers and symbolic interactionists. I thank Joseph Schneider for keeping me on the mark here.

References

Addelson, Kathryn. 1979. "Moral Revolution." In Julia Sherman and E. Beck, eds., *The Prism of Sex*. Madison: University of Wisconsin Press.

———. 1983. "The Man of Professional Wisdom." In Sandra Harding and Merrill B. Hintikka, eds., *Discovering Reality*. Dordrecht:, Netherlands: D. Reidel.

———. 1987. "Moral Passages." In Meyers and Kittay, 1987.

Addelson, Kathryn, and Elizabeth Potter. Forthcoming. "Making Knowledge." In Ellen Messer-Davidow and Joan Hartman (eds.), *Gender and Knowledge*.

Anscombe, G. E. M. 1957. *The Collected Philosophical Papers of G. E. M. Anscombe: Ethics, Religion, and Politics*. Vol. III. Minneapolis: University of Minnesota Press.

Baier, Annette. 1986. "Trust and Antitrust." *Ethics* 96 (January).

Baynes, Kenneth, J. Bohman, and T. McCarthy, eds. 1987. *After Philosophy: End or Transformation?* Cambridge, Mass.: MIT Press.

Becker, Howard S. 1970. *Sociological Work: Method and Substance*. Chicago: Aldine Publishing Co.

———. 1973. *Outsiders*. New York: The Free Press.

Bernstein, Richard. 1983. *Beyond Objectivism and Relativism: Sci-*

ence, Hermeneutics, and Praxis. Philadelphia: University of Pennsylvania Press.

Blumer, Herbert. 1969. *Symbolic Interactionism: Perspective and Method*. Englewood Cliffs, N.J.: Prentice Hall.

Bondi, Richard. 1984. "The Elements of Character." *Journal of Religious Ethics* 12, no. 2 (Fall):201–18.

Bruner, Jerome. 1986. *Actual Minds, Possible Worlds*. Cambridge, Mass.: Harvard University Press.

Clifford, James. 1988. *The Predicament of Culture: Twentieth-Century Ethnography, Literature, and Art*. Cambridge, Mass.: Harvard University Press.

Clifford, James, and George E. Marcus. 1986. *Writing Culture*. Berkeley: University of California Press.

Danto, Arthur. 1980. "Analytic Philosophy." *Social Research* 47(4): 615–16.

———. 1985. *Narrative and Knowledge*. New York: Columbia University Press.

Dye, Nancy Schrom. 1979. "Cleo's American Daughters: Male History, Female Reality." In Julia Sherman and E. Beck, eds., *The Prism of Sex*. Madison: University of Wisconsin Press.

Gilligan, Carol. 1982. *In a Different Voice: Psychological Theory and Women's Development*. Cambridge, Mass.: Harvard University Press.

GoffMass.n, Erving. 1961. *Asylums*. Garden City, N.Y.: Doubleday.

Gusfield, Joseph. 1984. "On the Side." In Joseph Schneider and John Kitsuse, eds., *Studies in the Sociology of Social Problems*. Norwood, N. J.: Ablex Publishing.

Hauerwas, Stanley. 1981. *A Community of Character*. Notre Dame, Ind.: University of Notre Dame Press.

———. 1977. *Truthfulness and Tragedy*. Notre Dame, Ind.: University of Notre Dame Press.

Hauerwas, Stanley, and Alasdair MacIntyre. 1983. *Revisions*. Notre Dame, Ind.: University of Notre Dame Press.

Jarvie, I. C. 1984. *Rationality and Relativism: In Search of a Philosophy and History of Anthropology*. London: Routledge and Kegan Paul.

Kohlberg, Lawrence. 1971. "From Is to Ought." In Theodore Mischel, *Cognitive Development and Epistemology*. New York: Academic Press.

Kuhn, Thomas. 1970. *The Structure of Scientific Revolutions*. 2nd ed. Chicago: University of Chicago Press.

Ladd, John. 1970. "Morality and the Ideal of Rationality in Formal Organizations." *The Monist* 54(4).

Lemert, Edwin. 1951. *Social Pathology: A Systematic Approach to the Theory of Sociopathic Behavior.* New York: McGraw-Hill.

MacIntyre, Alasdair. 1984. *After Virtue.* 2nd ed. Notre Dame, Ind.: University of Notre Dame Press.

Macklin, Ruth. 1985. "Standards in Philosophy." In Daniel Callahan, A. Caplan, and B. Jennings, eds., *Applying the Humanities.* New York: Plenum Press.

Martin, Mike. 1989. *Everyday Morality: An Introduction to Applied Ethics.* Belmont, Calif.: Wadsworth.

Meyers, Diane, and Eva Kittay. 1987. *Women and Moral Theory.* Totowa, N. J.: Roman and Allenheld.

Mills, C. Wright. 1963. *Power, Politics, and People.* Ed. I. L. Horowitz. New York: Ballantine Books.

Newton, Lisa. 1988. *Ethics in America: Source Reader.* Englewood Cliffs, N.J.: Prentice Hall.

Noddings, Nel. 1984. *Caring.* Berkeley: University of California Press.

Polkinghorne, Donald. 1987. *Narrative Knowing and the Human Sciences.* Ithaca, N.Y.: State University of New York Press.

Quine, Willard Van Orman. 1963. *From a Logical Point of View.* New York: Harper and Row.

———. 1969. *Ontological Relativity and Other Essays.* New York: Columbia University Press.

Rains, Prudence. 1971. *Becoming an Unwed Mother.* Chicago: Aldine.

———. 1975. "Imputations of Deviance." *Social Problems* 23 (October): 1–11.

RajchMan, John, and C. West, eds. 1985. *Post Analytic Philosophy.* New York: Columbia University Press.

Rawls, John. 1971. *A Theory of Justice.* Cambridge, Mass.: Harvard University Press.

Rock, Paul. 1979. *The Mass.king of Symbolic Interactionism.* Totowa, N.J.: RowMass.n and Littlefield.

Rorty, Richard. 1979. *Philosophy and the Mirror of Nature.* Princeton: Princeton University Press.

———. 1982. *Consequences of Pragmatism (Essays: 1972–1980).* Minneapolis: University of Minnesota Press.

Schneider, Joseph W. 1985. "Defining the Definitional Perspective on Social Problems." *Social Problems* 32: 214–27.

Smith, Dorothy. 1979. "A Sociology for Women." In Sherman, Julia, and E. Beck, eds. 1979. *The Prism of Sex.* Madison: University of Wisconsin Press.

———. 1987. *The Everyday World as Problematic: A Feminist Sociology.* Boston: Northeastern University Press.

Spector, Malcolm and John Kitsuse. 1977. *Constructing Social Problems.* Menlo Park, Calif.: Cummings.

Stacey, Judith. 1988. "Can There Be a Feminist Ethnography?" *Women's Studies International Forum* 11, no. 1:21–27.

Stacey, Judith, and Barrie Thorne. 1985. "The Missing Feminist Revolution in Sociology." *Social Problems* 32, no. 4 (April).

Strauss, Anselm L. 1987. *Qualitative Analysis for Social Scientists.* Cambridge: Cambridge University Press.

Velasquez, Manuel, and Vincent Barry. 1988. *Philosophy.* Belmont, Calif.: Wadsworth.

Whitbeck, Caroline. 1982. "The Moral Implications of Regarding Women as People: New Perspectives on Pregnancy and Personhood." In *The Concept of Person and Its Implications for the Use of the Fetus in Biomedicine.* Dordrecht, Netherlands: D.Reidel.

Winch, Peter. 1963. *The Idea of a Social Science and its Relation to Philosophy.* New York: Humanities Press.

———. 1972. "Understanding a Primitive Society." In *Ethics and Action.* London: Routledge, & Kegan Paul.

Woolgar, Steven and Dorothy Pawluch. 1985. "Ontological Gerrymandering: The Anatomy of Social Problems Explanations." *Social Problems* 32(2):14–27.

6 Art Worlds: Developing the Interactionist Approach to Social Organization
Samuel Gilmore

INTRODUCTION

Writing about symbolic interaction and the arts, one becomes immersed in issues of social organization. The development of an interactionist approach to social structure has greatly benefited from research in the arts, particularly the effort to construct a macro-level interactionist conception of society. Becker's work in the arts has been central in this area. In his analysis of art as "collective activity" (Becker 1974), and introduction of the concept of "art worlds" (Becker 1976), Becker has helped interactionists clarify the "social worlds" approach to social organization in specific applications (e.g., Strauss 1978, 1982, 1984; Kling and Gerson 1978; Unruh 1979). In *Art Worlds* (1982), Becker presents a comprehensive model of social organization in the arts and elaborates the processes through which collective artistic activity is transacted and resources distributed. *Art Worlds* illustrates how the use of a specific substantive context—the arts—to analyze an abstract conception—the interactionist approach to social structure—is more revealing than it is constraining.[1]

Becker's colleagues have also contributed to the development of an interactionist approach to social structure through research in a variety of artistic media. This includes the examination of the worlds of theater (Lyon 1974), photography (Rosenblum 1978), pop music (Bennett 1980), and concert music (Gilmore 1987). Although each art world analysis tends to emphasize different levels of social structure, from a predominantly micro focus on division of labor issues (e.g., Lyon), through mid-level organization (e.g., Rosenblum and Gilmore), to macro cultural and environmental influences (e.g., Bennett), they all try to integrate levels of behavioral and organizational analysis so as not to have analytically distinct micro and macro perspectives.

Such an emphasis on an integrated micro-macro analysis is the distinguishing feature of the interactionist approach to social organization. Both micro and macro levels of analysis are conducted through a "relational" mechanism, that is, interaction or exchange between specific people, not an "attribute" mechanism describing the distribution of individual attributes and their correlation with behaviors or attitudes. Interactionists tend to be most closely associated with a micro level of analysis using a relational mechanism to explain individual meaning and action. A similar relational approach provides interactionists with an acceptable way to conceptualize a macro level of analysis through the emergence of the "social world" concept.

In a social world, people's collaborative activity ties them into a set of direct relations that have meaning for them. The cluster of individuals who interact with each other produce a relatively stable aggregation of relations. This pattern of meaningful aggregated relations represents a social world. Such a "network" based conceptualization of social structure has proved attractive to interactionists if sufficient emphasis is put on the meaning of both an individual's direct and aggregate relations (see Maines 1977, Fine 1983, Hall 1987).

Interactionist research in art worlds has succeeded in producing both individually and collectively meaningful descriptions of social organization. The development of a truly organizational (i.e., relational) approach to examining artistic collective activity makes it easier to establish the connections between micro and macro levels of analysis. Macro relations are simply an extension of micro relations and vice versa. Artists are integrated into a social setting through the support networks in which they participate. The networks and social processes through which artists and support personnel interact help explain variation in collective forms of artistic expression. Stable patterns of networks and artistic processes establish these collective aesthetic interests. The explanatory focus is on social relations and interdependent activity.

In comparison, the traditional analysis of macro-level social influences on art uses a "reflection model" (Peterson 1979). Reflection models examine the broader social context in which artistic activity takes place (e.g., Hauser 1951, Kavolis 1968, Gay 1968, Schorske 1981). The level of analysis is the fit of the individual artist with the sociocultural environment. Explaining variation in artistic activity is primarily a matter of analyzing how political, economic, and cultural influences are internalized by artists living in a particular sociocultural context.

The relationship between micro behavior and macro context is more difficult to establish because the influence mechanisms are less concrete. The explanatory focus is on the shared attributes of individual and social context.

Differences between the interactionist and reflection models follow the split between a "relational or structural" approach to sociological explanation and "methodological individualism," a long-standing debate in the social sciences (Webster 1973, Mayhew 1980, Alexander et al. 1987). Much of the debate has centered around the relationship of micro and macro levels of analysis. While interactionists are generally comfortable with this relationship, that is, the social integration of the individual, they have been less comfortable with most macro-level conceptions of society. The difficulty stems from establishing the meaning of social structure to participants beyond direct, ego-centered relationships.

The development of the social world concept offers a solution to this problem. It does not rely simply on an ego-centered construct of social structure. Instead the social world provides a framework for an aggregated set of relations, be it a community following some substantive interest or a more formally organized production system that has a shared meaning for participants. This shared meaning guides the joint interests and activities of participants and also provides collective identities.

SOCIAL ORGANIZATION AND SOCIAL WORLDS

A social world consists of "common or joint activities or concerns tied together by a network of communication" (Kling and Gerson 1978:26). The concept has been theoretically developed in the interactionist literature by Shibutani (1955, 1962) and Strauss (1978, 1982, 1984), and has been applied to a variety of collective task and ideological arenas, including such disparate activities as surfing, coin collecting, nuclear disarmament, and homosexuality (see Strauss 1982, 1984). Common characteristics of these worlds include an amorphous and diffuse social form, without clear-cut spatial boundaries or a specified population of participants. As noted above, social worlds are useful as an interactionist unit of social organization because of the dual emphasis on structural and cultural elements.

This dual emphasis is illustrated by artistic participants' group construct of an "art world." Becker defines an art world as a production system comprised of producers, distributors, and consumers "whose cooperative activity, organized via their joint knowledge of conventional means of doing things, produces the kind of art works that art world is noted for." (Becker [982:x] Art world participants arrange their cooperative activity through networks of exchange that routinely form coalitions of like-minded producers, distributors, and consumers. Routine collective activity creates relatively stable patterns of interaction that act as social referents guiding future collective activity. An art world thus organizes and identifies artistic activity.

Participants' definitions of artistic activity are not haphazard individual claims to particular artistic statuses, but mutually interdependent claims produced through the coordinated and interdependent organization of artistic activity. Individual participants evaluate each other's claims and acknowledge them through their willingness to interact and exchange. The joint recognition of these individual claims is a collective definition of collective activity.

Social worlds acting as production systems are comparable to formal organizations in that they focus on collective products or events and have a significant degree of specialization, that is, task and social differentiation. A well-established division of labor forms the basis for a regular and routine exchange among cooperating participants in the art world. Collectively, these networks of exchange resemble a formal organization.

The difference in social world production systems is that exchange takes place through an "open system" (Thompson 1967, Scott 1981) in which collaborators are not specifically identified or linked before exchange takes place. This means social worlds don't designate an exclusive membership pool within which interaction is to take place. Instead, potential collaborators in an art world develop artistic skills and even prepare individual contributions to collective activity independently, with only a "generalized collaborator" in mind. When artistic exchange with a "specific collaborator" is planned (e.g., a commission), an effort is frequently made to align the activities of specific and generalized collaborators so as to avoid having to develop new skills for a single exchange.[2]

Another difference between social worlds and formal organizations is the lack of authority relations among participants in the former. The employment relation in formal organizations distinguishes elites who construct the goals and means of collaboration from subordinates who follow these directions. These elites form an administration that acts as a "coordination mechanism" (Thompson 1967). In social worlds, the absence of authority relations means participants must coordinate interdependent activities themselves during each and every transaction. Such a procedure is not only inefficient, but unwieldy for larger systems of exchange. A collective solution to coordinating exchange is called for.

When membership and authority relations are not present, the collective coordination mechanism in social organization shifts from designating the relations between people—an administration—to designating common practices that link interdependent activities—a convention. A convention is a common practice constructed through a tacit agreement process (Lewis 1969). Collaborators agree to conform to past practices because they expect other social world participants to do the same. This agreement facilitates exchange. Participants also use conventions to form identities that allow them to locate and to be located by compatible collaborators. In an art world, such artistic conventions help circumscribe the "style" of collaborative activity.

A focus on issues in social organization and the coordination of activities locates interactionist research in the arts in a research area Peterson calls the "production-of-culture" (1979). While some of the most visible research in this area emphasizes activity in the arts within formal organizations (e.g., Hirsch 1972; DiMaggio and Hirsch 1976; Peterson and Berger 1975; Adler 1979, Coser, Kadushin, and Powell 1982; Dubin 1987), often centering around issues of organizational rationality and the unpredictability of the arts, artistic processes take place in a variety of social contexts, some formally organized, some not. The interactionist concept of social worlds offers an alternative appproach to social organization that works with emergent forms of organization as well as relatively stable patterns of exchange and interaction. Social world research foci include issues of organizational efficiency in addition to the meaning of structure and social processes.

The body of this paper will review studies in the arts, clustered into production, distribution, and consumption stages, that are of interest to interactionists if not actually done by interactionist researchers. I treat these stages as a technical separation of activities, often not so clearly differentiated socially. Like Peterson, I prefer to define the "production" of culture in a generic sense, applicable to all three technical stages including "processes of creation, manufacture, marketing, distribution, exhibiting, inculcation, evaluation, and consumption" (Peterson 1976:672). Each social process has its own distinct effect on the collective construction of artistic activity.

WHAT'S ORGANIZATIONAL ABOUT THE ARTS?

One result of the interactionist approach to the arts is the debunking of the romantic myth of the socially isolated artist, struggling alone to produce his or her work in a cold, barren garret. The ubiquity of this myth is in part due to the artists themselves, who describe their alienation from mainstream society in biographies and autobiographies, which argue that one becomes a great artist by using one's inner resources to rise above social and institutional constraints. A position marginal to, but not entirely removed from, society permits the artist an opportunity to observe and be otherwise influenced by society, while maintaining sufficient social distance to construct characteristic aesthetic expression individually .

Linda Nochlin (1971) calls this psychologistic approach to explaining artistic influence the "golden nugget theory of artistic genius." It presumes the critical explanatory elements of artistic activity are cognitive. A picture of the isolated artist is thus quite satisfying.

Left out, however, are the more mundane, pragmatic aspects of organizing and supporting artistic activity, the processes through which all artists acquire resources and orient themselves to relevant conventions in an art world. Artists acquire financial resources to support themselves and their families, creative resources to help conceptualize aesthetic expression, material resources to actualize artistic work, distributional resources to establish contacts with an art world and exchange their work, and critical resources to legitimate their work and facilitate further resource acquisition. In *Art Worlds*, Becker illustrates these processes in a variety of artistic media including literature, the plastic arts (i.e., painting, sculpture, and photography), and the performing arts (i.e., music, dance, theater, and film). Some social support relationships are less obvious than others, for example, the contribution of Anthony Trollope's butler to Trollope's prolific output (see Becker 1982), but all serve to embed artistic activity socially.

Reviews of Becker's work, while generally laudatory, suggest that the art world model is most appropriate for "social" media like concert music, where there exists an artistic division of labor, and less applicable to more "solitary" media like poetry (e.g., Wilson 1983, Kavolis 1982). Others (e.g., Kimmel 1982, Lovell 1983) suggest that Becker at one point relies too strongly on an organizational level of analysis in explaining aesthetic meaning, then shifts abruptly to an individual level of analysis to explain artistic innovation and social change. Both criticisms misinterpret the interactionist approach to relating the individual and society.

First, the division of labor in artistic activity, as in most other activities, is historically relative and thus primarily determined through political and social processes. While technical considerations enter into the social construction of a division of labor, the social power of specialists often plays a more significant role in organizing collaboration (see Freidson 1976). A contemporary comparison of artistic disciplines indicates the performance arts are more specialized than the literary arts, but it is mistaken to assume this is an inherent aspect of each discipline. An interactionist analysis of the artistic division of labor in each medium explores the social processes and sociopolitical considerations establishing such an artistic social order, for example, differences in the composer-performer division of labor in classical music (Gilmore 1987). In addition, even where artistic activities appear to be socially isolated at one level, such as the conceptualization to articulation process in literature, potential social influences affect the literary act through a variety of resource systems (e.g., the creative, distribution, and critical systems mentioned above).

However, the art world approach does not insist that all artists in all media are equally well socially integrated. Becker (1976) describes how individual artists vary in degree of social integration in mainstream art worlds, from highly integrated "professionals" to partially integrated "mavericks" and ignored "naive" or "folk" artists. Many artists radically change their relationship to art world support systems over their careers. Ignored or similarly socially disenfranchised artists may try to cope independently or seek support from alternative support systems. Such resource-seeking activities produce the alternative art worlds which are the locus of highly innovative artistic activity.

In short, while individuals vary in their degree of social integration, artistic media also vary historically and socially in the collective arrangement of artistic activities. Thus the relationship of the individual artist and the art world is jointly produced. An emphasis on the art world in interactionist research in the arts works as a corrective to the individualistic myth of artistic activity, but is not intended to entail a simple mechanistic relationship between the artist and the art world.

ARTIST AND PRODUCTION RELATIONSHIPS

Many interactionist studies in the arts focus primarily on the analysis of artistic production. One reason is their theoretical emphasis on the organization of interdependent activity which, in production relationships, is displayed through the division of labor. Interactionist approaches to the division of labor (e.g., Freidson 1976, Strauss 1985) analyze collective activity on a micro level, seeking to distinguish what activities are involved, who participates, who does what and why, who is responsible for a given activity (i.e., accountability), who gets credit for the activity, how exchange is managed, and the stable patterns of organization that emerge from this negotiation. Though the division of labor in artistic production is clearly a complex process, it can be broken down into separate components for analysis. One relatively straightforward aspect of this process is exchange.

Exchange in artistic production is treated in a similar matter to exchange in industrial production, as a problem of coordination. As mentioned previously, coordination in artistic exchange takes place through artistic conventions. My own research analyzed variation in the processes of artistic exchange between composers and performers in the concert music world. Differences in the types of musical activities, division of labor, and aesthetic interests of participants all influenced the musical conventions used to organize concerts.

To examine these processes, I interviewed over one hundred composers, performers, and support personnel participating in the organization of concert activity, primarily in New York City, the central and largest location in the concert world. Responses differentiate three "subworlds" of concert organization: "Midtown," "Uptown," and "Downtown." Midtown refers to the major symphony orchestras, touring soloists, and chamber groups booked into such big performance halls as Lincoln Center and Carnegie Hall, and to the arts management and concert marketing organizations located on 57th street in Manhattan. Uptown refers to the composers and performers affiliated with universities, who use on-campus rehearsal and performance sites, and rely on academic resources and networks to help organize concerts. Downtown refers to musical nonspecialists, the combined composer/ performers living and performing in small lofts or in alternative performance spaces in Greenwich Village, Soho, and Tribeca. Each subworld is a wholly encompassed system of concert activities with a relatively distinct identity.

I analyzed the coordination of exchange between compositional and performance activities within each system and compared them, in order to develop a model of the relationship between organizational processes and aesthetic interests (see Gilmore 1987). Midtown is the largest and most visible of concert systems with the most complex system of concert organization including a rigid specialization of activities between composers and performers, a large number of potential participants for any given concert, an open, free-lance market system organizing temporary concert coalitions, frequent collaborative events, and direct economic pressures on musical transactions taking place in professional rehearsal contexts.

As a consequence, Midtown participants have a strong organizational interest in musical conventions with which to coordinate concert activities. Concert collaborators have rationalized the production process through the use of a performance "repertory" that standardizes musical notation, instrumentation, and performance techniques. These strong concert conventions create efficiency, but limit musical innovation. Midtown concerts thus primarily emphasize musical virtuosity as an aesthetic focus.

In comparison, Downtown concerts, the least visible in the concert world, are organized through relatively simple social processes. These include a collapsed division of labor between compositional and performance activities, a very small population of potential concert collaborators, musical exchange organized through interpersonal channels, infrequent concerts, and minimal economic pressure on collaboration.

Under this type of concert organization, Downtown participants have not standardized their activities. Musical notation is varied, where it exists at all, and is often open to interpretation. New instruments and radically new performance techniques are constantly being introduced. Such organizational flexibility suits the avant-garde sensibilities of Downtown concert participants well. The lack of strong conventions means concert collaboration is often laborious and inefficient, but such organization supports radical musical innovation and avant-garde aesthetic interests.

Between Midtown and Downtown, both organizationally and aesthetically, is the academic concert subworld, Uptown. Uptown is moderately visible to serious concertgoers, but does not have much national exposure. Concert organization is moderately complex, characterized by a clear-cut musical specialization between composers and performers, but with a joint commitment to a shared musically innovative aesthetic ideology, a large number of potential participants segmented into smaller campus-oriented communities, concert collaboration organized through membership in these communities and network ties, regular but not frequent performances, and indirect economic pressures on musical transactions.

This type of concert production system creates moderate organizational interests in conventionalizing activities. Uptown concert collaborators seek to maintain a degree of efficiency in coordinating musical transactions while leaving room for the introduction of some innovative practices. In this type of compromise, new performance practices are introduced, but on traditional instruments. Notation remains predominantly conventionalized, but new symbols are introduced to represent the new sounds. Uptown collaborators thus try to balance efficient organizational goals and innovative aesthetic interests.

While a complete explanation of the relationship between an artist's aesthetic interests and social organization is obviously more elaborate, the effects of artistic conventions are apparent. The elements that make up a musical convention serve as a form of musical social control. Musical decisions about notation, instrumentation, and performance techniques are embedded in the exchange context and distributional framework between compositional and performance activities. Musicians entering into collaborative activity through organized concert systems are disposed to adopt the conventional practices which make their participation attractive. In this way, interdependent musical activity is organizationally influenced.

This approach to analyzing artistic production works in nonperformance media as well. In one of the plastic arts, photography, Rosenblum (1978) shows how the variable organizational contexts through which different types of photographers produce their work play a significant role in determining what a photograph looks like. Rosenblum documented the conventions that guide collective activity in three areas of photography, news, advertising, and fine arts. Photographs from each area are readily identified. News pictures, in sharp focus, have a "specific range of content" (e.g., press conferences), with the key figure in the center of the composition. Advertising, in contrast, depicts people or objects in visually extraordinary ways. A particular effort is made to represent three dimensions through "short foregrounds, complex middlegrounds, and deadstop, horizonless backgrounds." Fine arts photography has a tremendous range of imagery that self-consciously manipulates "space, meaning, and light." There is a range of variation within each category, but there is enough homogeneity to make the category hold up.

The social organization of each sphere defines relationships between the photographer and participants in each social world which guide a significant degree of "stylistic" decision making. In the news world, editors choose assignments, the company allocates material resources including cameras, film, and film processing, photo editors select images to be published and crop or enlarge the print, and retouchers and typographers make technical decisions about how the picture will look in print. Rosenblum characterizes this organization as a highly rationalized, bureaucratic form in which the photographer has comparatively little discretion. Institutional priorities in journalism determine the conventions under which the news picture is shot and developed. This degree of standardization produces a stylistic category Cawelti (1970) calls a "formula" aesthetic.

In the advertising world, a free-lance photographer's work is organized by an advertising agency representing a client. This transitive relationship creates a complex process of communication in which the advertising agency seeks to control the vision of the photographer while representing the priorities of the client. An art director in the advertising agency negotiates the imagery of the photograph with the photographer through a "layout" of the proposed ad. After the layout is accepted, the photographer tries to distance the agency and the client in order to use his or her own technical skills and aesthetic sensiblities to make the shot, but is frequently "interfered with" in this process. The photographer, dependent upon a cooperative relationship with agencies for work, nevertheless resists losing control of the image. Rosenblum remarks that the photographer can be reduced to "technical labor" by this negotiation. As in news organizations, the result is a standardized imagery acceptable to social world participants which constrains innovative perspectives.

Finally in the world of fine arts photography, the stylistic conventions of the picture are largely determined by the relationship between the photographer and the dealer. This relationship (elaborated in the following section), channels feedback from a variety of sources, including museum curators, critics, and collectors. Rosenblum describes fine arts photographers as the most socially independent of the three types, but cautions against any interpretation that suggests that fine arts activities are not socially influenced. An extremely competitive market, controlling outlets for exposure and financial support, plays a significant role in setting trends for subject matter and compositional characteristics. As in the news and advertising contexts, the distribution of material, financial, and ideological resources integrates the photographer into a social world. One can seek alternative sources of support, but aesthetic discretion can be costly to photographers in time and effort. The fine arts photography world thus embeds even technically independent activities.

Analyses of the social determinants and effects of artistic conventions have been done in painting (Baxandall 1972), prints (Ivins 1953), and the film industry (Faulkner 1971, 1983) as well. All these studies document the organization of artistic production in order to explore socially based variation in artistic expression. The close fit of organization with a wide variety of artistic activities demonstrates the utility of the combined "structure and culture" interactionist approach to macro social structure. The social world concept has also been effectively utilized in related cultural fields, for example, exploring epistemological considerations in the sociology of science (e.g., Star and Gerson 1987 and Clarke and Gerson in this volume) and medical sociology (e.g., Strauss et al. 1985). This variety of cultural activities suggests the social world concept is robust, not limited to specific, socially elaborated, artistic activities.

ARTISTS AND DISTRIBUTION RELATIONSHIPS

The analysis of artistic relationships within a specific division of labor or organization is only one stage of an art world analysis. A second stage deals with art world distribution. As an extended aspect of the production stage, studies of distributional artistic organizations link production processes to distribution processes in order to examine transactions across organizational boundaries. These boundaries are even less clear in art worlds than they are in industrial organizations, where a formally designated membership exists. A revealing approach that combines elements of both cultural and industrial contexts is provided by Hirsch (1972), who focuses on distribution processes in "mass culture" industries. He emphasizes that distributional processes are in no way secondary to production processes in explaining variation in artistic activity.

Hirsch's research compares distributional processes in three mass culture industries: books, phonograph records, and motion pictures. Each industry provides insight on the strategies organizations use to adapt to "uncertainty" problems in cultural production. Uncertainty, the inability of managers to accurately predict organizational inputs and outputs, is a frequent problem in the rational administration of organizations. In cultural industries, the problem is considerably magnified. To examine the fit of "rational" management and "irrational" (i.e., uncertain) artistic activity, Hirsch compares the administration of "through-put" organizations linking the artist at one end of the production sequence to the mass audience at the other.

In all three industries, Hirsch finds a bureaucratic organizational form that has adapted to cultural production uncertainty by using "craft" administrative techniques (see Stinchcombe 1959). Artists (i.e., authors, singers, actors) are contracted for on a royalty basis which pays artists for their work contingent upon the number of books, records, or theater tickets sold when the product is released into the marketplace. If possible, artists are also hired on a temporary basis for work on specific products in order to minimize overhead. Independent contact men and women (i.e., agents) buffer artistic production activities from distributional manufacture and promotional activities. This encourages artists to work without direct financial risk to the organization.

Distributional organizations also "overproduce" artistic products so that they can pick the products with the most profit potential for increased promotion. The early success of any artistic product increases promotional attention significantly. Unsuccessful products are left to wither. Since promotional costs are much greater than manufacturing costs, differential investment in promotion leads to greater profitability. At the same time, distributional organizations try to "coopt" such promotional sources as radio stations (in the recording industry) to contain promotional costs where possible. These strategies allow distributional organizations to lay off some of the risk of cultural production on personnel outside the organization.

In-depth analyses of publishing organizations reveal a similarly significant role for distribution organizations in the literary process. Coser, Kadushin, and Powell (1982), in a comprehensive study of the contemporary publishing industry, argue that writers are only the "junior partners" in the literary world, where publishers and editors reign supreme. They remark that writers are often ignorant of the process through which book publishing and promotion decisions are made. Although some writers are made "stars" by the promotional system and appear to wield significant artistic power in the literary world, most writers operate in highly constrained circumstances determined by the commercial priorities of the publishing house. Coser, Kadushin, and Powell also note that few industries have been as heavily taken over by conglomerates as book publishing. As a consequence, many artistically significant financial decisions are not even made within the distribution organization.

This kind of distributional influence on the literary process is not only a contemporary phenomenon. Sutherland (1976) describes how the serial publication of Victorian novels in weekly issues affected their length and style. For example, the plots of Charles Dickens's novels retained readers' interest within each weekly chapter, as well as in the novel as a whole. As long as the weekly issues sold, the publisher continued to issue chapters, which partially accounts for the length of Victorian novels.

Nor is distributional influence simply a function of mass production contingencies in the literary arts. A number of the most interesting studies on distributional influence have focused on the plastic arts, mainly painting. These include White and White's examination of nineteenth-century French painting, *Canvases and Careers* (1965), Moulin's study of the contemporary French painting world, *The French Art Market* (1967, 1987), Simpson's study of painters and galleries in a New York neighborhood, *Soho* (1981), and Crane's comparative analysis of seven contemporary artistic movements, *The Transformation of the Avant-Garde* (1987). All focus on artists and their complex relationships with dealers and critics to explain artistic perspectives.

White and White document and discuss the change in French painting from a classically oriented style to impressionism. To explain this transformation socially, White and White concentrate on the changes in the institutional support system controlling the selection, socialization, recognition, and distribution of paintings in French society. The institution in operation prior to the stylistic change, which they call the "academic system," has historical roots in the craft guilds organized in the Middle Ages. By royal edict guilds established a monopoly of privilege over any craft for their members. In 1670, a similar edict established the Royal Academy with control over painting in France. The Royal Academy had a monopoly on the teaching of painting "from life" (i.e., models) and forced all formerly "free" painters to become part of the organization. By the nineteenth century, painting was controlled from a centralized location in Paris. A rigid aesthetic ideology delineating subject matter, imagery, composition, and other characteristic elements of style was enforced.

The Royal Academy also controlled artistic legitimation and distribution processes. Legitimation focused on such competitions as the Prix de Rome, which each year designated a historical or mythological subject to be painted in the classical style by all painters in the competition. The winner of the competition received considerable attention from patrons and other collectors interested in purchasing prestigious work. At the Paris Salon, the important distributional event of the year, hundreds of paintings lined the walls of the exhibition hall from floor to ceiling to attract buyers. This annual public exhibition brought thousands into contact with the Academy's "best" paintings. The Salon was juried and good sales established a painter's career.

By the 1860s, demographic changes in the French art world began to seriously strain the capacity of the academy system. From 500 new paintings a year in 1803, the Academy was handling 5000 paintings a year by 1863. In addition, there were over 3000 Academy recognized painters in 1863 plus 1000 more in the provinces, a dramatic increase from the 100 recognized in 1800. At the same time, thousands of older paintings entered the market, as aristocrats sold the family heirlooms to support themselves. White and White estimate that 200,000 canvases were available to the French market in 1863. As a result, the centrally organized academy system began to break down.

In its place emerged a decentralized "dealer-critic" system. All sales had previously been conducted through the Academy, but it was extremely difficult for a centralized system to process 200,000 unique canvases. The dealer-critic system shifted the marketing focus from unique canvases to linked canvases produced in the career of a given artist. In the hands of independent dealers, often recruited from the ranks of minor painters, the distribution system was organized around speculative practices that contracted young painters when they were relatively unknown, and made a killing if they became reputable. The emergence of new painters was favored under this type of marketing system. Critics played a new role, promoting new theories of paintings and helping to identify new "schools" for marketing purposes. Thus the new distributional system facilitated the emergence of such new styles as impressionism, in which the aesthetic focus shifted from line to color.

The organization of a dealer-critic system is also the focus of Moulin's study (1967, 1987) of the contemporary French art market. Particularly interested in the relationship of aesthetic and economic value, Moulin examined this relationship in interviews with dealers, critics, collectors, and painters in the Parisian art world and collected data on changes in the prices of paintings. Her interviews indicate clearly that the art market operates through what she characterizes as "artificial manipulation" (i.e., nonmarket forces) by the participants involved. Dealers set prices arbitrarily, indicated by the widely varying prices of comparable works by the same artist, and manipulate supply strategically to stimulate interest in a painter they represent. Critics "discover" new artistic geniuses weekly in a promotional role that plays a critical part in the distribution of paintings to sophisticated buyers who would not dream of being influenced by advertising. Collectors buy and sell to influence other collectors and thus increase prices in their own collection, exactly as they might buy and sell stock on Wall Street. Artists consciously increase and slow down production in relation to the economic value of their paintings in the market. Each group acts to serve its own special interests in the joint construction of aesthetic and economic value.

Even more emphatic on the leading role of critics in the art world is Tom Wolfe's essay on the New York art scene from the fifties to the seventies (1975). Wolfe, a journalist, argues that, in the contemporary art world, painters watch critics rather than the other way around, as a way of defining styles and guiding their own aesthetic activities. Wolfe describes the aesthetic-defining activities of the three "Bergs," Clement Greenberg, Harold Rosenberg, and Leo Steinberg, the major art critics of the period, and their association with the emergence of such major contemporary art movements as abstract expressionism, minimalism, pop art, op art, photorealism, and conceptual art. Wolfe claims that the primacy of "artistic theory" over "artistic representation" reached a logical end with the acceptance of conceptual art by the art world. The major theory makers, the critics, thus established themselves as the most powerful group in the construction of aesthetic value.

Also analyzing the New York art market, Simpson (1981) and Crane (1987) document the art world "constituencies" (Crane 1987:35) contemporary painters must collaborate with to establish a market for their work. Simpson focuses on the role of the professional dealer or gallery owner in Soho who acts as gatekeeper to the contemporary New York art world. The major activity of the dealer is matching collectors and painters. Like independent agents spanning organizational boundaries in the recording industry, dealers seek artistic "talent" in one group and corresponding buyers in a different group. The successful Soho artist is one who recognizes the privileged "entrepreneurial" position of the dealer and listens to the appropriate feedback about the aesthetic sensibilities of the dealer's clients.

Crane's argument similarly acknowledges that, for painters in emerging artistic movements (i.e., the avant garde) to make themselves familiar to the art-buying public, they must establish links to three types of groups: organizational patrons, both private and public, who provide legitimacy and direct financial support; art experts, such as critics and curators, who also provide legitimacy and publicity; dealers and private collectors, who act as opinion leaders. Crane terms these groups "sponsors" of an artistic movement. In her historical analysis, Crane finds that none of emerging art movements between 1940 and 1985 made it until the participant painters established these sponsorship relations. Expanding Wolfe's analysis of the role of major art critics, she shows that each movement had its own artistic legitimators.

Like the cultural mass production process in publishing and recording, the dealer-critic system organizes the distribution and legitimation of unique artistic products by seeking to tie the transaction of artistic commodities to an effective promotional procedure. This complex balancing process maintains the independence of the critical-legitimation activity while orienting that activity to the distributional transaction. There is a significant degree of mutual interdependence between the critical and distributional processes that may be overtly coopted (as in Hirsch's example of the recording industry) but is often more subtly connected through discreet interaction as in the French and New York art markets. In either case, the artistic distribution system has a major influence on artistic expression. Interactionist oriented research has made important contributions to examining this relationship.

ARTISTS AND CONSUMPTION RELATIONSHIPS: AUDIENCES

Interactionists, like most researchers in the production-of-culture perspective, have tended to emphasize the production and distribution stages of artistic organization, while leaving the analysis of artistic consumption to the humanities. One factor explaining this bias is the mainstream social scientist's discomfort with the "internal" construction of expressive symbols and cultural meaning. When social scientists do analyze artistic consumption, they tend to do so through "external" behavioral indicators (e.g., the effect of television on children's aggressive actions towards others) (Comstock 1975, Gerbner and Gross 1976).

Hirsch (1978) points out that the dichotomization of internal and external effects represents an arbitrary intellectual division of labor between the disciplines. He argues that social scientists ignore cultural meaning because they are not trained to analyze it, rather than because of any inherent limitations in the sociological perspective. He argues further that social scientists are limiting themselves by ignoring cultural meaning and suggests they overcome this limit by embedding the analysis of artistic content in the social characteristics of the artistic medium. Hirsch regards this type of interdisciplinary cross-fertilization as quite promising for a more integrated study of cultural activity.

From this standpoint, it is surprising that more interactionist research on the meaning of artistic consumption has not been done. Interactionists, of course, have considerable experience in analyzing the social context of cultural meaning, but I am unaware of empirical interactionist studies on aesthetic response.[3] One of the problems stems from the difficulty of ascertaining commonly held artistic beliefs among consumers. This problem has both methodological and conceptual elements.

Methodologically, it is difficult to identify and locate the audience for a given artistic medium other than at the time the artistic product is purchased or consumed (e.g., the audience at a concert or film, the buyers of a book in a bookstore, the attendees at a gallery or a museum). If researchers can get access to these transactional situations, they can face the alternative problem of collecting data from participants directly involved in artistic transactions, a process requiring an extreme amount of consumer cooperation.

On the other hand, collecting data from consumers not directly involved in artistic transactions is best accomplished through survey techniques (i.e., sampling and structured questionnaires). While these techniques can provide interesting results on types and degrees of participation in the arts by the general public (see the National Endowment for the Arts supported patterns of cultural choice studies, e.g., Peterson 1983, Robinson 1985), these methods are not relational, and it is difficult to obtain complex information on artistic response through such techniques. It is not surprising that there are longstanding interactionist biases against such types of data collection (Blumer 1969, Glaser and Strauss 1967, Denzin 1971).

Conceptually, the difficulty lies in determining the degree to which artistic consumption is interdependent with artistic production. When treated as a straightforward transaction between artist and consumer, the goal is simply effective communication, and the approach is to articulate the shared conventions both parties to the transaction use to coordinate their exchange. This approach parallels that used in the production and distribution stages of artistic activity, but the conventions are specific to consumption practices.

The analysis of aesthetic response, however, indicates that the consumption of art is a more complex transaction entailing a subtle balance of hiding and revealing information (Dewey 1934, Langer 1953, Gombrich 1960). The skill with which the artist handles the balance of hidden and revealed information is an indication of the art work's aesthetic potential. An effective balance requires artistic consumers to organize information cognitively so that they can interpret aesthetic expression. Artistic conventions are used to establish appropriate "mind-sets." Several interesting analyses using such an approach to examine aesthetic response in different media are described below.

Meyer's *Emotion and Meaning in Music* (1956) is a detailed examination of the cognitive elements that make an aesthetic response by listeners to classical music possible. Meyer argues that even average listeners have a fairly sophisticated level of musical knowledge that allows them subconsciously to predict where a given sequence of notes, rhythmic pattern, or chordal progression is leading, based on prior experience in listening. Meyer suggests that the listener in this state of expectation responds emotionally to the resolution of musical patterns. The resolution can be satisfying even when known, that is, on repeated hearing of the same piece, because the state of musical expectation is produced by a subconscious organization of musical elements. When the resolution of the musical pattern is innovative, for example, a transposition to an unusual musical key from a composition's primary key, a successful aesthetic response is still possible if a link is made with the previous musical sequence. What is temporarily innovative is integrated into a conventional pattern.

Recognition of these musical patterns is a function of musical socialization, but no formal knowledge of compositional theory is necessary. Future classical concert goers experience and cognitively organize basic harmonic and melodic conventional patterns when listening to music throughout their audio-cultural environment (e.g., nursery songs, television, advertising jingles), not simply in music appreciation classes. The ability to organize and interpret more sophisticated musical patterns is explained by more intensive and extensive listening. Shared concert audience conventions thus grow out of a common socialization experience in a given musical culture.

In a different but related medium, Smith's study of how poems end, *Poetic Closure* (1968), develops a parallel argument for literary aesthetic response. Smith examines the structure of poetic form in a variety of styles, from Elizabethan lyric through free verse to concrete poetry. In each style, she isolates the characteristic elements constituting poetic form by focusing on what readers perceive as relevant. For example, Smith treats the "line" as the fundamental unit in poetry and identifies an initial structural element by examining the metrical pattern in which four lines hang together, producing a quatrain. The fourth line in this pattern receives added emphasis, imparting a sense of closure. A simple convention is consequently identified.

Likewise in the sonnet, which Smith characterizes as perhaps the most familiar form in the history of literature, the conventional structure of closure is established formally through a terminal rhyming of the couplet. Such a common convention is recognized immediately by sophisticated readers, but even among "naive" readers (i.e., readers without experience in reading sonnets), the closure of the sonnet is effectively imparted through the rhyming pattern in a first-time reading. Conventional knowledge is learned directly through the experience of consumption.

Meyer's and Smith's analyses of aesthetic response take very similar approaches to examining conventional knowledge among artistic consumers. Both have a gestalt orientation to pattern recognition in artistic expression, both involve artistic media that are read in a linear form, thus defining a sequence leading to a resolution, and both treat people's socialization to conventional knowledge as a function of experience with artistic consumption, not formal training in the medium. Their most significant difference is in the artistic socialization process. Meyer sees musical socialization as a function of cultural environment while Smith focuses on more direct artistic experience. Nevertheless, for both, conventions are applied subconsciously in organizing and responding to artistic input.

Michael Baxandall, in his extraordinarily detailed work on Florentine painters, *Painting and Experience in Fifteenth Century Italy* (1972), analyzes aesthetic response to painting as a conscious process. Like Meyer, he looks to the larger sociocultural environment for sources of conventional socialization. He focuses directly on these social processes to show that the conditions of everyday social life directly effect how the people of a given society perceive and "read" paintings. In particular, he explores the effect of the Catholic church on the ability of Florentines to understand the story and symbols of religious painting, and shows how the rise of an active merchant class in Florentine society produced skills enabling educated "Quattrocento man" to perceive sophisticated pictorial composition.

The Church in Florentine society was the major patron of the arts. Not surprisingly, then, most paintings had ecclesiastical subject matter intended to assist the Church's ideological mission. Although the Scriptures were the main teaching tool of religious training, most

Church members were illiterate. The Church solved this problem by using paintings to describe biblical stories that impressed the lessons of pious behavior upon the faithful. The actual messages were transmitted through visual symbols readily interpretable by a public already familiar with most stories through oral teachings. The posture of a body or hand, the presence of a tree branch or bird, all served to remind the public of specific points in a sermon. Regular encounters at the church with religious paintings had the same pedagogical effect as reading the Scripture.

Baxandall remarks that it was easier for the public to learn artistic conventions than to learn to read because they were already practiced at the "internal visualization" of biblical stories. Painters simply provided an "external visualization." Developing visual literacy with religious symbols was basically a matter of experiencing the paintings in conjunction with relevant sermons. Prior experience with one's own visual representations provided the cognitive skills needed to make such an association.

The Florentines also developed skills in reading a painting in the context of commercial life. Florentine merchants needed basic mathematical skills to conduct commercial transactions. The universal arithmetic tool, the "rule of three," enabled traders to calculate equivalent ratios (i.e., 7 is to 9 as 5 is to what number?) quickly and easily. Florentines who could solve this problem in ratios developed parallel skills regarding geometric proportions in art.

Baxandall indicates that Florentines especially appreciated proportion, which enabled them to gauge ratios while calculating them. Local painters utilized this appreciation of proportions in their pictorial composition by paying close attention to the ratio of head and body parts (e.g., Leonardo da Vinci), and to the size and placement of figures. The same gauging and calculating skills that worked in commercial transactions were used in artistic transactions.

Like Meyer and Smith, Baxandall describes the cognitive organization of artistic consumers and analyzes the social conditions that explain this organization. Audience consumption transactions, in a process similar to production and distribution transactions, rely on cognitive gestalts to guide aesthetic orientation. Effective artistic communication occurs when artists and audiences share some degree of common aesthetic orientation. It is clear, however, that in many art forms, particularly in the avant garde, artist and audiences share relatively little knowledge (see for example, Meyer 1967 on composers leaving the audience behind in music). Variation in artistic knowledge among different types of consumers is not assessed by these cognitive studies. This research is still to be undertaken.

ARTISTS AND CONSUMPTION RELATIONSHIPS: AESTHETICIANS

An alternative to examining artistic knowledge among audiences is to examine the artistic knowledge of critics and aestheticians. One advantage of a focus on these highly visible consumers is that researchers have easier access to knowledge standards through such published materials as a critic's newspaper columns or books. There also tends to be less variation in the type and degree of artistic knowledge of critics and aestheticians than of the public at large, but that depends on the internal organization of critical activities, including the selection, socialization, and interaction of participants. A sociological perspective on aesthetics thus differs from a philosophical perspective in that researchers in the arts examine variation in organizational factors to determine how aesthetic points of view are constructed. This perspective holds even though sociological analysis does not grant aestheticians any special position in determining immanent artistic knowledge.

For example, Becker treats aesthetics as an activity, no different from any other artistic activity, produced collectively by specialists in the art world. The purpose of aesthetics is "value-making" (Becker 1982, chapter 5), which includes the identification of objects with aesthetic value (i.e., the "What is art?" question), and the evaluation of the relative aesthetic merit of artistic objects (i.e., the "What is good art?" question). These questions are addressed indirectly by everyone in the art world through their daily activities, but critics and aestheticians directly develop complex theories to articulate the criteria under which aesthetic decisions are made. These theories are then used by members of the art world to evaluate and legitimate artistic activities.

The "institutional theory of art" (Danto 1964, Dickie 1975) takes just such a sociological approach to addressing evaluation and legitimation questions. In brief, a work of art is defined in practice, through the activities of participants in the art world. Any recognized participant in the art world may confer artistic status upon an object in the collective activity of the art world. This "labeling" process is then socially confirmed through further interdependent activity, or may be resisted by art world participants who don't recognize either the aesthetic qualities of the object or the person conferring status. The dominant aesthetic theory is one with adherents in influential artistic institutions, such as prominent critics and museum curators. Although some sociologists have expressed doubts that sociology can take aesthetic questions seriously, even when treating aesthetics as a socially constructed activity, as "a discipline with a social history" (Wolff 1983:105), the institutional theory suggests an empirical and compatible alternative.

A more Marxist approach to the analysis of dominant aesthetic theories is taken by Raymond Williams (1977, 1980). He argues that dominant aesthetic theories need to be analyzed in the context of larger socio-economic institutions external to the art world. He elaborates a well-known Marxist, two-component model to explain the relationship between the art world and the political economy of a society. Essentially the model states that "base" (economic organization) has a determining role in the composition of "superstructure" (cultural activities) although more technically the relationship between the two is "dialectical," so that each component plays a significant role in the composition of the other. Hence the cultural activities of any society are developed in the context of legitimating dominant economic practices and ideology (e.g., capitalism). Aesthetic theory also serves in this capacity.

The influence of the economic base on the aesthetic ideology of an art world can be quite direct, as in the flow of corporate patronage to artists and museums. This process has been well documented by the artist Hans Haacke (1975), who demonstrates how patronage to a museum (he quotes a corporate manager referring to art as a "social lubricant" [120]), affects the organization and aesthetic appreciation of an exhibition of 19th century portraits of the American upper class. Using quotes from an exhibition catalog, Haacke makes clear how the aesthetic values of that exhibition are deeply embedded in the economic relationship of the museum and the corporate world.

Economic influences on aesthetic ideology can also be indirect, operating through the "hegemony" of a pervasive capitalist ideology. Hadjinicolaou's work *Art History and Class Struggle* (1978:95) explains how the "visual ideology" of a painting reflects such capitalist ideology. In an analysis of the works of Rembrandt and David, he argues that formal aesthetic appreciation of these paintings is not a function of the individual painter's background. Nor does the "visual ideology" or style of each painter remain consistent across all of his or her work. Instead, each painting is produced and appreciated in particular social and historical circumstances. The aesthetic values of the work are determined by the political and economic ideology of artists, patrons, audiences, and other participants in the art world. The task of the art historian is to articulate these circumstances for each work.

Wolff (1983) seeks to temporize this strongly deterministic marxist position, while maintaining an explanatory relationship between the art world and society at large. She contends that the production of aesthetic values is clearly embedded in historical socio-economic contexts, but that the analysis of aesthetic values needs also to acknowledge what she terms "the specificity of art" (1983:85), that is, internal aesthetic issues that are not reducible to external political and economic issues. An analysis of the relationship of these internal and external issues is subtle, entailing a recognition of the relative autonomy of specific artistic practices as well as an awareness of potential external ideological considerations. Wolff does not provide any completely successful examples of such an analysis, instead presenting her position as an injunction for future work in the sociology of aesthetics. Her injunction could encourage an integration of interactionist and Marxist positions that would include both the internal issues of "institutional theories" and the external focus of analysts such as Williams and Haacke. In any case, Wolff supports a sociological approach to deciphering what have been in the past predominantly philosophical issues.

ARTISTS AND CONSUMPTION RELATIONSHIPS: CLASS

The effect of artistic activities on the class position of consumers is one of the most frequently asked questions in research on art's audiences. This focus partially stems from Weber's classic analysis of "status groups" (Weber 1968), which use cultural resources to identify members, create and maintain group solidarity, and exclude outsiders. Artistic activities are an important component of these cultural resources that tend to show significant variation in consumption patterns across stratified populations. The clustering of related artistic activities help group members identify a parallel cluster of participants with distinct social and economic privileges. Thus class and artistic activities are directly related.

Much of the work in this field has been published relatively recently. However, one of the earlier studies of artistic stratification processes is also one of the most frequently cited, Herbert Gans's *Popular Culture and High Culture* (1974). Gans develops the concept of a "taste culture," cultural activities linked by the fact that they are liked by the same people, and the parallel concept of a "taste public," or the aggregate of people who define the taste culture. He argues that a relationship among cultural choices exists because such choices are based on similar values or aesthetic standards. Taste cultures thus differentiate the mass public into more homogeneous categories that can help identify socio-economic strata and related values.

Using this approach, Gans describes the choices of five taste cultures: high, upper-middle, lower-middle, lower, and quasi-folk low culture, and delineates their respective taste publics. High culture participants tend to be the creators and critics of the cultural world and to choose complex, innovative, and abstract cultural activity. Upper-middle and lower-middle taste cultures represent the majority of Americans and differentiate the middle class into those who tend to focus on the large-scale, mainstream artistic institutions for cultural resources (e.g., metropolitan museums and orchestras) versus the mass media. Lower and quasi-folk cultures represent smaller, more marginal social categories made up of older, more ethnic and more rural populations who tend to focus on local and traditional cultural resources. These taste publics roughly correspond to political and ideological values and thus influence patterns of social interaction. As such, cultural choices appear to have real social consequences.

Interest in how people make cultural choices and what they choose has produced an enormous amount of arts consumption data. Most of this data, however, has not been collected explicitly to analyze class. Instead, arts consumption research has been largely funded and organized by arts organizations seeking to expand their audiences and justify government patronage (see DiMaggio, Useem, and Brown 1978 for a collection of 270 survey studies). While it is still not clear what strategies best attract arts audiences, as evidenced by a steady decline in arts attendance across the general population, the analysis of arts consumption data for the identification of class categories has been more successful. DiMaggio and Useem used the above-mentioned studies to document the fact that indicators of social class, such as education and income, are very good predictors of attendance at classical music concerts and arts museum attendance (DiMaggio and Useem 1978). The higher the social class indicators, the higher the frequency of arts activities. They conclude that while there is an inexact fit between arts activities and social class, nevertheless, art consumption plays a significant role in stratification processes.

The work of Pierre Bourdieu, particularly the social reproduction effects of public education (e.g., Bourdieu 1973), has had a strong theoretical influence on arts and social class research. Bourdieu approaches the arts as "cultural capital," as resources individuals use to establish elite class membership in educational and occupational processes. Those recognized as members of the upper class are evaluated better than those who lack the appropriate cultural capital. *Distinction* (Bourdieu 1984) presents an extensive empirical analysis of various cultural activities and social status processes in France that has been widely acclaimed as a milestone in arts consumption research.

Another study by DiMaggio (1982) on American stratification processes also provides support for Bourdieu's thesis. Self-report survey data collected from over 2900 high school students in 1960 indicate a clear relationship between a student's high school grades and different levels of artistic knowledge and participation. Interestingly, the effect on girls is much stronger than on boys, which DiMaggio suggests is a function of the fact that high culture activities are more clearly prescribed for girls than boys. DiMaggio concludes that these direct indicators of cultural capital have a greater influence on stratification processes than such past proxies for cultural activity as family background. In sum, the relationship of class position and art consumption is well documented.

CONCLUSIONS

I've made three points about interactionist research in the arts. First, art world research need not be marginalized to those with substantive interest in the arts. As shown, interactionist research in the arts addresses many sociologically central issues, including fundamental questions about organization, coordination, and control processes. It should not be necessary to abstract art world models in a formal way to demonstrate their utility. Already used in related research in science, medicine, and work, social world approaches are suitable to many types of collective ideological activity.

Second, examples from a variety of different artistic media indicate that the interactionist approach is appropriate for all artistic activity, despite technological differences among media. While nonsociological factors certainly influence the division of labor in any kind of interdependent activity, granting these factors causal priority in the arts ignores the remarkable extent of organizational variation in artistic activity. Following the distinction between genotype and phenotype variation in biological models, I don't dismiss technology, but rather emphasize organizational flexibility.

Finally, the interactionist perspective is entirely compatible with developing elaborate organizational models. This renders the micro-macro problem of such interest to contemporary sociological theory irrelevant. I agree with Maines (1983) that this unnecessary distinction is largely a function of methodological individualist approaches to theories of action. By using relations and interaction as an explanatory mechanism at both organizational and individual levels of analysis, interactionists can develop sociological models that operate with consistency. While some of the research examined above is not done by interactionists per se, it is all pertinent to the interactionist approach to social organization.

NOTES

1. In the research tradition of Robert Park, Everett Hughes, and the "Chicago School," symbolic interactionists develop theory in close proximity to substantive contexts. Thus it is not surprising that interactionist research in organization is tied to the arts and several other substantive fields (see Hall 1987).

2. In comparison, a long-term exclusive relationship between specific artistic collaborators tends to promote the development of exchange specific skills, depriving those involved of alternative outlets.

3. There have certainly been a number of attempts at developing a more finely grained analysis of the social object. See Denzin (1987) for a phenomenological approach integrating semiotics and symbolic interaction.

REFERENCES

Adler, Judith. 1979. *Artists in Offices*. New Brunswick, N.J.: Transaction Books.

Alexander, Jeffrey, et al. 1987. *The Micro-Macro Link*. Berkeley: University of California Press.

Baxandall, Michael. 1972. *Painting and Experience in Fifteenth Century Italy*. Oxford: Oxford University Press.

Becker, Howard S. 1974. "Art as Collective Activity," *American Sociological Review* 39:767–76.

———. 1976. "Art Worlds and Social Types," *American Behavioral Scientist* 19:703–18.

———. 1982. *Art Worlds*. Berkeley: University of California Press.

Bennett, H. Stith. 1980. *On Becoming a Rock Musician*. Amherst: University of Massachusetts Press.

Blumer, Herbert. 1969. *Symbolic Interactionism*. Englewood Cliffs, N.J.: Prentice Hall.

Bourdieu, Pierre. 1973. "Cultural Reproduction and Social Reproduction," in *Knowledge, Education, and Cultural Change*, Richard Brown (ed.). London: Tavistock.

————. 1984. *Distinction.* Cambridge, Mass.: Harvard University Press.

Cawelti, John. 1970. *The Six-Gun Mystique.* Bowling Green, Ohio: Bowling Green University Popular Press.

Comstock, George. 1975. "The Effect of Television on Children and Adolescents," *Journal of Communications* 25:25–34.

Coser, Lewis, Charles Kadushin, and Walter Powell. 1982. *Books: The Culture of Commerce and Publishing.* New York: Basic Books.

Crane, Diana. 1987. *The Transformation of the Avant-Garde.* Chicago: University of Chicago Press.

Danto, Arthur. 1964. "The Artworld," *Journal of Philosophy* 61:571–84.

Denzin, Norman K. 1971. "The Logic of Naturalistic Inquiry," Social Forces. 50:166–82.

————. 1987. "On Semiotics and Symbolic Interactionism," *Symbolic Interaction* 10:1–19.

Dewey, John. 1934. *Art as Experience.* New York: G. P. Putnam.

Dickie, George. 1975. *Art and the Aesthetic: An Institutional Analysis.* Ithaca: Cornell University Press.

DiMaggio, Paul. 1982. "Cultural Capital and School Success," *American Sociological Review.* 47:189–201.

DiMaggio, Paul, and Paul Hirsch. 1976. "Production Organizations in the Arts," *American Behavioral Scientist* 19:735–49.

DiMaggio, Paul, and Michael Useem. 1978. " Social Class and Arts Consumption," *Theory and Society* 5: 141–61.

DiMaggio, Paul, Michael Useem and Paula Brown. 1978. *Audience Studies of the Performing Arts and Museums.* Research Division Report 9. Washington, D.C.: National Endowment of the Arts.

Dubin, Steven. 1987. *Bureaucratizing the Muse.* Chicago: University of Chicago Press.

Faulkner, Robert. 1971. *Hollywood Studio Musicians.* Chicago: Aldine.

————. 1983. *Music on Demand.* New Brunswick, N.J.: Transaction.

Fine, Gary. 1983. "Symbolic Interaction and Social Organization," *Symbolic Interaction* 6:69–70.

Freidson, Eliot. 1976. " The Division of Labor as Social Interaction," *Social Problems* 23:304–13.

Gans, Herbert. 1974. *Popular Culture and High Culture.* New York: Basic Books.

Gay, Peter. 1968. *Weimar Culture.* New York: Harper and Row.

Gerbner, George, and Larry Gross. 1976. "Living with Television: The Violence Profile," *Journal of Communications* 26:172–99.

Gilmore, Samuel. 1987. "Coordination and Convention: The Organization of the Concert World," *Symbolic Interaction* 10:209–228.

Glaser, Barney, and Anselm Strauss. 1967. *The Discovery of Grounded Theory.* Chicago: Aldine.

Gombrich, E. H. 1960. *Art and Illusion*. Princeton, N.J.: Princeton University Press.

Haacke, Hans. 1975. *Framing and Being Framed*. New York: New York University Press.

Hadjinicolaou, Nicos. 1978. *Art History and Class Struggle*. London: Pluto Press.

Hall, Peter. 1987. "Interactionism and the Study of Social Organization," *Sociological Quarterly* 28:1–22.

Hauser, Arnold. 1951. *The Social History of Art*. New York: Vintage.

Hirsch, Paul. 1972. "Processing Fads and Fashions: An Organization Set Analysis of Culture Industry Systems," *American Journal of Sociology* 77:639–59.

———. 1978. "Production and Distribution Roles among Cultural Organizations," *Social Research* 45:315–330.

Ivins, William. 1953. *Prints and Visual Communications*. Cambridge, Mass.: MIT Press.

Kavolis, Vytautas. 1968. *Artistic Expression: A Sociological Analysis*. Ithaca: Cornell University Press.

———. 1982. "Review of *Art Worlds*," *Journal of Aesthetic and Art Criticism* 41:226.

Kimmel, Michael. 1983. "Review of *Art Worlds*," *American Journal of Sociology* 89:733.

Kling, Rob and Elihu M. Gerson. 1978. "Patterns of Segmentation and Intersection in the Computing World," *Symbolic Interaction* 1:24–43.

Langer, Susanne. 1953. *Feeling and Form*. New York: Charles Scribner's Sons.

Lewis, David. 1969. *Convention*. Cambridge, Mass.: Harvard University Press.

Lovell, Terry. 1983. "Review of *Art Worlds*," *Sociological Review* 31:561.

Lyon, Eleanor. 974. "Work and Play," *Urban Life and Culture* 3:71–97.

Maines, David. 1977. "Social Organization and Social Structure in Symbolic Interactionist Thought," *Annual Review of Sociology*. 3:235–59.

———. 1983. "In Search of Mesostructure," *Urban Life* 11:267–79.

Mayhew, Bruce. 1980. "Structuralism vs. Individualism: Part I," *Social Forces* 59:335–75.

Meyer, Leonard. 1956. *Emotion and Meaning in Music*. Chicago: University of Chicago Press.

———. 1967. *Music, the Arts and Ideas*. Chicago: University of Chicago Press.

Moulin, Raymonde. [1967] 1987. *The French Art Market.* New Brunswick, N.J.: Rutgers University Press.

Nochlin, Linda. 1971. "Why have there been no great women artists?," in *Art and Sexual Politics,* Thomas Hess and Elizabeth Baker, eds. New York: Collier Macmillan Publishers.

Peterson, Richard. 1976. "The Production of Culture: A Prolegomenon," *American Behavioral Scientist* 19:669–84.

———. 1979. "Revitalizing the Culture Concept," *Annual Review of Sociology* 5:137–166.

———. 1983. "Patterns of Cultural Choice: A Prolegomenon," *American Behavioral Scientist* 26:422–38.

Peterson, Richard, and David Berger. 1975. "Cycles in Symbol Production: The case of popular music," *American Sociological Review* 40:158–73.

Robinson, John. 1985. *Public Participation in the Arts: A Project Summary.* College Park, Md.: University of Maryland Survey Center.

Rosenblum, Barbara. 1978. "Style as Social Process," *American Sociological Review* 43: 422–38.

Schorske, Carl. 1981. *Fin-De-Siecle Vienna.* New York: Vintage Books.

Scott, W. Richard. 1981. *Organizations: Rational, Natural, and Open System.* Englewood Cliffs, N.J.: Prentice Hall.

Shibutani, Tomatsu. 1955. "Reference Groups as Perspectives," *American Journal of Sociology* 60: 562–69.

———. 1962. "Reference Groups and Social Control," in *Human Behavior and Social Control,* ed. A. Rose. Boston: Houghton Mifflin.

Simpson, Charles. 1981. *Soho.* Chicago: University of Chicago Press.

Smith, Barbara H. 1968. *Poetic Closure.* Chicago: University of Chicago Press.

Star, Susan L. and Elihu Gerson. 1987. "The Management and Dynamics of Anomalies in Scientific Work," *Sociological Quarterly* 28: 147–69.

Stinchcombe, Arthur. 1959. "Bureaucratic and Craft Administration of Production: A comparative study," *Administrative Science Quarterly* 4:168–187.

Strauss, Anselm. 1978. "A Social World Perspective," *Studies in Symbolic Interaction* 1:119–28.

———. 1982. "Social Worlds and Legitimation Processes," *Studies in Symbolic Interaction* 4:171–90.

———. 1984. "Social Worlds and their Segmentation Processes," *Studies in Symbolic Interaction* 4:123–39.

———. 1985. "Work and the Division of Labor," *Sociological Quarterly* 26:1–19.

Strauss, Anselm L., et al. 1985. *The Social Organization of Medical Work.* Chicago: University of Chicago Press.

Sutherland, J.A. 1976. *Victorian Novelists and Their Publishers.* Chicago: University of Chicago Press.

Thompson, James. 1967. *Organizations in Action.* New York: McGraw-Hill.

Unruh, David. 1979. "Characteristics and Types of Participation in Social Worlds," *Symbolic Interaction* 2:115–29.

Weber, Max. 1968. *Economy and Society.* Berkeley: University of California.

Webster, Murray. 1973. "Psychological Reductionism, Methodological Individualism, and Large-Scale Problems," *American Sociological Review* 38:258–73.

White, Harrison and Cynthia White. 1965. *Canvases and Careers.* New York: John Wiley.

Williams, Raymond. 1977. *Marxism and Literature.* Oxford: Oxford University Press.

———. 1980. *Problems in Materialism and Culture.* London: Verso.

Wilson, Robert. 1983. "Review of *Art Worlds, Society* 20:94.

Wolfe, Tom. 1975. *The Painted Word.* New York: Bantam Books.

Wolff, Janet. 1983. *Aesthetics and the Sociology of Art.* London: George Allen and Unwin.

7

Symbolic Interactionism in Social Studies of Science
Adele E. Clarke and Elihu M. Gerson

INTRODUCTION

Over the past decade, both the sociology of science and the interdisciplinary field of science studies have grown rapidly. Scholars from many traditions have entered the fray. This paper provides an overview of recent symbolic interactionist and related contributions focused largely on scientific work organization. It also draws attention to efforts of historians and philosophers in ways traditional to science studies.[1]

Before the 1930s, questions about the nature of science were usually linked to the development of the sociology of knowledge and to philosophical debates (R. Collins and Restivo, 1983). Many philosophical perspectives were used to frame and argue about the social nature of the sciences, and echoes of these debates can still be heard (Star, 1988a). The pragmatist philosophers who laid the basis for symbolic interactionism were particularly interested in the nature of scientific inquiry, methodologies, and approaches (Peirce, 1877, 1878; Dewey, 1929; Mead, 1917; Bentley, 1954; Veblen, 1932). But these concerns were largely ignored in the interactionist sociological tradition.

While the history and philosophy of science began to develop as independent disciplines at the turn of this century, sociological approaches to science emerged in the 1930s through the work of British Marxist and American functionalist scholars. Work in both these traditions has continued ever since. However, neither Marxists nor functionalists examined the actual content or work of science. Marxists focused on the social determination of ideas, on relations of science to elites, and on issues in science policy development (e.g., Bernal, 1967; Wersky, 1978; Zilsel, 1941).

Merton (1938, 1973) led the American functionalist tradition in sociology of science. Functionalists have taken it for granted that modern 179 science is the standard for objective inquiry and assumed that scientific knowledge is somehow special and different from other kinds of knowledge. Functionalist studies have focused largely on norms and stratification within science (e.g., career patterns, status and reward structures, priority disputes, and women in science), forms of social control in scientific domains, and values issues. A related line of sociological work has centered on bibliographic citation analyses (e.g., Mullins, 1973) from which the term "invisible colleges" emerged, referring to informal but highly significant networks among scientists (Crane, 1972).

Since the early 1970s several other approaches to science studies have been developed by scholars in both the United States and Europe. This new work includes neo-Marxist (e.g., Levidov and Young, 1981; Rose and Rose, 1976; Lewontin and Levins, 1985; Nowotny and Rose, 1979), conflict (e.g., Restivo, 1988), feminist (e.g., Abir-Am and Outram, 1987; Fee, 1983; Keller, 1982, 1985; Merchant, 1980), social constructionist (e.g., Latour and Woolgar, 1979; Callon, Law, and Rip, 1986; H. M. Collins, 1983; Knorr-Cetina and Mulkay, 1983; Mulkay, 1977; Pickering, 1984; Law and Lodge, 1984; Shapin, 1982), and ethnomethodological approaches (e.g., Garfinkel, Lynch, and Livingston, 1981; Lynch, 1985a, 1985b).[2] These works were integral to the broader challenge to functionalism characteristic of the era, and many were in dialogue with Kuhn's (1962) pivotal work on paradigms and the structure of scientific revolutions. While there was a small spate of science studies by symbolic interactionists in the 1960s (e.g., Becker and Carper, 1956; Bucher, 1962; Bucher and Strauss, 1961; Glaser, 1964; Marcson, 1960; Reif and Strauss, 1965; Strauss and Rainwater, 1962), no further efforts emerged until the 1980s.

All of the recent symbolic interactionist science studies to date have drawn upon the work and organizations concerns of the tradition (e.g., Park, 1952; Hughes, 1958, 1971; Blumer, 1969; Becker, 1970; Freidson, 1976; Strauss, 1975). They focus on science as work rather than science as "knowledge," refusing to divorce knowledge from interaction and social organization. They have not been concerned with selves or individuals, but instead with all other scales of work organization from research projects to laboratories to disciplines to political and economic relations in the wider society. They are often at what Maines (1982; 1977; Maines and Charlton, 1985) has called the meso scale of organizations, but focus equally intently on linkages across micro, meso, and macro scales. In fact, interpenetration across scales is a standard starting point for most interactionist science studies. That is, while focus may be especially at one scale, relations across scales are also invariably analyzed. It is assumed that micro, meso and macro scales interpenetrate—the macro is inextricably in the macro and vice versa. Indeed, for some interactionists these distinctions dissolve.

We begin our review with a brief discussion of the assumptions shared by current interactionist sociologists of science. We next review studies of scientific work processes at the work site, and of alliances and going concerns at meso scales of organization. Last, we describe studies of larger scale scientific social worlds and their interactions.[3] We organized the paper in this manner to facilitate entrée into science studies for readers who may be unfamiliar with this cultural area. In conclusion, we discuss topics and questions for additional research and the necessity for interdisciplinary approaches to them.

Rather than focusing on a few studies in depth, we scan the full range of interactionist science studies. We also include parallel approaches and results in the sociology of science to underscore some important convergences between interactionism and related traditions. While this paper reviews research findings, many salient methodological issues and connections with early Chicago sociology and pragmatist philosophy and politics are discussed elsewhere (Clarke, 1989a; Fujimura, Star, and Gerson, 1987; Star, 1988a, 1989).

Assumptions in Interactionist Science Studies

The first assumption interactionists in science studies make is that all scientific facts, findings, and theories are socially constructed. We see these "things as the products of people doing things together" (Becker, 1986:1). In recent years, this assumption has become conventional in many approaches to science studies and is not exclusively interactionist by any means (e.g., Callon, Law and Rip, 1986; Cambrosio and Keating, 1988; Knorr-Cetina, Krohn, and Whittley, 1980; Knorr-Cetina, 1981; Latour and Woolgar, 1979; Latour, 1986; Law and Lodge, 1984; Law, 1984, 1986; Lynch, 1982, 1985a,b; Traweek, 1984).

Second, we assume that knowledge represents and embodies work, a particular way of organizing the world through a series of commitments and alliances. It is here, in making no distinction between cognitive and social aspects of knowledge, that interactionist approaches diverge from most others. That is, while many in science studies share commitments to the social construction of scientific knowledge, for some other constructionists the central issue is the construction of knowledge per se. Their studies focus largely on the concrete processes of knowledge construction in laboratories, developing the notion that knowledge cannot be understood without looking at practice (e.g., Latour and Woolgar, 1979; Knorr-Cetina, 1981; Lynch, 1985a). In general, these other constructionists do maintain the distinction between knowledge and social organization, although Latour (1983, 1984, 1987) does not. For interactionists, ideas are commitments, ways of allocating resources and responding to constraints. In this regard, we draw directly upon Dewey ([1916] 1953).

The third basic assumption made by interactionists currently in science studies is that science is best approached as a matter of work, organizations, and institutions. These emphases provide natural ties to historians of science who study how scientists go about their business (e.g., Borell, 1987a,b; Geison, 1987; Kimmelman, 1983, 1987; Maienschein, 1988; Rainger, Benson, and Maienschein, 1988; Pauly, 1984, 1987). Fourth, we endorse the assumption that scientific work, institutions, and knowledge are not essentially different from other kinds, nor in any way sociologically special. Again, this assumption has become routine in many science studies. In sum, the major differences to date between symbolic interactionist and other constructionists is in making no distinction between knowledge and work and in the intensity of focus on work and its organization.

SCIENTIFIC WORK ORGANIZATION
AT MICRO AND MESO SCALES

Beginning with Latour and Woolgar's (1979) now classic study of a neuroendocrinology laboratory, other social constructionists have conducted many studies focused on work in laboratories through extensive observations and interviews with people who work in them. Such studies, reflecting many traditions of sociological thought, have become a staple of current research in the sociology of science (e.g., Knorr-Cetina, 1981; H. Collins, 1985; Traweek, 1984; Garfinkel, Lynch, and Livingston, 1981; Lynch, 1982, 1985a,b).

These studies successfully established the legitimacy of systematically examining work organization as a way of understanding how scientific results are constructed. The major lesson drawn from them concerns the inherently problematical, contingent, and negotiated character of technical research results. Latour and Woolgar (1979:236) refer to the "slow, practical craftwork by which inscriptions [documents] are superimposed and accounts backed up or dismissed." In a similar vein, the "shift from art to science" in the development of monoclonal antibody techniques has been studied in the laboratory by Cambrosio and Keating (1988). They found that the local and tacit parts of scientific practice—the "hands-on know-how," "art," or "magical" aspects of daily work with complex techniques and materials—are also subject to discussion, negotiation and construction by scientists. Of concern here was the means by which "hands-on know-how" was made adequately explicit for replication in other laboratories.

These studies raise the classic problem of replicability of scientific results. On this point, H. M. Collins (1985) points out that descriptions of work provided in the published literature often do not, in fact, permit unaided replication. Rather, scientists who wish to replicate results of others' research must be intimately familiar with the techniques employed or have direct assistance from the originating laboratory.

Extending this work into technology studies through an account of a British military aircraft project, Law and Callon (1988) detail the fundamentally interconnected character of the social and the technical and how they are jointly created in a single process. They assert that while the social nature of the technical may be counterintuitive to many sociologists, engineers have never experienced a rupture between the two domains. Moreover, the context in which a technical object such as an aircraft is created is subsequently internalized in it, or, in their network analysis terminology, the local network contains the global network.

These studies all emphasize the importance of immediate work circumstances in the construction of scientific facts. They also alert us to how both material objects and intellectual commitments can be hotly debated. Prior resolved debates are often present at current research sites in the form of "black boxes" that were, once upon a time, socially constructed (Latour and Wolgar, 1979; Bijker, Hughes, and Pinch, 1987). Such "black boxes" include now taken-for-granted instruments, materials, procedures, and theories.

Several interactionist studies focus on scientific work at the small scale and complement this emergent tradition of laboratory and related studies. Emphases have been on processes of making commitments and negotiating constraints and opportunities (Becker, 1960; Gerson, 1976; Strauss, 1979). In science, framing and solving the research problems immediately at hand shape and organize the work commitments and conventions or "standard operating procedures" of actors (Becker, 1970:261–74, 1982; Kling and Gerson, 1977, 1978). The problems are the touchstone against which all decisions are ultimately made and around which essentially all conflicts are fought.

In order to solve their research problems, scientists make commitments to theories and methods, to each other, to sponsors, and to various organizations. Understanding this pattern of commitments is the central problem for an interactionist analysis of scientific work organization. For example, Star and Gerson (1987) consider the negotiated character of anomalies both across a variety of scientific researches and through studying the career of one anomaly in neuroscience research since 1870. They define anomalies as interruptions to routine, generalizing Hughes's (1971) concern with mistakes at work. They point out that anomalies in scientific work do not exist in any absolute sense but are always relative to a specific local or institutional context: "Nothing except the negotiated context of work organization itself compels any scientist to correct or even take into account an anomalous event of any magnitude" (Star and Gerson, 1987:148). The content of science is not separable from its organization, refuting the cognitive versus social distinction about knowledge. Anomalies must therefore be studied by looking at the circumstances of work in which they arise and are negotiated. First it must be established that there is, "in fact," an anomaly; next it must be classified (mistake or accident, artifact, discovery, or impropriety); last it must somehow be managed vis-à-vis the work and the problem structure of the science.

A related study examines the robustness of findings, a problem philosophers have traditionally handled without analyzing the actual conditions of work. Drawing on the efforts of philosopher of science Wimsatt (1980, 1981), Star (1986) examined the triangulation of various research results to increase robustness in the neurosciences. Discussions of triangulation have largely ignored the structural conditions of work, daily work contingencies, histories and traditions of lines of work, and the concrete processes of actually collating different lines of evidence. Such omissions can lead to interlocking biases, buried uncertainties, the deletion of local considerations, and pseudo-robustness, as scientists often "believe" the results of other lines of work when it is in their interests to do so, and vice versa. Star found these were frequent problems in efforts to triangulate clinical and basic research in the neurosciences.

Structural Constraints and Opportunities

The commitments which scientists can make are, of course, restrained by the contexts in which they work. Farberman's (1975) and Denzin's (1977) studies of criminogenic market structures focused on constraints in the automobile and liquor industries. They analyzed how the organization of these industries and their market structures shaped how participants did their work. Both emphasized the structural nature of the pushes toward criminal activities in order to survive—to stay in business. Becker's (1982) and Gilmore's (this volume) studies of art worlds and Riemer's (1979) study of construction work all develop this theme of institutional constraints on commitments in yet other work settings. Gilmore's study vividly demonstrates how constraints vary across sub-worlds. A number of interactionist science studies share and extend this aspect of the symbolic interactionist tradition, focusing on both the constraints and opportunities engendered by structural conditions.

Specific kinds of constraints often lead to deletion of accounts of the actual work involved from scientific reports (Star, 1983). Scientists present partial or schematic results by deleting qualifications and elaborate descriptions from their papers. These simplifications of work occur in the presence of particular constraints: inadequate time to process all of the data; incompatible demands for intelligibility and brevity from multiple audiences; and time pressures from journals, funding agencies, and university departments. Specific kinds of formatting and deleting regularly "got the work done" in the face of such constraints and became standard operating procedures in the neuroscience fields Star studied.

Constraints of various kinds also shape scientific problem selection processes. Extending Strauss's (1988; Strauss et al., 1985) work on articulation in medical worlds to scientific worlds, Fujimura (1986b, 1987) introduced the concept of doable problems in scientific research. Doable problems require successful alignment across several scales of work organization: the experiment as a set of tasks; the laboratory as a bundle of experiments and other often administrative tasks; and the scientific social world as the work of laboratories, colleagues, sponsors, regulators, and other players all focused on the same family of problems. Doability is achieved by articulating alignment to meet the demands and constraints imposed at all three scales simultaneously: a problem must provide doable experiments, feasible within the parameters of immediate constraints and opportunities in a given laboratory, and be viewed as worthwhile and supportable work within the larger scientific world.

In the contemporary cancer research world, for example, oncogene research offers an array of doable problems. But investigators must align the actions of antibodies, techniques, personnel, laboratories, companies, stockholders, venture capitalists, private suppliers, protein chemists, molecular biologists, EMBO and NIH data banks, and even Congress. Doability is increased under conditions relatively free of constraints: abundant resources, a clear division of labor, a modular task structure, and standardized tasks. In cancer research, certain standardized tasks are now common—described in handy molecular biological "cookbooks" such as Cold Spring Harbor's (Maniatis, Fritch, and Sambrook, 1982) *Molecular Cloning: A Laboratory Manual* (cf. Cambrosio and Keating, 1988).

Doable problems must, of course, be constructed and reconstructed many times as the work proceeds. Fujimura (1986a,b) examines these processes as problem paths: the changes in problems addressed as scientists meet contingencies in the course of their work over time. Scientists work around constraints, take detours, decompose problems, abandon problems, and construct new problems to take advantage of new techniques, materials, discoveries, or personnel. The problem path concept permits analytic incorporation of all the activities, conditions, and contingencies involved in constructing doable problems over time (e.g., lack of markets, resource constraints, mistakes, and unanticipated articulation work). Fujimura offers a notational scheme for mapping problem paths which might well be of use in other areas of sociological investigation.

Appropriate materials for research are requisite for pursuit of doable problems. Clarke (1987) studied how scientists organized research materials during the early decades of this century. As more physiologically oriented approaches to life sciences research spread, investigators confronted a serious constraint upon their work because these approaches required large quantities of live and fresh materials which were not readily available. For example, when reproductive scientists initially incorporated these new approaches into their daily work, they were obliged to "do it themselves": literally run to abattoirs for fresh sow ovaries, pull on cows' labia to induce urination to supply hormone assays, trudge through the snow to feed their monkeys on Sundays, and dash to hospitals in the middle of the night to preserve human embryos discarded during emergency surgeries. Eliminating as many of these constraints as possible by routinizing access to supplies of specialized materials was part of the development of the infrastructure that supports modern scientific work. Gradually the biological supplies industry emerged to meet some of these needs, and on-site colonies of laboratory animals (new phenomena) were established to meet others. Easy access to usable materials then created new opportunities for research and shaped research itself. That is, once a given organism or material was easily available at a given site, researchers tended to use it again and again, at times shaping their research problems to fit the available materials (one facet of doability).

All these studies demonstrate the inseparability of scientific knowledge and the work organization that produces it. From framing problems to acquiring materials, to using others' research as evidence, handling anomalies, and writing reports, research consists of betting on how things will turn out. Scientists manage their constraints and opportunities by committing their available resources to constructing and solving doable problems.

Research as a System of Going Concerns

Another focus of interactionist and related science studies has been on meso scale work organization. Analysis here focuses on larger-scale patterns of commitment organization as they are formed by negotiation of alliances among participants, and the development of conventional procedures and arrangements. Hughes (1971:53–64) provides us with the generic term "going concerns" to refer to groups of people sufficiently committed to something to act in concert over time. These occur in great variety in many forms and stages of development. For Hughes (1971:54), going concerns

> have a present existence and an historical dimension; discovery of the relations between the two is one of our chief sociological tasks. This requires that we try to make some sort of order out of the various contingencies to which going concerns are subject and the kinds of changes that occur in them as they survive . . . these contingencies (joinings of events and circumstances).

Such efforts are at the heart of interactionist science studies.

Latour, Callon, and their colleagues at the Center for the Sociology of Innovation at the Ecole des Mines in Paris led the way in developing a framework for understanding these phenomena in the sciences. The starting point is Latour's study of Pasteur (1983, 1984, 1988b). In 1881, Pasteur organized the first demonstration of vaccination against anthrax in cattle. He invited a wide array of potential allies, including the press, farmers, and government officials, to observe the effectiveness of his center's work. As the uninoculated cows keeled over and died, the inoculated ones calmly chewed their cud and stared healthily at the crowd. Potential alliances were actualized here as Pasteur demonstrated to his audiences that their varied interests could all be well served by his center's work. As Pasteur enrolled increasing numbers of allies in his cause, his group became more and more important in French public health, agriculture, and other industries. Thus, Pasteur and his group became a "center of authority."

For a research program to become such a center, the concerns of different audiences must be translated or reinterpreted to mesh with the purposes of the program and vice versa. Moreover, the center must become the gatekeeper (an "obligatory point of passage") in these negotiations (Callon, Law, and Rip, 1986; Callon, 1985; Latour, 1987). These translation or reconstruction processes funnel diverse concerns into a relatively centralized and coherent system of new commitments which then shape and constrain the conduct of the center and its allies.

Some specific strategies for building such centers are examined in Star's (1985, 1989) studies of the work of late nineteenth-century British neurophysiologists. The scientists who supported localizationist theories of brain function built a successful research program through several strategies: by gaining control of relevant journals, hospital practices, teaching posts, and other means of knowledge production and distribution; by screening out those who held opposing points of view from print and employment; by linking a successful clinical program with both basic research and a theoretical model; and by uniting against common enemies with powerful scientists from other fields (e.g., joining with others to form the first professional physiological association to fight antivivisectionists).

Interactionists have also elaborated on the notion of centers using social worlds theory (Strauss, 1978; Becker, 1982; Gerson, 1983a). They assert that a center's allies come from different social worlds and hold differing perspectives on the work at hand. This approach draws upon Park's (1952) early interactionist concerns with intersections of human communities, which Hughes (1971) extended by conceiving of the workplace as "where [diverse] peoples meet." For example, Star and Griesemer (1986) studied relations among hobbyists, collectors, and researchers in Berkeley's Museum of Vertebrate Zoology before World War II. The success of this enterprise was critically dependent upon the comparability of large numbers of specimens, which made the researchers dependent upon the hobbyists and collectors. The researchers' goal was therefore to convince collectors and hobbyists to meet the researchers' standards for preparing and handling specimens. Such negotiations were, of course, only part of the system of overlapping negotiations in which the Museum was engaged as researchers sought to solve technical problems, build disciplines, and maintain a stable funding base.

The process of building centers of authority has also been examined by historians. Geison (1981, 1987) has focused on the development of specialties, research schools and centers. His more recent paper draws on quantitative publications counts to construct an intriguing set of "social maps" of American centers of physiology c1880–1940. Maienschein (1987, 1988) and Pauly (1987, 1988) analyze the development of one subworld of American biology as it centered in two institutions: the Woods Hole Marine Biology Laboratory and the University of Chicago. A particular style of scientific work in biology emerged at these tightly linked organizations at the turn of the century, inspired by the alliance-building efforts of zoologist Charles Otis Whitman. These and related studies of the Chicago–Woods Hole axis provide the most detailed picture of center building that we have to date. Further research is also in progress on biologists' work at the University of Chicago and their alliances with Chicago social scientists and philosophers.[4] All were focused on the problem of organization during the first half of this century (e.g., Redfield, 1942).

Contemporary science is now so large and widely distributed that a center of authority seldom exists as a single geographical or institutional entity. Building a going concern under these conditions requires the commitments of many laboratories, organizations, and institutions. Fujimura's (1986a, 1988b) study of the molecular biological bandwagon in cancer research analyzes the development of a line of research as a going concern through the mobilization of such widely distributed commitments. This mobilization placed the package of oncogene theory (on the molecular genetic origins of cancer) and recombinant DNA and other molecular biological technologies at the center of authority. This package of a theory and technologies to develop it became a transportable center of authority.

The new package was marketed as a means of constructing highly doable problems in multiple research centers, well aligned with funding, organizational, material and other constraints upon research and as a means for attacking long-standing problems in many biological disciplines. By persuading scientists, organizations, and institutions to use this package to restructure laboratories, lines of research, and lines of work, molecular biologists and tumor virologists created a going concern of oncogene and other molecular biological approaches to cancer. By the 1980s, this going concern had grown into a bandwagon, a scientific social movement. A scientific bandwagon exists when large numbers of people, laboratories, and organizations commit their resources to one approach to scientific problems. Fujimura found no grand marshal orchestrating the movement toward molecular genetic approaches, but rather a cascading series of decentralized choices, changes, exchanges, and commitments.

A similar bandwagon occurred historically when the practical interests of American agricultural scientists and eugenists encouraged early attention to Mendelian, biometric, and cytological studies (Kimmelman, 1983, 1987). This resulted in rapid and widespread adoption of such methods by American scientists throughout the more applied agricultural research system as well as in elite universities, which subsequently cohered into the discipline of genetics. "Marketing Mendelism" was easy across these diverse sites because Mendelism made immediate sense to practical breeders as it explained their experience vividly, while it also appealed to the theoretical bent of scientific elites (Paul and Kimmelman, 1988).

The common thread across these studies is how going concerns get going and maintain themselves in the face of many kinds of challenges and uncertainties and how they manage to take advantage of unique opportunities for entrenchment and expansion.

Scientific Social Worlds

Another major thrust of interactionist science studies centers on relations among scientific social worlds and on their relations with nonscientific worlds. Disciplines, specialties, and research traditions are social worlds—interactive groups with shared commitments to certain activities, sharing resources to achieve their goals (Strauss, 1978; Bucher and Strauss, 1961; Bucher, 1962, 1988; Becker 1982; Kling and Gerson, 1977, 1978; Shibutani, 1955, 1962). The major processes of social worlds formation and development (segmentation, intersection, and legitimation) characterize scientific social worlds as they do others (Strauss, 1982a,b, 1984; Gerson, 1983a).

The social worlds concept is especially useful in science studies in at least two ways. First, it temporarily or permanently mutes the problem of distinguishing between various kinds and scales of scientific work organization: disciplines, specialties, subspecialties, "invisible colleges," and so on. This conceptual hierarchical nesting can often be misleading, whether or not there is socially meaningful hierarchy is an empirical question. By taking a social worlds perspective, we see only worlds, their subworlds, and their relations with other worlds. These relations can therefore be handled as a matter of empirical study, rather than prior analytic necessity.

Second, the notion of social world allows us to distinguish between disciplines and professions (Gerson, 1987b). Both are social worlds organizing their interaction around a common subject matter. However, professions are organizations for building, controlling, and regulating markets for a class of technical services, a way of organizing an occupational labor market (Freidson, 1977, 1982; Larson, 1977). In contrast, disciplines are social worlds organized around topics and methods of inquiry. They divide intellectual labor and organize work on research problems. Other differences lie in the primary audiences of work performed, the foci of codes of ethics, relations with "amateurs," career structures, the role of government, and the organization of day-to-day work.

Interactionists conceptualize interaction among disciplines (and other worlds) as a matter of analyzing patterns of negotiation and commitment among them (e.g., Becker, 1982; Strauss, 1982a). Thus, for every discipline, the other scientific and nonscientific worlds with which it interacts are a set of audiences (the generic term) which attend to its work, make use of its results, and provide it with findings, materials, equipment, raw data, and money (Gerson, 1987a). Each audience holds unique expectations of a discipline, makes a different pattern of demands upon its research, and offers a different pattern and amount of resources in return. Different audiences' expectations may even be incompatible with one another, and sometimes they are incompatible with the basic research problems that scientists seek to pursue (e.g., antivivisectionists). Hence audiences may act as constraints on the work of each discipline as well as providing resources or opportunities. Disciplines keep the goodwill and support of an audience by addressing its particular concerns. Thus the concerns of audiences and disciplines are complexly linked and constantly renegotiated. Such "marriages of convenience" between disciplinary research programs and the concerns of sponsors and consumers are (and were) at the core of the relations between disciplines and the larger society.

Disciplines must find (or create) a suitable "stable" of audiences that will provide the full range of support the discipline needs while refraining from crippling demands. This typically means gaining partial support from many different audiences for different programs and problems. It also means playing audiences off against one another. Thus every discipline is constantly engaged in a complex juggling act, balancing research problems and techniques with the ever-changing demands of supporting, competing, and even antagonistic audiences.

Interactionist studies of scientific social worlds have framed larger scale work organization in terms of discipline formation, interaction with other scientific and nonscientific worlds. They also attend to relations between disciplines and the larger society.

Discipline Formation and Interaction

There has recently been considerable historical and sociological interest in discipline formation and development and several such studies have been undertaken from interactionist perspectives.[5] Volberg (1983) focused on the development of American botany at the turn of the century as economic and political constituencies interested in agricultural and natural resources development demanded government support and expertise to solve their problems. Farmers, for example, sought means of improving both the quality and quantity of their crops. As a result of such pressures, the federal government funded a network of state agricultural research and dissemination organizations linked to the land-grant universities. Technical direction of botanical and crop research work then moved increasingly out of the hands of hobbyists and collectors and into those of university-based scientists.

Like many other disciplines, botany was characterized by the segmentation of several different types of research whose practitioners competed for resources (e.g., sites, funding, and personnel). Those approaches best able to package (produce, organize, and deliver) their work to address narrowly defined technical problems were most successful in obtaining resources. Skillful research entrepreneurs also established niches within existing organizations and built these into going concerns. The most successful lines of work were generally committed to new types of experimental research. Nonexperimental lines of work, such as classification, were segmented off into narrowed specialties with their own restricted institutional and professional bases.

The emergence and coalescence of reproductive science in the United States, c1910–1940, was the focus of another study (Clarke, 1985, 1989a, 1989b). Disciplinary status was defined here as the construction of a distinctively reproductive problem structure plus the work organization to pursue it. This new discipline emerged from a previously undifferentiated nexus of problems in heredity, development, and reproduction after the turn of the century. What Clarke called the trilateral segmentation of disciplines from this nexus became the basis for genetics, developmental embryology, and reproductive science. Research on problems of reproduction was then undertaken in biological, medical, and agricultural settings with considerable interaction among them, making reproductive science an intersectional enterprise.

Reproductive scientists successfully coped with the illegitimacy of this sexuality-laden and therefore suspect research field in their negotiations with various audiences (Clarke, 1985, 1989a, 1989b). First, with scientific and funding worlds, they emphasized reproductive endocrinology which linked their endeavor with cutting-edge biochemical approaches in the life sciences. Second, despite pressures, they eschewed open alliances with controversial birth control advocacy groups before World War II. Third, they convinced major foundation sponsors, who had initially sought studies of human sexuality, to support biological studies of sex using animal models instead of psychosocial studies of humans.

Disciplinary and professional worlds may also be in competition with one another for limited or scarce resources. For example, at the turn of the century, zoology fared best at institutions where the development of medical schools was slow and problematic (Pauly, 1984, 1987, 1988). Conversely, on other campuses vigorous medical schools succeeded in capturing talent and resources, typically preempting development of an independent zoology there. Historian Pauly has both charted the mechanisms of early victories of medicine over biology and pioneered in investigating local institutional influences on disciplinary and professional formation and growth.

This competition between medicine and biology took place during a broader reorganization of disciplines throughout the life sciences at the turn of the century (Gerson, 1983b). The basic lines of specialization in classical natural history were along taxon lines (i.e., the kinds of organisms studied such as ornithology and entomology) and by geographic region. By the end of the century, specialization by taxon had become finer-grained, and a new line of cleavage among disciplines began to emerge—organizing work by analytical topic rather than by taxa and regions. For example, the analytic problem of heredity became the work of genetics, while growth and development are the focus of developmental embryology.

Gerson finds that the analytic disciplines that emerged in this way fell into two clear groups: on the one hand those that deal with single organisms and parts of organisms which he calls "organism disciplines" (e.g., cytology, histology, embryology, cytogenetics) and, on the other hand, those that deal with groups and classes of organisms, which he calls "population disciplines" (biogeography, ecology, population genetics, paleontology, systematics). As each specialty developed, it formed its own pattern of relationships with sponsors and other influential audiences. Thus, as these disciplines emerged and coalesced, contact across this great divide tended to diminish. The institutional consequence of this realignment was a pattern of many small, relatively weak basic research disciplines. Most had their own scholarly machinery of departments, journals, and learned societies, while there were few umbrella professional organizations (Appel, 1987, 1988).

In contrast, Fujimura (1986a, 1988b) studies the blurring and collapsing of contemporary disciplinary boundaries across a host of biological disciplines. One consequence of the molecular biological bandwagon in cancer research is that very similar types of research on cancer are now done by developmental biologists, tumor virologists, molecular biologists, biochemists, immunologists, and microbiologists. When asked, these researchers cannot give a clear answer about which discipline they belong to. Oncogene research is thus one example of a wider arena of conjoint research including such areas as normal growth and differentiation, retroviruses, and chemical hormonal and radiation carcinogenesis. Thus the concept of a bandwagon is useful for analyzing the actions of multiple worlds (disciplines, lines of work, and lines of research).

Science in Society

Questions about the nature of large-scale changes in the sciences lead researchers to examine relationships between scientific institutions and the larger society. Most of the interactionist work in this vein focuses on relationships between science and the economy, although a few studies also consider relations with government.

One government and science study analyzes how American academic oceanographers are alienated from much of the work on the cutting edge of their discipline because the most sophisticated research techniques are under the exclusive jurisdiction of the Defense Department (Mukerji, 1987). Oceanographers in academia are thus cut off from participation in this work and do not even know where the boundaries of their discipline currently lie.

Relationships between science, the economy, and the larger society are often studied as intersections of scientific worlds with various industries. From an interactionist perspective, industries are also social worlds, organized around the production of a group of related goods or services (Kling and Gerson, 1977, 1978). In this view, markets are intersections between worlds. A key question here is, "[W]hat is the pattern of markets in which the world is engaged, and how do these 'map' onto the pattern of intersections among subworlds?" (Kling and Gerson, 1978:42). The relationships between disciplines and industries are complex, however, and cannot be analyzed as simple buyer/seller relations. Rather, disciplines appear as sources of skill, knowledge, and technology which are bought and sold by other organizations, most notably universities, professions, and industries. Untangling the details of these complex relationships remains a major area for further research.

For reproductive science, for example, the applied domains of animal agriculture and obstetrics and gynecology were obvious consumers (Clarke, 1985, 1989a, 1989b). Moreover, as reproductive science developed over this century, it became largely if not exclusively identified with its applied medical and agricultural domains. This was in part because its applications (such as birth control and infertility treatment in humans and artificial insemination in farm animals) were so controversial yet lucrative. Gradually but clearly, American centers of reproductive science in biological institutions waned as those in applied, productive, and profitable agricultural and medical settings came to predominate. Here we see how the economy shapes the academy.

Drawing upon earlier work (Busch, 1981, 1984), Busch and Chatelin (in prep.) argue more generally that certain kinds of science best serve capital accumulation goals and that, over time, these have become the kinds of sciences that are done—instrumental sciences. Such sciences serve the development of commodity and technological production, indeed are more and more central parts of it, through its instruments, materials, practices, and results. Certain features of capitalist societies make them particularly supportive vehicles for the development of instrumental sciences. Like Veblen (1932), Busch and Chatelin view the relation between the two as mutually supportive rather than causal, although instrumental sciences are now virtually indispensable to capitalism.

To be instrumental, science must be applied in production processes. This involves a complex web of organizational arrangements sustained over time (e.g., Etzkowitz, 1983), generally conceived as an economic sector. Sociologically, a sector is a domain including all the organizations producing similar products or providing similar services along with all the other organizations providing support and funding, serving as regulatory agencies, and those that use or consume the products or services produced (Clarke, 1988b).[6] Each participant in a sector must itself become a going concern as well as articulate successfully with other participants. Clarke is using the concept of a life sciences industrial sector to better understand the durability of relationships among life sciences disciplines, related industries, research universities, philanthropists and foundations, disciplinary and professional associations, and governments. She analyzes how the life sciences became going concerns and sector participants. In the "start-up" era c1890–1917, activities in the life sciences centered around building an adequate research infrastructure. In the consolidation era c1917–1940, activities centered on developing adequate scientific management mechanisms to manage growth and expansion, including fuller articulation with other participants in the life sciences industrial sector.

The anticipated impacts of biotechnology on the agricultural sector are also under scrutiny, drawing upon earlier work on relations of agricultural science and scientists with their audiences, sponsors, and consumers within the framework of negotiated order theory (Busch, 1981, 1982, 1984; Busch and Lacy, 1983, 1986). The application of biotechnologies to plant breeding will lead to fundamental changes (Busch and Lacy, 1986; Hansen et al., 1986; Lacy and Busch, 1988, 1989). Agricultural research will cease to be an isolated "island empire" as it is linked, in new and hitherto unnecessary ways, with medicine, pharmacy, and basic biology. We could move from a world where industry depends on agriculture to one where agriculture depends on industry. But varied outcomes are possible from place to place and from commodity to commodity. These outcomes will be shaped by the institutional structure which itself will be shaped in interactions between the U.S. Department of Agriculture and the land-grant universities focused on resource allocation. The fundamental tension here, as elsewhere in biotechnology, is between public and private development.

Another study of the application of instrumental science examines changes over the past century in the social organization of human reproduction through the introduction of industrial conceptual approaches and techniques (Clarke, 1988a). Different patterns of industrialized development have characterized different reproductive processes from menstruation to contraception to menopause and so on. For some processes, commodity development came first, for example in the development of female hygiene products. For others, the reorganization and professionalization of service delivery was primary, as in the management of childbirth by physicians and its movement into hospitals. For yet other reproductive processes, technological development was and remains first and foremost, as in contraception and infertility treatments. The overall pattern is one of market saturation with increasingly industrialized approaches to all reproductive processes, now spreading to male reproduction.

Several studies have focused on the role of the instrument industry in linking scientific institutions to the economy. Historian Borell (1987a,b), for example, focuses on the growing importance of instruments in physiological research over the past century. Demand grew for large quantities of instruments as hands-on learning innovations were initiated for teaching purposes in expanding universities. This led late nineteenth-century Harvard physiologist William Townsend Porter to redesign and invent instruments and to establish the Harvard Apparatus Company to mass produce them using standardized, interchangeable parts. This company became a model for others in the emergent American scientific instruments industry.

Through an analysis of advertisements for scientific instruments, Busch and Marcotte (1987) illuminate Bourdieu's perspective that the work of science resembles and shares values with capital accumulation. The values claimed to be embodied in the instruments and the values of industrial capitalists coincide—accuracy, speed, and cost efficiency. They conclude that as the instruments industry has matured, the means of factual accumulation have superseded the ends of enhanced scientific understanding.

Issues of the power of science and power in science are raised in Latour's (1984, 1987, 1988b) studies of microbes. Sciences create new sources of power in society, such as the power to control disease or improve agricultural production. In interactionist science studies, explicit attention is increasingly being given to questions of who participates in creating that knowledge and in deciding how such power is used (e.g., Star, 1989; Clarke, 1988b).

All of these studies at the meso-macro scale are thus concerned with the articulation of parts, with specifying the nature and structure of relations between sciences and other organizational entities. Hopefully they will extend the boundaries of interactionist theories of organizations in some of the directions Hall (1985, 1987) anticipated.

CONCLUSIONS: DOING INTERACTIONIST SCIENCE STUDIES

The sciences are good "laboratory animals" for basic sociological research, especially for interactionist approaches focused on work, organizations, and social worlds. For the sciences are easily accessible, routinely keep extensive records of their operations, vary widely across many dimensions of interest, and change both quickly and slowly, providing temporal variation. In addition, their organization makes it relatively easy to trace connections among organizational scales from face-to-face interaction in the laboratory to large-scale institutional structures. Extensive local variation and the international character of scientific work also facilitate comparative studies at various scales. The sciences thus provide an ideal body of materials for building cohesive models of institutional organization out of the concepts of negotiated order and commitments, the organization of work, and social worlds.

Another exciting and continually provocative aspect of doing science studies is its interdisciplinary nature. Interactionist sociologists regularly collaborate with researchers from other schools of sociological thought, with historians, with philosophers, and with scientists from the traditions we study. The most striking reason for active collaboration with researchers from other schools of thought is provided in the work of Latour, Callon, Law, and their associates. Their work is not simply important in its own right; it also illuminates and challenges interactionist thinking in significant ways. For example, Latour (1984, 1987, 1988a,b) insists, correctly we believe, that we view all participants in a setting as actors, not just humans. For example, microbes were major actors in the rise of the germ theory of disease and the Pasteur Institute. Door-closers are actors in both scientific and non-scientific contexts. This point is an important extension to basic interactionist principles and ties to issues of meaning and action which Mead (1932) explored philosophically.

A similar point applies to the work of some philosophers. In the half century since Mead's death, philosophical research has made progress on many problems he addressed. It would be sadly ironic if the pragmatist tradition of sociological research enshrined the work of Mead and Dewey as final authority rather than using it as a springboard to new discoveries. The work of Wimsatt (1974, 1980, 1981, 1985) on robustness, bias, heuristics, reductionism and problem decomposition is especially useful and important. So too is that of Griesemer (1988, in press; Griesemer and Wade, 1988) on laboratory models, museums as models, and kinds of causal explanation, and that of Magnus (1989) on issues of natural history such as speciation.

At the conference that led to this volume, a number of participants asked how much science one needs to know to do sociology of science. Given that we are not going to become competent in these disciplines by ourselves, we routinely enroll scientists from the fields we study as advisors and teachers. But how competent we need to become depends very much on our specific research questions. The more technical these are the more science we need to know to understand what is going on, and vice versa. However, there is not a one-to-one relationship between the amount of science known and the quality of science studies. For example, many researchers now in science and technology studies of various kinds were, at earlier stages of their careers, scientists, physicians, or engineers. While in some ways this gives them tremendous advantages and makes their work invaluable to us, it can also act as a potent constraint. For they are vulnerable to all the pitfalls of "going native," especially loss of a broader perspective on the work. As sociologists generally lacking formal training in the sciences we study, we are in the reverse situation which also has its potent strengths and weaknesses.[7]

One thing sociologists of science do not have to worry about is making certain their respondents' voices are heard, a point raised in this volume by McCall and Wittner especially. Scientists' voices and cultures are quite strong. We do, however, have to be careful to keep doing our sociology rather than getting caught up in their science to which we may bring the raw enthusiasm of neophytes. This is the same risk Hall (this volume) discusses in historical sociology—the risk of getting lost in doing history rather than doing historical sociology.

But science studies must attend to history for several reasons. First, many important phenomena (e.g., disciplinary emergence and realignment) typically occur over many years. Second, studies of contemporary practice using traditional field observation and interviewing techniques can make better sense of those practices by understanding how things came to be the way they are. Third, depending upon one's research problem, there can be distinct advantages in science studies to doing research on areas where key issues are relatively settled. It is easier to avoid "going native" and being drawn into hot scientific debates about who is right or wrong. Fourth, our concerns with larger scale organization naturally pull us toward historical approaches as we seek comparative data about contrasting conditions and circumstances. Indeed, it is difficult to see how adequate research at larger organizational scales could be performed without using historical data.

But a historical orientation also poses methodological problems. Participant observation and interviewing are of only limited use in studying the work of dead scientists. While we have successfully used grounded theory approaches with historical materials,[8] several serious problems remain: (1) how to manage the vast amounts of materials characteristic of historical research; (2) how to speed up gaining an adequate grasp of the historical story so that one can do the sociology of it; and (3) how to fuse historical and philosophical considerations into the ordinary flow of our sociological work.

We continually struggle with these challenges. For example, Gerson and Griesemer are involved with a continuing program of research on biology in California before World War II. Gerson is compiling an analytic computerized data base of "fact and figure" information on the major biological research organizations and individuals in California, which will document long-term conjoint patterns of scientific and institutional change (Gerson, 1986). The focus on a single, narrowly defined body of data over a long period of time is somewhat unusual for an interactionist approach, but he has high hopes that it will be fruitful.

The future possibilities for interactionist science studies are virtually infinite. They include an array of approaches not addressed here, such as research on symbolic or ideological dimensions. Much of the current and planned work of interactionists already in the field is centered around heterogeneous worlds coming together at work. This reflects early interactionist concerns with intersections of human communities (e.g., Park, 1952), extended by Hughes (1971) to focus on the workplace "where [diverse] peoples meet."

For example, in the sociology of technological design, Star (1988c) is developing a theory of cooperation in scientific work where collaborating heterogeneous groups must reconcile their differences to solve problems and create technologies. The flow of information and the consequences of organizational structure in the design of computer chips by engineers is a related problem (Star, 1988b). At times, however, differences are not resolved and mavericks emerge—marginal people whose work can be highly controversial or largely ignored (Fujimura, 1988b). The institutional construction of mavericks in science also extends traditional interactionist concerns.

Others are studying the Museum of Vertebrate Zoology at Berkeley, founded in 1908, and now housing a major research collection of birds, mammals, and amphibians. They seek to understand the ways in which the organizational history of the Museum was shaped by the technical concerns of its staff on the one hand, and the constraints imposed by its setting at the intersection of many disciplinary and other worlds on the other hand (Gerson, 1987a; Griesemer, in prep.; Star and Griesemer, 1986).

While peoples meet in the workplace, the workplace itself must be constructed. Many things must be in place for science to be done. Concrete infrastructure for the specific kind of work must be constructed, managed, and changed to keep up with developments. These include materials, instruments, and techniques along with personnel. How this was done across an array of life sciences disciplines wrestling with varied problems is also being explored (Clarke and Fujimura, in press).

In summary, the major thrust of interactionist research in sciences studies to date has been on examining multiple scales of work organization. At the micro/meso scale, research has focused on daily work, on its material requirements, on negotiating local and wider constraints, opportunities, and resources, on the local nature of the construction of knowledge and what is done to make knowledge transportable (e.g., simplification), on doability, and on problem paths over time.

At the meso scale, scientific research has been conceived as a network of going concerns or enterprises. Emphasis has been on how centers of research establish and maintain themselves through ongoing negotiations with a stable of audiences and alliances, and through gaining control over resources and means of knowledge production and distribution. Several studies have been done on discipline formation and development through both segmentations and intersections. And scientific bandwagons have been studied as a kind of social movement.

At the meso/macro scale are several studies of the relations of disciplines as social worlds with the larger society, which share a focus on political and economic market concerns. These fit well with the analysis that those disciplines that succeed are more instrumental, productive, and ultimately profitable. Studies here have focused on the industrialization of human reproduction, scientific instruments, biotechnology in agriculture, and the development of a life sciences—based industrial sector.

While these studies all center on scientific work organization at different scales, they simultaneously focus on dynamics across scales. Thus this work is equally about linkages across multiple scales of scientific work organization and the interpenetration of the micro, meso and macro categories, despite the format of this paper. Indeed, the paper could have been written to highlight these aspects of the research, for it is a figure/ground phenomenon. Instead, we conclude by drawing attention to them.

The very act of developing an adequate research site immediately draws scientists into a web of relationships that cross-cut micro, meso, and macro categories. Obtaining materials and instruments, learning techniques, and organizing skilled personnel are concrete infrastructural dimensions. To do this reasonably, scientists must construct doable problems—must align resources, interests, and activities across multiple scales from the experiment to the laboratory to wider scientific social worlds and beyond.

In an important sense, the concepts of audiences, markets, and sectors offer a framework for understanding doability over time. To sustain a research endeavor requires considerable stability of both local arrangements and relations with wider audiences including sponsors and consumer markets. Routinely maintained yet flexible relationships create an organizational framework for institutionalizing doability. As these relations endure and elaborate, a science-based economic sector may emerge, a very complex going concern.

Interactionist science studies have been highly organizational and structural in their vision of the working arrangements and commitments of science without losing sight of the symbolic interactions through which knowledge is constructed.

NOTES

1. We are grateful to our colleagues H. S. Becker, J. H. Fujimura, J. R. Griesemer, S. L. Star, and A. L. Strauss for their many contributions to the work discussed here. We are also grateful to M. S. Gerson, K. Charmaz, M. Little, and A. Hazan for advice and comments on earlier versions. Clarke's efforts were supported by an NIMH postdoctoral fellowship in the Department of Sociology, Stanford University. David Wake, Barbara Stein, and the staff of the Museum of Vertebrate Zoology at Berkeley have been generous with their time and gave permission to examine the Museum's archives. Clarke also thanks Dr. M. C. Shelesnyak for ongoing assistance with her research on reproductive science.

2. For more ambitious and thorough maps of this terrain, see Knorr-Cetina and Mulkay (1983), R. Collins and Restivo (1983), and Maienschein (1985).

3. Because of the slow pace of publication and to make this paper bibliographically useful for as long as possible, we cite some works currently under review (without, of course, noting the journals).

4. A volume to be edited by Gregg Mitman, Adele Clarke, and Jane Maienschein is anticipated for 1992.

5. For work from other perspectives, see for example Cambrosio and Keating (1983), Chubin (1976), Graham, Lepenies, and Weingart (1983), Law (1980), Lemaine et al. (1976), Light (1983), Rosenberg (1976, 1979), and Whitley (1976, 1984).

6. Clarke draws here upon both recent work on institutional aspects of organizations (e.g., Scott and Meyer, 1983; Scott, 1987) and on social worlds and arenas theory (Strauss, 1978, 1982a).

7. For a more in-depth discussion of the problems of "insider histories" and strategies for using them as data, see Clarke (1985:469–71). Even scientists

themselves question the validity of scientists doing histories of their own fields (M. C. Shelesnyak, personal communication, 1988).

8. On grounded theory, see Glaser and Strauss (1968), Glaser (1978), and Strauss (1987). For discussion of how these approaches were concretely used in historical research, see Clarke (1986) and Star (1989).

REFERENCES

Abir-Am, Pnina G., and Dorinda Outram, eds. 1987. *Uneasy Careers and Intimate Lives: Women in Science, 1789–1979.* New Brunswick, NJ: Rutgers University Press.

Appel, Toby A.1987. "Biological and Medical Societies and the Founding of the American Physiological Society." Pp. 155–76 in Gerald L. Geison (ed.), *Physiology in the American Context, 1850–1940.* Bethesda: American Physiological Society.

———. 1988. "Organizing Biology: The American Society of Naturalists and its 'Affiliated Societies,' 1883–1923." Pp. 87–120 in Ronald Rainger, Keith R. Benson, and Jane Maienschein, eds., *The American Development of Biology.* Philadelphia: University of Pennsylvania Press.

Becker, Howard S. 1960. "Notes on the Concept of Commitment." *American Journal of Sociology* 66:32–40.

———. 1970. *Sociological Work: Method and Substance.* New Brunswick, NJ: Transaction Books.

———. 1982. *Art Worlds.* Berkeley: University of California Press.

———. 1986. *Doing Things Together.* Evanston: Northwestern University Press.

Becker, Howard S., and James Carper 1956. "Development of Identification with an Occupation." *American Journal of Sociology* 61:289–98.

Bentley, Arthur F. 1954. *Inquiry into Inquiries: Essays in Social Theory.* Boston: Beacon Press.

Bernal, J. D. 1967. *The Social Function of Science.* Cambridge: MIT Press.

Bijker, Wiebe E., Thomas P. Hughes, and Trevor Pinch, eds. 1987. *The Social Construction of Technological Systems.* Cambridge: MIT Press.

Blumer, Herbert. 1969. *Symbolic Interactionism: Perspective and Method.* Englewood Cliffs, NJ: Prentice Hall.

Borell, Merriley. 1987a. "Instrumentation and the Rise of Modern Physiology." *Science and Technology Studies* 5:53–62.

———. 1987b. "Instruments and an Independent Physiology: The Harvard Physiological Laboratory, 1871–1906." Pp. 293–322 in Gerald L. Geison (ed.), *Physiology in the American Context, 1850–1940.* Bethesda: American Physiological Society.

Bourdieu, Pierre. 1975. "The Specificity of the Scientific Field and the Social Conditions of the Progress of Reason." *Social Science Information* 14:19–47.

Bucher, Rue. 1962. "Pathology: A Study of Social Movements within a Profession." *Social Problems* 10:40–51.

———. 1988. "On the Natural History of Health Care Occupations." *Work and Occupations* 15:131–47.

Bucher, Rue, and Anselm L. Strauss 1961. "Professions in Process." *American Journal of Sociology* 66:325–334.

Busch, Lawrence, ed. 1981. *Science and Agricultural Development.* Montclair, NJ: Allanheld, Osmun.

———. 1982. "History, Negotiation and Structure in Agricultural Research." *Urban Life* 11:368–84.

———. 1984. "Science, Technology, Agriculture and Everyday Life." *Annual Review of Rural Sociology and Development* 1:289–314.

Busch, Lawrence, and Yves Chatelin. In preparation. *Voyage to the Southern Seas: Science, Utopia and Development.*

Busch, Lawrence, and William B. Lacy, eds. 1983. *Science, Agriculture and the Politics of Research.* Boulder, CO: Westview.

———. 1986. *The Agricultural Scientific Enterprise: A System in Transition.* Boulder, CO: Westview.

Busch, Lawrence, and Paul Marcotte. 1987. "Instruments and Values in Science." Paper presented at meetings of the Society for Social Studies of Science, Worcester, MA.

Callon, Michel. 1985. "Some Elements of a Sciology of Translation: Domestication of the Scallops and the Fishermen of St. Brieuc Bay." Pp. 196–233 in J. Law (ed.), *Power, Action, and Belief: A New Sociology of Knowledge?* Sociological Review Monograph 32. London: Routledge and Kegan Paul.

———. 1986. "The Sociology of an Actor-Network: The Case of the Electric Vehicle." Pp. 19–34 in Michel Callon, John Law, and Ari Rip, eds., *Mapping the Dynamics of Science and Technology.* London: Macmillan.

Callon, Michel, John Law, and Ari Rip, eds. 1986. *Mapping the Dynamics of Science and Technology.* London: Macmillan.

Cambrosio, Alberto, and Peter Keating. 1983. "The Disciplinary Stake: The Case of Chronobiology." *Social Studies of Science* 13:323–53.

———. 1988. "Going Monoclonal: Art, Science and Magic in the Day-to-day Use of Hybridoma Technology." *Social Problems* 35:244–60.

Chubin, Daryl E. 1976. "The Conceptualization of Scientific Specialties." *Sociological Quarterly* 17:448–76.

Clarke, Adele E. 1985. "Emergence of the Reproductive Research Enterprise: A Sociology of Biological, Medical, and Agricultural Science in the United States, 1910–1940." Doctoral dissertation, University of California, San Francisco.

———. 1986. "Methods Issues in the Historical Sociology of Science." Paper presented at the Pacific Sociological Association, Denver.

———. 1987. "Research Materials and Reproductive Science in the United States, 1910–1940." Pp. 323–350 in Gerald L. Geison (ed.), *Physiology in the American Context, 1850–1940.* Bethesda: American Physiological Society.

———. 1988a. "The Industrialization of Human Reproduction, c1890–1990." Plenary address, U.C. Systemwide Conference of Women's Programs, Davis, CA.

———. 1988b. "Getting Down to Business: The Life Sciences as Start-Up and Consolidating Industries in the U.S., c1890–1940." Paper presented at the meetings of the Society for Social Studies of Science. Amsterdam, November.

———. 1989a. "A Social Worlds Research Adventure: The Case of Reproductive Science." In Thomas Gieryn and Susan Cozzens, eds., *Theories of Science in Society.* Bloomington: University of Indiana Press.

———. 1989b. "Controversy and the Development of Reproductive Science." *Social Problems* 36. In press.

Clarke, Adele E., and Joan H. Fujimura, eds. In press. *The Right Tools for the Job: Materials, Instruments, Techniques and Work Organization in Twentieth Century Life Sciences.*

Collins, H. M. 1983. "The Sociology of Scientific Knowledge: Studies of Contemporary Science." *Annual Review of Sociology* 9:265–85.

———. 1985. *Changing Order: Replication and Induction in Scientific Practice.* Beverly Hills: Sage.

Collins, Randall and Sal Restivo. 1983. "Development, Diversity, and Conflict in the Sociology of Science." *Sociological Quarterly* 24:185–200.

Crane, Diana. 1972. *Invisible Colleges: The Diffusion of Knowledge in Scientific Communities.* Chicago: University of Chicago Press.

Denzin, Norman K. 1977. "Notes on the Criminogenic Hypothesis: A Case Study of the American Liquor Industry." *American Sociological Review* 42:905–20.

Dewey, John. [1916] 1953. *Essays in Experimental Logic.* New York: Dover.

———. 1929. *The Quest for Certainty: A Study of the Relation of Knowledge and Action.* New York: Minton, Balch.

Etzkowitz, Henry. 1983. "Entrepreneurial Scientists and Entrepreneurial Universities in American Academic Science." *Minerva* 21(2–3):198–233.

Farberman, Harvey A. 1975. "A Criminogenic Market Structure: The Automobile Industry." *Sociological Quarterly* 16:438–57.

Fee, Elizabeth. 1983. "Women's Nature and Scientific Objectivity." Pp. 9–27 in Marian Lowe and Ruth Hubbard, eds., *Woman's Nature*. New York: Pergamon.

Freidson, Eliot. 1976. "The Division of Labor as Social Interaction." *Social Problems* 23:304–313.

———. 1977. "The Futures of Professionalization." Pp. 14–40 in M. Stacey, M. Reid, C. Heath, and R. Dingwall, eds., *Health and the Division of Labor*. New York: Prodist.

———. 1982. "Occupational Autonomy and Labor Market Shelters." Pp. 39–54 in P.L. Stewart and M.G. Cantor, eds., *Varieties of Work*. Beverley Hills: Sage.

Fujimura, Joan H. 1986a. "Bandwagons in Science: Doable Problems and Transportable Packages as Factors in the Development of the Molecular Genetic Bandwagon in Cancer Research." Doctoral dissertation, University of California, Berkeley.

———. 1986b. "Problem Paths: An Analytical Tool for Studying the Social Construction of Scientific Knowledge." Paper presented to the Society for Social Studies of Science, Pittsburg.

———. 1987. "Constructing Doable Problems in Cancer Research: Articulating Alignment." *Social Studies of Science* 17:257–93.

———. 1988b. "The Institutional Construction of Mavericks in Science." Paper presented at meetings of the Society for Social Studies of Science. Amsterdam, November.

———. 1988b. "The Molecular Biological Bandwagon in Cancer Research: Where Social Worlds Meet." *Social Problems* 35:261–83.

Fujimura, Joan H, S. Leigh Star and Elihu M. Gerson. 1987. "Methodes de Recherche en Sociologie des Sciences: Travail Pragmatisme et Interactionisme Symbolique." *Cahiers de Recherches Sociologique* 5:65–85.

Garfinkel, H., M. Lynch and E. Livingston. 1981. "The Work of Discovering Science Construed with Materials from the Optically Discovered Pulsar." *Philosophy and Social Science* 11:131–58.

Geison, Gerald L. 1981. "Scientific Change, Emerging Specialties and Research Schools." History of Science XIX:20–40.

———. 1987. "International Relations and Domestic Elites in American Physiology, 1900–1940." Pp. 115–54 in Geison, ed., *Physiology in the American Context, 1850–1940*. Bethesda: American Physiological Society.

Gerson, Elihu M. 1976. "On Quality of Life." *American Sociological Review* 41:793–806.

———. 1983a. "Scientific Work and Social Worlds." *Knowledge* 4: 357–77.

———. 1983b. "Styles of Scientific Work and the Population Realignment in Biology, 1880–1925." Paper presented at the Society for the History, Philosophy, and Sociology of Biology, Granville, Ohio.

———. 1986. "Where Do We Go from Here?" *Qualitative Sociology* 9:208–12.

———. 1987a. "Audiences and Allies: The Transformation of American Zoology, 1880–1930." Paper presented at meetings of the Society for the History, Philosophy and. Sociology of Biology, Blacksburg, VA.

———. 1987b. "Disciplines and Professions." Paper presented at meetings of the Society for Social Studies of Science, Worcester, MA.

Glaser, Barney G. 1964. *Organizational Scientists: Their Professional Careers.* Indianapolis: The Bobbs-Merrill Co., Inc.

———. 1978. *Theoretical Sensitivity: Advances in the Methodology of Grounded Theory.* Mill Valley, CA: Sociology Press.

Glaser, Barney G., and Anselm L. Strauss 1968. *The Discovery of Grounded Theory: Strategies for Qualitative Research.* New York: Aldine.

Graham, Loren, Wolf Lepenies, and Peter Weingart, eds. 1983. *Functions and Uses of Disciplinary History.* Dordrecht, Netherlands, and Boston: D. Reidel Kluwer.

Griesemer, James R. 1988. "Causal Explanation in Laboratory Ecology: The Case of Competitive Indeterminacy." *Philosophy of Science Association* I:337–44.

———. In press. "Modeling in the Museum: On the Role of Remnant Models in the Work of Joseph Grinnell." *Biology and Philosophy.*

Griesemer, James R., and Michael Wade. 1988. "Laboratory Models, Causal Explanation, and Group Selection." *Biology and Philosophy* 3:67–96.

Hall, Peter M. 1985. "Asymmetric Relationships and Processes of Power." Pp. 307–44 in H. Farberman and R. S. Perinbanayagam, eds., *Foundations of Interpretive Sociology.* Studies in Symbolic Interaction, Supplement 1. Greenwich, CT: JAI Press.

———. 1987. "Interactionism and the Study of Social Organization." *Sociological Quarterly* 28:1–22.

Hansen, Michael, Lawrence Busch, Jeffrey Burkhardt, William B. Lacy, and Laura R. Lacy. 1986. "Plant Breeding and Biotechnology: New Technologies Raise Important Social Questions." *BioScience* 36: 29–39.

Hughes, Everett C. 1958. *Men and Their Work*. Glencoe: Free Press.
———. 1971. *The Sociological Eye*. Chicago: Aldine Atherton.
Keller, Evelyn Fox. "Feminism and Science." 1982. *Signs* 7(4):589–602.
———. 1985. *Reflections on Gender and Science*. New Haven: Yale University Press.
Kimmelman, Barbara A. "The American Breeders' Association: Genetics and Eugenics in an Agricultural Context, 1903–1913." *Social Studies of Science* 13:163–204.
———. 1987. "The Progressive Era Discipline: Genetics at American Agricultural Colleges and Experiment Stations, 1890–1920." Doctoral dissertation, University of Pennsylvania. 1983.
Kling, Rob and Elihu M. Gerson. 1977. "The Dynamics of Technical Change in the Computing World." *Symbolic Interaction* 1:132–46.
———. 1978. "Patterns of Segmentation and Intersection in the Computing World." Symbolic Interaction 2:25–43.
Knorr-Cetina, Karen. 1981. *The Manufacture of Knowledge: An Essay on the Constructivist and Contextual Nature of Science*. Oxford: Pergamon Press.
Knorr-Cetina, Karen, and Michael Mulkay, eds. 1983. *Science Observed: Perspectives on the Social Study of Science*. London and Los Angeles: Sage.
Knorr-Cetina, Karen, Roger Krohn and Richard D. Whitley, eds. 1980. *The Social Process of Scientific Investigation*. Sociology of the Sciences Yearbook 4. Boston: Reidel.
Kuhn, Thomas 1962. *The Structure of Scientific Revolutions*. Chicago: University of Chicago (second edition, 1970).
Lacy, W.B. and L. Busch, eds. 1988. *Biotechnology and Agricultural Cooperatives: Opportunities and Challenges*. Lexington, KY: Kentucky Agricultural Experiment Station.
———. 1989. "The Changing Division of Labor between the University and Industry: The Case of Agricultural Biotechnology." In Joseph J. Molnar and Henry Kinnucan, eds., Social and Institutional Impacts of Biotechnology on Agriculture: Now and in the Future. Boulder, CO: AAAS and Westview Press.
Larson, Magali Sarfatti. 1977. *The Rise of Professionalism: A Sociological Analysis*. Berkeley: University of California.
Latour, Bruno. 1983. "Give Me a Laboratory and I Will Raise the World." Pp. 141–70 in Karen Knorr-Cetina and Michael Mulkay, eds., *Science Observed: Perspectives on the Social Study of Science*. Beverly Hills: Sage.
———. 1984. *Les Microbes: Guerre et Paix suivi de Irreduction*. Paris: A. M. Metaillie.
———1986. "Visualization and Cognition: Thinking with Eyes and Hands." Pp. 1–40 in Henrika Kuklick and Elizabeth Long, eds.,

Knowledge and Society: Studies in the Sociology of Culture Past and Present, Vol. 6. Greenwich, CT: JAI Press.

———1987. *Science in Action*. Cambridge: Harvard University Press.

———1988a. "Mixing Humans and Nonhumans Together: The Sociology of a Door-Closer." *Social Problems* 35:298–310.

———1988b. *The Pasteurization of France*. Cambridge: Harvard University Press.

Latour, Bruno, and Steve Woolgar 1979. *Laboratory Life: The Social Construction of Scientific Facts*. Beverly Hills: Sage.

Law, John. 1980. "Fragmentation and Investment in Sedimentology." *Social Studies of Science* 10:1–22.

———. 1984. "How Much of Society Can the Sociologist Digest at One Sitting? The "Macro" and the "Micro" Revisited for the Case of Fast Food." *Symbolic Interaction* 5:171–96.

———. 1986. "Laboratories and Texts." Pp. 35–50 in Michel Callon, John Law and Ari Rip, eds., *Mapping the Dynamics of Science and Technology*. London: Macmillan.

Law, John, and Michel Callon. 1988. "Engineering and Sociology in a Military Aircraft Project: A Network Analysis of Technological Change." *Social Problems* 35:284–97.

Law, John, and Peter Lodge. 1984. *Science for Social Scientists*. London: Macmillan.

Lemaine, G., R. Macleod, M. Mulkay and P. Weingart, eds. 1976. *Perspectives on the Emergence of Scientific Disciplines*. The Hague Chicago: Mouton Aldine.

Levidow, Les and Bob Young, eds. 1981. *Science, Technology and the Labour Process*. London: CSE Books.

Lewontin, Richard C. and Richard Levins 1985. *The Dialectical Biologist*. Cambridge: Harvard University Press.

Light, Donald W. 1983. "The Development of Professional Schools in America." Pp. 345–66 in Konrad Jarausch (ed.), *The Transformation of Higher Learning, 1860–1930*. Chicago: University of Chicago Press.

Lynch, Michael. 1982."Technical Work and Critical Inquiry: Investigations in a Scientific Laboratory." *Social Studies of Science* 12:499–533.

———. 1985a. *Art and Artifact in Laboratory Science: A Study of Shop Work and Shop Talk in a Research Laboratory*. London: Routledge and Kegan Paul.

———. 1985b."Discipline and the Material Form of Images: An Analysis of Scientific Visibility." *Social Studies of Science* 15:37–66.

Magnus, David 1989. "In Defense of Natural History: David Starr Jordan and the Role of Isolation in Speciation." Doctoral dissertation, Stanford University.

Maienschein, Jane. 1985. "History of Biology." *Osiris* (second series) I:147–62.

——, ed. 1987. *Defining Biology: Lectures from the 1890's.* Cambridge: Harvard University Press.

——1988. "Whitman at Chicago: Establishing a Chicago Style of Biology?" Pp. 151–84 in Ronald Rainger, Keith R. Benson and Jane Maienschein, eds., *The American Development of Biology.* Philadelphia: University of Pennsylvania.

Maines, David R. 1977. "Social Organization and Social Structure in Symbolic Interactionist Thought." *Annual Review of Sociology* 3:235–59.

——. 1982. "In Search of Mesostructure: Studies in the Negotiated Order." *Urban Life* 11:267–79.

Maines, David R., and Joy C. Charlton. 1985. "The Negotiated Order Approach to the Analysis of Social Organization." Pp. 271–306 in H. Farberman and R. S. Perinbanayagam, eds., *Foundations of Interpretive Sociology.* Studies in Symbolic Interaction, Supplement 1. Greenwich, CT: JAI Press.

Maniatis, T., E. F. Fritch, and J. Sambrook. 1982. *Molecular Cloning: A Laboratory Manual.* Cold Spring Harbor, NY: Cold Spring Harbor Laboratory.

Marcson, Simon. 1960. *The Scientist in American Industry.* New York: Harper.

Mead, George Herbert. 1917. "Scientific Method and the Individual Thinker." In J. Dewey et al., eds., *Creative Intelligence: Essays in the Pragmatic Attitude* New York: Henry Holt.

——. 1932. *The Philosophy of the Present.* Chicago: Open Court.

Merton, Robert K. [1938] 1970. "Science, Technology and Society in Seventeenth Century England." *Osiris,* Studies on the History and Philosophy of Science 4, Part 2. New York: Fertig.

1973. *The Sociology of Science: Theoretical and Empirical Investigations.* Chicago: University of Chicago Press.

Merchant, Carolyn 1980. *The Death of Nature: Women, Ecology, and the Scientific Revolution.* San Francisco: Harper and Row.

Mukerji, Chandra. 1983. *From Graven Images.* New York: Columbia University Press.

——. 1987. "The Alienating Character of Technique in Science." Presented at Society for Social Studies of Science, Worcester, MA.

Mulkay, Michael J. 1977. "Sociology of the Scientific Research Community." In Ina Spiegel-Rosing and Derek deSolla Price, eds., *Science, Technology and Society: A Cross-Disciplinary Perspective.* Beverly Hills: Sage.

Mullins, Nicholas 1973. *Theory and Theory Groups in Contemporary American Sociology.* New York: Harper and Row.

Nowotny, Helga, and Hilary Rose. 1979. *Counter-Movements in the Sciences: The Sociology of Alternatives to Big Science.* Boston: D. Reidel.

Park, Robert Ezra. 1952. *Human Communities.* Glencoe: Free Press.

Paul, Diane, and Barbara Kimmelman. 1988. "Mendel in America: Theory and Practice, 1900–1919." Pp. 281–310 in Ronald Rainger, Keith Benson, and Jane Maienschein, eds., *The American Development of Biology.* Philadelphia: University of Pennsylvania Press.

Pauly, Philip J. 1984. "The Appearance of Academic Biology in Late Nineteenth Century America." *Journal of the History of Biology* 17:369–97.

———. 1987. *Controlling Life: Jacques Loeb and the Engineering Ideal in Biology.* New York: Oxford University Press.

———. 1988. "Summer Resort and Scientific Discipline: Woods Hole and the Structure of American Biology, 1882–1925." Pp. 121–50 in Ronald Rainger, Keith Benson, and Jane Maienschein, eds., *The American Development of Biology.* Philadelphia: University of Pennsylvania Press.

Peirce, C.S. 1877."The Fixation of Belief." *Popular Science Monthly* 12:1–15.

———. 1878. "How to Make Our Ideas Clear." *Popular Science Monthly* 13:286–302.

Pickering, Andrew. 1984. *Constructing Quarks: A Sociological History of Particle Physics.* Chicago: University of Chicago Press.

Rainger, Ronald, Keith R. Benson, and Jane Maienschein, eds. 1988. *The American Development of Biology.* Philadelphia: University of Pennsylvania Press.

Redfield, Robert (ed.) 1942. *Levels of Integration in Biological and Social Systems.* Lancaster, PA: Jacques Cattell Press.

Reif, F., and Anselm L. Strauss. 1965. "The Impact of Rapid Discovery upon the Scientist's Career." *Social Problems* 12:297–310.

Restivo, Sal. 1988. "Modern Science as a Social Problem." *Social Problems* 35:206–25.

Riemer, Jeffrey. 1979. *Hard Hats: The Work World of Construction.* Beverley Hills: Sage.

Rose, Hilary, and Stephen Rose, eds. 1976. *Ideology ofın the Natural Sciences.* Boston: G. K. Hall and Schenkman.

Rosenberg, Charles E. 1976. *No Other Gods: On Science and American Social Thought.* Baltimore: The Johns Hopkins University.

———. 1979. "Toward an Ecology of Knowledge: On Discipline, Contexts and History." Pp. 440–55 in Alexandra Oleson and John Voss, eds., *The Organization of Knowledge in Modern America*. Baltimore: Johns Hopkins University Press.

Scott, W. Richard. 1987. "The Adolescence of Institutional Theory." *Administrative Science Quarterly* 32:493–511.

Scott, W. Richard, and John W. Meyer. 1983. "The Organization of Societal Sectors." Pp. 129–54 in John W. Meyer and W. Richard Scott, eds., *Organizational Environments: Ritual and Rationality*. Beverly Hills: Sage.

Shapin, Steve. 1982. "History of Science and Its Sociological Reconstructions." *History of Science* 20:157–211.

Shibutani, Tomatsu. 1955. "Reference Groups as Perspectives." *American Journal of Sociology* 60:562–9.

———. 1962. "Reference Groups and Social Control." Pp. 128–45 in Arnold Rose (ed.), *Human Behavior and Social Processes*. Boston: Houghton Mifflin.

Star, S. Leigh. 1983. "Simplification in Scientific Work: An Example from Neuroscience Research." *Social Studies of Science* 13:208–26.

———. 1985. "Scientific Work and Uncertainty." *Social Studies of Science* 15:391–427.

———. 1986. "Triangulating Clinical and Basic Research: British Localizationists, 1870–1906." *History of Science* 24:29–48.

———. 1988a. "Introduction: The Sociology of Science and Technology." *Social Problems* 35:197–206.

———. 1988b. "Layered Representations: A Comparison of Computer Chip Design and Maps of the Brain." Paper presented at meetings of the Society for Social Studies of Science, Amsterdam.

———. 1988c. "The Structure of Ill-Structured Solutions: Boundary Objects and Heterogeneous Distributed Problem Solving." Paper presented at the Eighth AAAI Conference on Distributed Artificial Intelligence. Technical Report, Department of Computer Science, University of Southern California.

———. 1989. *Regions of the Mind: Brain Research and the Quest for Scientific Certainty*. Stanford: Stanford University Press.

Star, S. Leigh, and Elihu M. Gerson. 1987. "The Management and Dynamics of Anomalies in Scientific Work." *Sociological Quarterly* 28:147–69.

Star, S. Leigh, and James R. Griesemer 1986. "Institutional Ecology, 'Translations' and Coherence: Amateurs and Professionals in Berkeley's Museum of Vertebrate Zoology, 1907–1939." Paper presented at Society for Social Studies of Science meetings, Pittsburg.

Strauss, Anselm L. 1975. *Professions, Work, and Careers*. New Brunswick, NJ: Transaction Books.

————. 1978. "A Social Worlds Perspective." Pp. 119–128 in Norman K. Denzin (ed.), *Studies in Symbolic Interaction*Vol. 1.

————. 1979. *Negotiations: Varieties, Contexts, Processes, and Social Order.* San Francisco: Jossey Bass.

————. 1982a. "Social Worlds and Legitimation Processes." Pp. 171–90 in Norman Denzin (ed.), *Studies in Symbolic Interaction* Vol. 4.

————. 1982b. "Interorganizational Negotiation." *Urban Life* 11: 350–67.

————. 1984. "Social Worlds and Their Segmentation Processes." Pp. 123–39 in Norman K. Denzin (ed.), *Studies in Symbolic Interaction* Vol. 5.

————. 1985."Work and the Division of Labor." *Sociological Quarterly* 16:1–19.

————. 1987. *Qualitative Analysis for Social Scientists.* Cambridge: Cambridge University Press.

————. 1988. "The Articulation of Project Work: An Organizational Process." *Sociological Quarterly* 29:163–178.

Strauss, Anselm L., Shizuko Fagerhaugh, Barbara Suczek, and Carolyn Weiner. 1985. *The Social Organization of Medical Work.* Chicago: University of Chicago Press.

Strauss, Anselm L., and Lee Rainwater 1962. *The Professional Scientist: A Study of American Chemists.* Chicago: Aldine.

Traweek, Sharon. 1984. "Nature in the Age of Its Mechanical Reproduction: The Reproduction of Nature and Physicists in the High-Energy Physics Community." Pp. 94–116 in C. Belisle and B. Schiele, eds., *Les Savoirs dans les Practiques Quotidiennes: Recherche sur les Representations.* Paris: Edition du C.N.R.S.

Veblen, Thorstein. 1932. *The Place of Science in Modern Civilization and Other Essays.* New York: Viking Press.

Volberg, Rachel A. 1983. "Constraints and Commitments in the Development of American Botany, 1880–1920." Doctoral dissertation, University of California, San Francisco.

Wersky, Gary. 1978. *The Visible College: The Collective Biography of British Scientific Socialists of the 1930s.* New York: Holt, Reinhart and Winston.

Whitley, R. 1976. "Umbrella and Polytheistic Scientific Disciplines and Their Elites." *Social Studies of Science* 6:471–97.

————. 1984. *The Intellectual and Social Organization of the Sciences.* New York: Oxford University Press.

Wimsatt, William. 1974. "Complexity and Organization." Pp. 67–86 in K. Schaffner and R. Cohen, eds., *Proceedings of the Philosophy of Science Association.* Boston: D. Reidel.

————. 1980. "Reductionist Research Strategies and their Biases in the

Units of Selection Controversy." Pp. 213–59 in T. Nickles (ed.), *Scientific Discoveries: Case Studies.* Boston: D. Reidel.

———. 1981. "Robustness, Reliability and Overdetermination." Pp. 124–62 in M.B. Brewer and B.E. Collins, eds., *Scientific Inquiry and the Social Sciences.* San Francisco: Jossey Bass.

———. 1985. "Forms of Aggregativity." Pp. 259–91 in A. Donagan, A.N. Perovich, and M.V. Wedin, eds., *Human Nature and Natural Knowledge.* Boston: D. Reidel.

Zilsel, Edgar. 1941. "The Sociological Roots of Science." *American Journal of Sociology* 47:544–60.

8

Fit for Postmodern Selfhood

Barry Glassner

The dead are the only people to have permanent dwellings.

Rita Mae Brown

A widespread interest in the pursuit of fitness has been documented among the middle and upper classes in national surveys (Gurin and Harris, 1987; Glassner, 1988) and in the market success of magazines such as *American Health, New Body, Prevention,* and *Self.* Yet the popular explanations for this interest prove rather anemic. Those who market fitness programs and products, for instance, along with commentators in the media, often put forward a biosocial realist account. They maintain that Americans are merely accepting the well-confirmed scientific evidence for the adaptive and aesthetic superiority of a strong, fat-free body.

In actuality, reviews of the research literature raise serious doubts as to whether exercise (Solomon, 1985; Hughes, 1984; Folkins and Sime, 1981; LaPorte, Dearwater, et al., 1985), weight control (Schwartz, 1986; Brody, 1987; Ritenbaugh, 1982), or changes in diet (Becker, 1986; Goodman and Goodman, 1986) do improve longevity or afford significant protection against disease and psychological distress.

More likely, it is not the sheer force of truth that has propelled Americans toward fitness pursuits, but rather the manner in which purported facts are conveyed and the role of such information in the culture. The countless images of idealized bodies Americans see every day in television, magazine, and billboard advertising have become dominant symbols, thanks to their pivotal position in structures of social exchange. They channel capital and serve as a common resource for judging the adequacy of self and others.

Ultimately, though, this sort of cultural-economy argument, even if thoroughly developed (see Turner, 1984; Featherstone, 1982; Ewen and

For helpful comments on earlier drafts I thank Peter Conrad, Julia Loughlin, Steven Mailloux, Mark Mizruchi, Robert Perinbanayagam, Barry Schwartz, David Silverman, Manfred Stanley, David Sylvan, and participants at the SSSI Symposium, in particular, Howard S. Becker, Marjorie DeVault, Michal McCall and Fred P. Pestello.

Ewen, 1982; O'Neill, 1985), also will not suffice as an explanation for the fitness furor. While there is no denying that a general commodification of society and of the bodies within it (human, political, knowledge, etc.) has taken place (Glassner, 1988, chaps. 2 and 9)[1], analysis of that state of affairs does not in itself permit an answer to the question: Why fitness? Why is this particular package of acts and ideas so appealing to participants, and why has it sold so well in recent years?

REGARDING "FITNESS" AND "POSTMODERN"

A first step in answering this question is to examine the concept itself, whereupon one notices that "fitness" refers to more than might be assumed. A mélange concept in its current usage, "fitness" references not only exercise or the effects thereof, but the general state of a person's psycho-physical well-being. The subtitle of *American Health* magazine is "Fitness of Body and Mind." A direct mail advertisement from Time-Life Books for a series of volumes on exercise, diet, stress, and toning proclaims that "if you're ready to enter the new age of fitness . . . ," with their help, "[y]ou'll go beyond exercise to experience a dimension of health, vitality and confidence you've never known before."

A special issue of *Life* magazine (February, 1987) entitled "The American Way of Fitness" consisted of the following articles (in order of their appearance): weight-loss plans, a California spa where people take mud baths to relieve stress, aerobic exercise programs for seniors, others for babies, obesity in adolescence, bulimia, a triathlete, the Framingham Heart Study, workouts by Hollywood stars of the 1930s and 1940s, how Christie Brinkley got "back into shape" after the birth of her daughter (workouts, mineral baths, massages, etc.), and swimwear.

The hybridization of potentially independent matters can also be found in many of the most successful commercial programs in the body improvement industry. A major selling point in Weight Watchers advertisements has been their Quick Start Plus Exercise Plan; and Nautilus, the manufacturer of exercise machines, markets to health clubs its Nautilus Diet, which "consists of three-times-per-week supervised Nautilus workouts combined with a descending-calorie diet."

So although some fitness enthusiasts distinguish between "fitness" and "health," the two have become generally synonymous in everyday usage. Each of the acts referenced (diet, exercise, etc.) solicits the others. The longer expression, "health and fitness," is invoked primarily when the speaker wants to draw attention specifically to nonexercise

components. Packages of Nabisco Shredded Wheat, for example, recently featured a mail-in coupon for an exercise video by Jane Fonda.
The ad referred to Fonda as "one of America's favorite health and fitness advocates." In so doing, Nabisco made an association to their own
product, which is positioned as a health(ful) food. ("It's the natural
goodness of whole wheat and has no added sugar or salt.")[2]

Therein lies one reason I refer to fitness as a postmodern activity—it
is pastiche, a borrowing from diverse imagery, styles, and traditions,
including both "high" and "low," mundane and special, and past, present and future, wherever these seem usable: a form of contextless
quotation (see Jameson, 1984; Clarke, 1985; Venturi, 1966; Venturi,
Brown, and Izenour, and 1972).

The pastiche quality of fitness is evident even where the concept is
used to refer primarily to exercise. More than mere movement is typically involved, after all, in exercise programs. The typical exercise
video (like its live counterparts at health clubs) involves also dance, as
well as either nostalgic or futuristic imagery, and commercial tie-ins.
One video, selling briskly when this paper was prepared, "Esquire's
Dance Away—Get Fit with the Hits of the 50's," includes on the side
cover, without explanation, the Tampax tampons emblem. The tape
itself features workouts performed to songs including "Rock around
the Clock" and "Blue Suede Shoes."

Before I suggest some of the implications of fitness as pastiche (in
particular as regards selfhood), I want to discuss briefly the other contentious term in my title.

Rather than define "postmodern," I am going to use it pragmatically
to understand the cultural phenomenon at hand. Any definition one
might propose would only conflict with others in the vast and confusing literature. That fact does not necessarily imply, however, that the
concept is confusing or unhelpful. Perhaps, as Hebdige (1986:78–79)
has proposed in a discussion of postmodernism, "the more complexly
and contradictorily nuanced a word is, the more likely it is to have
formed the focus for historically significant debates, to have occupied
a semantic ground in which something precious and important was felt
to be embedded" (see also McRobbie, 1986:108; Glassner and Moreno,
1982).[3] I do have in mind something resembling a period in American
culture, one that I along with others (e.g., Trachtenberg, 1985:263–
291; Huyssen, 1986:178–221; Herron, 1987–88:73; Jameson, 1983)
date as having begun in roughly the early 1960s, with efforts at resistance and innovation in the arts and living arrangements. Then, during
approximately the early 70s through early 80s, postmodernism took on

a positive rather than merely oppositional stance, as evidenced by trends in the arts to "counter the modernist litany of the death of the subject by working toward new theories and practices of speaking, writing and acting subjects" (Huyssen, 1986:213), and in daily life to devise alternatives to an alienated, inactive stance towards one's own physical and emotional reality (cf. Freund, 1982).[4]

While participation in (even access to) the postmodern is concentrated in the middle and upper classes, against Daniel Bell (1978: 353–54), I see more in postmodernity than nihilism, narcissism, and "anything goes"(ism). Rather, taking a symbolic interactionist perspective, I see a collocation of attempts to reconstruct the self (and in particular, the self-body relationship) in a manner that is more felicitous to life in contemporary American culture.

SYMBOLIC INTERACTIONS WITH THE MODERN

Modernity resulted in the first place, according to a Weberian analysis, from the collapse of religious authority and the rise of a rationalized, bureaucratic social order. Within this order, separate groups of professionals, each with special technical abilities, are granted responsibility for separate spheres of activity. Scientists oversee nature, lawyers administer justice, critics orchestrate taste, physicians regulate health, and so forth. The hope, beginning with the philosophers of the Enlightenment, was that this specialization and rationalization "would promote not only the control of natural forces, but would also further understanding of the world and of the self, would promote moral progress, the justice of institutions, and even the happiness of human beings" (Habermas, 1981:9). Instead, from the point of view of many middle-class Americans of the 1960s and 1970s, the activities of modernity resulted in a *loss* of control over nature (as evidenced by the prevalence of heart disease and cancer, the emergence of AIDS, and leaking nuclear plants), a loss or splintering of selfhood, built-in immorality in public institutions, and ever-inflated false promises of consumer happiness.

Charles Jencks, a popular proponent of postmodern architecture, identifies the symbolic death of modernism as 3:32 p.m. on July 15, 1972, when the Pruitt-Igoe housing project in St. Louis was dynamited. "The modern machine for living, as Le Corbusier had called it with the technological euphoria so typical of the 1920s, had become unlivable, the modernist experiment, so it seemed, obsolete" (quoted in Huyssen, 1986:186).

Of course, not only with regard to housing were people giving up on machine age science and technology and recognizing that, "[t]hough founded on the *historic* emergence of science," in the second half of the twentieth century, "modernity lives only at the level of the _myth of science_" (Baudrillard, 1987:71). This sentiment extended widely, as can be seen in the critiques of medicine (e.g., Illich, 1975; Szasz, 1966) and in belief systems based around axioms such as "small is beautiful" and buzzwords like "lite." Indeed, responses to the losses and disappointments of modern culture have appeared widely throughout American culture; _many forms of disyoking and disinheriting could be named_. These are perhaps most apparent in the arts and in some varieties of left politics, but none of the efforts—whether in architecture, the visual arts, fiction, or political mobilizing—afforded the general public such an encompassing attempt to disengage the negative effects of life in modern culture as did the fitness movement.[5] Fitness programs promise direct control over the effects of nature, as well as freedom from medical professionals, and the achievement of personal morality. And they offer outcomes one can feel almost every day of one's life.

In her analysis of the social factors that sent people to the streets in jogging suits beginning about two decades ago, Muriel Gillick (1984: 369–87) underlines two:

> First was the realization that modern medicine, for all its sophistication, could not prevent death. Even the coronary care unit, one of the great technological developments of the '60s, saved at most a few lives; and 60 percent of deaths from heart attacks occur before the victims ever reach medical attention. . . . The collapse of the liberal consensus—the belief that the strength and virtue of America had created peace abroad and harmony at home—coming on top of a shattered faith that American medicine could render the world safe from disease, led to the view that America was morally sick, in need of spiritual renewal. . . . The pursuit of physical fitness was seen by some as a means by which individuals could improve America. By ridding us of the stress and tension, the competitiveness and sleeplessness which are ruining our society, so the argument goes, running can help us pull ourselves up by our bootstraps.

I quote this passage at length because it points up several of the ways in which the fitness movement is postmodern rather than primarily anti-modern (cf., Venturi and Brown, 1984:115) or nostalgic.

Retained is the modernist idea of <u>renewal</u>, but the meaning of renewal has changed from what it was in previous health-and-exercise movements in the United States. At the end of the nineteenth century and beginning of the twentieth, progressiveness served as a guiding motif: those advocating exercise and healthful diets spoke of "regeneration" and preparing Americans for a bright new day. They also evoked notions—which had been deployed in health movements earlier in the 1800s—of a citizenry that had recently been strong and virtuous but was going flabby as the result of too much affluence (Green, 1986; Schwartz, 1986).

In contrast to those earlier movements, the fitness talk of the late 1960s through 1980s is not primarily about a happier recent past, progress, or the perils of wealth. Rather, what must be exorcised now are the deficiencies of the modern era. <u>Fitness is sold as an escape route from the characteristic ills of modern culture.</u> Biographical vignettes such as the following from *Weight Watchers Magazine* about thirty-five-year-old Kathy Smith (whom *Time* called "The Beverly Hills Fitness Guru") are standard fare in articles and books promoting exercise:

> When she was in college, her parents died within a year and a half of each other—her father of a heart attack, her mother in a plane crash. "My whole emotional foundation had been destroyed. It was the lowest point in my life," she recalls. Always outgoing and bubbly before, Smith withdrew into a shell of confusion, depression and fear. Unfortunately, there was no one to crack that shell—her only living relative, a sister, turned to drugs and alcohol for solace. At first, Smith turned to food to ease her despair: She'd binge on sweets one day, then, feeling guilty, fast the next day. . . . Running eventually helped her to climb out of her depression. "I found solace, real peace while running," she says. (Fain, 1987:47)

The article goes on to describe how Smith has brought exercise to the aid of others who suffer with the problems she and her relatives experienced. "When she's not working out, Smith keeps her mind off the bathroom scale by joining in the fundraising efforts of such nonprofit organizations as the American Heart Association and Fitness Against Drug Abuse" (47).

Or for another example, consider the premise of Chris Pepper Shipman's book, *I'll Meet You at the Finish!* (1987): that in these times of high divorce rates and marital unhappiness, couples who exercise together stay together. She details how her own marriage went from bad to great once she took up marathon running with her husband.

Let me also suggest a more subtle way in which the ideology of the contemporary fitness movement departs from earlier, truly modernist health movements. To paraphrase an observation Andreas Huyssen (1986:180) made about postmodern artists, fitness activists hold an "ostentatious self-confidence" that there can be "a realm of purity" for the body outside of the horrible degradations it has had to face in technological society. Unlike an earlier generation of exercisers and healthy eaters, the current practitioners of fitness frequently disengage their bodies rather than put them directly to the service of building a better America.[6] They do believe they are improving America, but indirectly, by way of the side effects of their endeavor—by becoming more productive and less of a burden to society in their old age, for instance (see Glassner, 1988).

FITNESS AND THE MEADIAN SELF

Not the salvation of the nation so much as of the *self* is at stake for the contemporary fitness enthusiast. In order to appreciate the melioration of selfhood which fitness activities and ideologies afford, consider the following statement Mead makes in *Mind, Self, and Society* (1934:136):

> We can distinguish very definitely between the self and the body. The self has the characteristic that it is an object to itself, and that characteristic distinguishes it from other objects and from the body. It is perfectly true that the eye can see the foot, but it does not see the body as a whole. We cannot see our backs; we can feel certain portions of them, if we are agile, but we cannot get an experience of our whole body.

It is precisely that experience—of an intimate and holistic marriage between self and body—which fitness in its postmodern guise is said to offer. The twin victims of Cartesian culture reconcile their differences at long last. The self "in touch with," "caring for," "in control of" the body, no longer need experience the body as but another object out in the world (Mead, 1934:164).

Moreover, and owing to the signal position of the fit body in contemporary American culture—as locus for billions of dollars of commercial exchange and a site for moral action (Stein, 1982; Crawford, 1984)—the following claim may no longer hold true:

> Our bodies are parts of our environment; and it is possible for the individual to experience and be conscious of his body, and of bodily sensations, without being conscious or aware of him-

self—without, in other words, taking the attitude of the other toward himself. (Mead, 1934:171)

In front of the television set, washed in torrents of disconnected images of exemplary talking bodies prescribing health clubs, fiber-enriched cereals, and mini-skirts, the individual has little time or space to experience "his" body as apart from generalized, insistent others.

The body that is fit or in the process of becoming so is no longer an "object to which there is no social response which calls out again a social response in the individual" (Mead, 1938:292, and see 445–53). Fitness activities frequently are performed with others in public programs, such that the body becomes a focus of interaction and hence a key constituent of the "me," of the experience of self in which the vision of the community is vitally present (Mead, 1934, sections 22 and 25). Nash (1980) has suggested about running, for example, that it is through conversations and running lore that joggers—who think of their activity as a solitary endeavor—learn to experience the "highs" and other benefits of running.

Even where fitness is pursued privately, in one's own home, the body is commonly experienced by way of looking glasses—by how it is interpreted in disciplines such as medicine (cf. Foucault, 1970, 1977) and in comparison to images of bodies in the media (cf. Brown and Adams, 1979), and sooner or later, by how it is commented upon by significant others.

If in modernity, "[t]hrough self-consciousness the individual organism enters in some sense into its own environmental field; its own body becomes a part of the set of environmental stimuli to which it responds or reacts" (Mead, 1934:172), in postmodern culture this encounter has been radicalized. The consciousness of body is always enthralled by the environment of perpetually repeating images (see Baudrillard, 1987:70–72), from the time the self-less infant is first narcotized by the moving bodies in the exercise video its mother watches.

Ironically, though, the more nearly bodies become present to selves in primarily third-hand ways, the more ostensibly intrinsic to selfhood they become.[7] A statement such as the following, made by Joe Daddona, mayor of Allentown, Pennsylvania, no longer seems preposterous: "I began to wonder, how well can I possibly manage a city when I do such a lousy job managing my health."[8]

As Stone (1962:101) suggested, "in appearances . . . . selves are established and mobilized," and through fitness, selves are truly *embodied*. The physique becomes a cardinal sign of the self in a way that add-ons such as fashion and cosmetics (the appearance-enhancer signs of modernity) no longer can. People do not "have" fitness, like they do a "look" (or, for that matter, "the flu"), they *are* fit. Fitness is totalizing, it has no opposite.[9] Hence, to ask what a fit body means, or the meaning fitness has for those who seek or admire it, would be to miss the postmodern context within which it exists (see Hinkson, 1987:128). A characterization made about MTV, that "it *is*, it *does* but it does not *mean*" (Fiske, 1986:77), describes fit bodies as well.[10]

Within postmodern culture meaning has imploded. The self, suspicious anyway of the possibility of any truth lasting more than a short while, is confronted with so many diverse, conflicting and compounded types of information, that instead of seeking meaning, or more or deeper meaning, it seeks to neutralize, reduce, or contain meaning (Baudrillard, 1980).[11]

The body in particular has been imagined to be overfull of meaning. When germ theory held sway, people pictured their bodies as occupied by miniature invaders, but our current entrancement with computers has us envisioning our bodies occupied by tiny information units. From biotechnology we've received the idea that the body houses trillions of bits of genetic information, available in principle for resplicing, and precoded to produce future cancers, heart disease, or mental illness (Hayles, 1987). The crucial problem with this situation was stated succinctly in a novel by Botho Strauss (1980, quoted in Wellbery, 1985:237):

> In everything there is information and language, from the tiny bacterial cell to the most secret end of a dream, we are overfilled with microtexts, codes and alphabets everywhere, and everywhere the rule of law and alien orders. Where in all this might there be room for an I?

One answer to that question—a place where the "I" does stand a chance, where one can both participate in and respond to the informational overbearance of the body—is, of course: in fitness. The information a person gives off by being fit is both economical and globally favorable for the self, in the manner upon which Goffman (1963:35) remarked in a different context:

> Although an individual can stop talking, he cannot stop communicating through body idiom; he must say either the right thing or the wrong thing. He cannot say nothing. Paradoxically, the way in which he can give the least amount of information

about himself—although this is still appreciable—is to fit in and act as persons of his kind are expected to act.

A fit body can be counted upon to perform competently and reliably; it bespeaks a contemporary version of what Goffman called "bureaucratization of the spirit."[12] Not merely a well-oiled machine (as modernists understood it), the fit body-cum-self is an information-processing machine, a machine that can correct and guide itself by means of an internal expert system.[13] When information from the medical and psychological sciences is received from exercise and diet instructors or health-beat reporters in the media, the self-qua-information-processor is able to use that information to change its own behavior for the better. It may change its exercise protocol, for instance, or reduce its exposure to stress, or consume more fish oil.

A commitment to fitness puts in perspective, too, the phenomenal information contents of the body itself. Aches, pains, and wrinkles are, if not meaningful each in their own right, at least occasions for constructive further action.

Taken to its logical limit, this version of selfhood virtually equates the self with fitness activities—as can be seen in autobiographical accounts by fitness-obsessed people (e.g., Sabol, 1986; Elman, 1986). In a less extreme way, this is also the vision of the self in the mass-market magazine, *Self*. Not only are many of the articles in *Self* about how to exercise and diet, but those articles that address other topics often resolve matters by means of fitness. In a recent issue, the lead article on the page devoted to pop psychology is headlined, "How staying in shape yourself can help keep your relationship in shape, too." In the same issue, atop the page on parenting appears an article and photograph on how to strap an infant safely to one's chest in preparation for riding a stationary bicycle. And a fashion feature answers the question, "How to fit your fitness life into a decent-size bag that's *not* a dingy duffel?"

The advertisements, too, treat the tasks of everyday life as fitness affairs. The ad for Lubriderm, a skin cream, lists as "the bare necessities" for arising in the morning—exercise, soap, and Lubriderm. A new pad from Kotex says it stays in place in "your shortest shorts, latest leotards, and active afternoons." Even the cigarette advertisers, who are required by law to include a warning from the surgeon general about health risks of smoking, evoke fitness imagery. Their products are called "Lights" or "Ultra Lights," the copy is about low "tar" content, and the photographs feature models in sporting clothes or engaged in active endeavors.

Needless to say, some fitness partisans bristle at the sight of cigarette advertising in magazines devoted to healthy living. But viewed from the perspective I have suggested in this paper, the inclusion of such advertisements is unexceptional. In a modernist context, one expects consistency and a clear distinction between good and bad, positive and negative, pure and dirty. In a postmodernist context, on the other hand, contradiction and complexity (Venturi, 1966) are the order of the day. Lyotard (1986:6) has described the postmodern condition as one of "complexification": "a destiny towards a more and more complex condition."

The self of the fit person, meanwhile, strives to locate itself in a safety zone within this cultural ferment. For the remainder of this paper, I want to concentrate upon two ways in which this is accomplished: by means of a distinctive form of temporal reasoning; and by certain forms of disengagement from the compelling polarities of modernity.

TENSED IMAGERY

While the future is important to postmoderns (Huyssen, 1986: 188–206), they depart from the modernist's faith that the future will bring progress (Hebdige, 1986:79–88; Lyotard, 1984). The linearity of human life assumed in modernity (Baudrillard, 1987) is frequently breached in postmodernity. On the one hand, it is breached in ways taken to be positive: biotechnology speeds up evolution; and a person can take up running at age fifty and become fitter than the average twenty-year-old. On the other hand, there are negative potential breachings of temporal linearity—a nuclear war might at any moment destroy all human life, a person might learn that a previous sexual encounter that at the time was physically and psychologically enhancing will cause him or her to die of AIDS.

Under such conditions, so runs the reasoning of the postmoderns, the best one can do is to try to heighten, strengthen and prolong what is presently safe and attractive. Robert Venturi, in his call for the type of architecture that has come to be called postmodern, expressed sentiments akin to those I heard from fitness enthusiasts I interviewed when they compared their lives now to what they'd been "in the 60s," or when they commented on accusations from current activists that they were turning inward and avoiding social problems. Venturi (Ven-

turi, Brown, and Izenour, 1972:1) decried the "progressive, if not revolutionary, utopian, and puristic" bent of modernist architects on the
grounds that, for all their would-be purity, they "have preferred to
change the existing environment rather than enhance what is there."

Exclaims the fitness buff: let's make ourselves as beautiful and
healthy as best we can today, for our own sake and for that of those
with whom we interact (to say nothing of anonymous others who will
benefit from our good health by paying lower insurance bills). If our
current diets or exercise proclivities turn out to have been mere fads,
let them be the finest fads available: jogging not heroin, walking not
crack.

If the postmodern imagination in literature is marked by "its refusal
to fulfill causally oriented expectations, to create fictions (and in extreme cases, sentences) with beginnings, middles, and ends" (Spanos,
1987:15), so, too, do fitness buffs try to write their lives outside the
plot that begins with birth, moves too quickly to boredom and decay,
and ends with inevitable death. By means of proper diet and exercise
they try to stay youthful and prolong their lives.

A second point about temporality. In postmodernity there is not
a dominant tense. The temporality of modernity has been characterized as the "perpetual present" (Jameson, 1983:125;[14] ; Frisby, 1986:
38–108; Baudrillard, 1987) and in that way contrasted with the perpetual past of premodernity (Habermas, 1981:5; Mead, 1938). Modernity lives in—and economically off of—newness;[15] premodernity
abides on tradition. Postmodernity, on the other hand, continues the
modernist passion for the present and for historical discontinuity, but
without omitting the past. Rather, the past is embraced iconographi-
cally: "The past has become a collection of photographic, filmic, or
televisual images. We . . . are put in the position of reclaiming a history
by means of its reproduction" (Bruno, 1987:73–4).[16]

Images have become, one could even argue of postmodern culture,
more real than the "real" things they reference (see Baudrillard, 1983).
Kim Sawchuk (1987) offers a bit of empirical evidence to that effect in
an essay where she recalls a startling experience in a shopping mall
in Toronto. She suddenly noticed that the mannequins she'd been
walking past were actually "flesh and blood women imitating replicas
of real women" (52)—a device used to gain the attention of blasé
consumers.

Live mannequins, Sawchuk rightly observes, "do not startle us simply because these women have been reified into a stationary position;

they shock us precisely because we are living in an age which antici-
pates an image. The present era, the age of the postmodern, marks a
collapsing of the space of these borders" (60).[17]

The advantage for the present discussion in recognizing the power of
the image (Kuhn, 1985; Hinkson, 1987) is that it permits one to explain, without resorting to notions such as narcissism and inauthentic-
ity, the role that vanity plays in the pursuit of fitness. For all their talk
of health, what fitness participants achieve on their Nautilus machines
and fat-free diets is an *image of healthiness* (cf., Klotz, 1984; Doubiet,
1984). They reshape their bodies to exhibit the visual indicators of
health demanded by the photographs in the glossy magazines and
by the numbers in the Metropolitan Life weight tables. As Stone
(1962:100) noted in his classic paper: "Appearance *substitutes* for past
and present action and, at the same time, conveys an *incipience* per-
mitting others to anticipate what is about to occur."

Talk of appearances (or of presentations of self) will not, however,
ultimately serve to describe the complex achievement of a fit person.
In postmodernity, a fit body is a special kind of image within a culture
that is teeming over with images: it is an afterimage—the shadow that
remains in mind when the thing itself has already left the screen. Specifically, the fit body is an afterimage of modernity, and not only because, as noted, it represents a response to the aspirations and failings
of modernist culture. A fit body is an afterimage of modernity also
by virtue of the acts involved in its construction. Green (1986) and
Schwartz (1986) have documented that much of what appears at first
glance to be unique to the contemporary fitness "revolution" (e.g.,
aerobic dance, fiber fetishism, particular exercise machines, popular diet plans) was present in the health and exercise movements of
nineteenth-century America.

Importantly, though, the fitness aficionado of the 1970s or 1980s
does not merely reproduce previous practices or styles, but enacts
them in ways befitting a postmodern context. Trachtenberg's (1985:7)
characterization of postmodern art—that it is "performative rather
than revelatory, superficial rather than immanent, aleatory rather than
systematic, dispersed rather than focused"—describes also some con-
trasts between how current fitness devotees engage in exercise and di-
eting as compared to their counterparts in the previous century.

In a modernist cultural context, the person still hoped to construct
patterns of action so well designed that they held a kind of perma-
nence. In a postmodernist context, on the other hand, the creating per-

son (or organization) assembles fragments, available from earlier or discarded objects and styles, into something that itself will be borrowed from, written over, or cast aside for later use.

A fit body is, in that regard, a postmodern object par excellence, its image perpetually reconstructed of pieces and colorations added on then discarded:[18] small waists and breasts for women in the late 70s and early 80s, voluptuous proportions more recently; a non-warrior look for men throughout much of the 70s, the return of muscles in the 80s; tanned skin when such is deemed healthy- or wealthy-looking, pale when cancer fears have been heightened.

Nor is there any vested interest in the continuity of particular fitness *practices* for more than a season or two. Although the fitness ideology always calls for exercise, for instance, the preferred types and amounts of exercise vary from year to year. Consider some statistics from 1986 by way of illustration. According to national sporting goods associations, 28 percent more Americans were walking for exercise that year than in 1985, while 12 percent fewer were running, and the sale of running shoes dropped by $46 million while the sale of walking shoes increased by at least that much (Shabe, 1987; Topousis, 1987; and information provided by the Sporting Goods Manufacturers Association).

A particularly graphic illustration of shifts in exercise practices is provided by Jane Fonda's career in the fitness industry. Early in this decade she was selling books, classes and videos favoring high-impact aerobics, then mid-decade she shifted to low-impact, and more recently she's produced a video on walking and another of free weights.

In such modulations one can recognize the modernist demand for newness and the structural requirement of capitalism to create markets, but there is a distinctly postmodern cast to the ever-fluid fitness ideals. Not merely fashion is involved here, but a special sort of after-image, what literary critics have termed simulacra:[19] images for which there are no originals because they are made by combining features from other images. The models in the advertisements, and stars like Fonda when they appear in fitness videos and magazine and book spreads, are specially lighted, posed, and made up in ways the viewers will never actually achieve no matter which exercise or diet regimens they undertake.[20] Moreover, the clothing and makeup the models wear, the poses they hold, and the environments in which they are filmed are borrowed from other contexts. The ideals of the fit body to which the viewer refers in (re-)designing his or her own body reference not actual people, but simulacra.

A familiar aspect of the experience of selfhood in postmodern culture is the sense that one's consciousness floats among images. No longer positioned as mere outsiders looking in, we feel ourselves to be parts of the swept-along confusion (Hayles, 1987:27–28). This experience is fictionalized in postmodern novels such as DeLillo's *White Noise,* in films such as *Desperately Seeking Susan* and *Blade Runner* (see Bruno, 1987), and in MTV videos (see Chen, 1986). And in their own daily lives, many Americans also live out an imagistic existence. They refer to photos of seemingly fit models in *GQ* or *Working Woman* as they prepare their attire, makeup, and comportment for going into the corporate office; from the Evian or Nike ads for going to the health club; from *Details* or *Cosmo* or *Miami Vice* for an evening out.

The "image-conscious" person of the 1970s and 8190s constructs his or her physique and dress in a manner reminiscent of the pop artists of the 60s such as Warhol, Lichtenstein and Wesselman, whose creations were copies of commercial art and advertising (Paoletti, 1985; and see Crimp, 1980 and Bowman, 1985 on postmodern photographers such as Sherrie Levine and Richard Prince, whose works involve rephotographing old photographs or advertising[21]).

Of course, most Americans cannot or do not afford the designer clothing, hairstylings, and makeup the models use, but instead rely upon imitations available at their local shopping malls. To get themselves "into shape," they use home videos or work out at local gyms, not with personal trainers and the latest equipment (cf. Sabol, 1986).

The lower middle class do not as a consequence rely upon more (or more extreme) simulacra in their pursuit of fitness, however, than do wealthier Americans. The exercise equipment at up-market health clubs is often highly derivative as well. A graphic artist who works with Precor, one of the leading makers of up-market exercise machines, described to a writer for an architecture magazine the thinking behind a new line his company had produced:

> We went for a new look ... tighter, cleaner, more sophisticated details. Subtle details. Grooves in the surfaces. We looked at what was happening in winter skiwear, in motorcycles— they're fashion conscious, more trendy than we could afford to be—and we saw a movement toward white and red. We brought out the red, played down the anodized-aluminum look, gave the machines a powder coating. (Jacobs, 1987:95)

Exercise machines are, like the bodies to which their users aspire, copies of copies. Stationary bicycles look rather like ordinary bikes and sometimes give a similar feel when one "rides" them, but they do not achieve the traditional function of a bicycle; and newer "ergometers," which involve the same motions, often look more like metal ducks than traditional bikes. As for rowing machines: "People who are serious about rowing don't own rowing machines," says a designer of these contrivances (Jacobs, 1987:95), so far from the original experience is the simulation.

Some popular machines are nearly pure simulacra: they bear almost no resemblance to their ancestors. The Bow-Flex, for instance, is a sort of bench with "power rods" atop, each of which provides a different amount of tension. By copying the postures provided in the instruction manual, the Bow-Flex can be used like a bench press, rower, or skiing device, and for several dozen other types of movements as well. "In a sense, what the Bow-Flex does is simulate other simulators" (Jacobs, 1987:98).

POSTDUALISTIC SELFHOOD

The Bow-Flex would seem to meet many of the requirements for a postmodern object as listed by Venturi in his book, *Complexity and Contradiction* (an augural work which became a sort of manifesto for postmodern architecture):

> I like elements which are hybrid rather than "pure," compromising rather than "clean," distorted rather than "straightforward," ambiguous rather than "articulated," perverse as well as impersonal, boring as well as "interesting," . . . accommodating rather than excluding, redundant rather than simple, vestigial as well as innovating, inconsistent and equivocal rather than direct and clear. (1966:22)

These descriptors attach nicely to much of the subjective and material content of life inside a health club, whether the club features postmodern equipment such as the Bow-Flex or more modernist machinery. Consider the Nautilus machines, for instance. As already noted, such machines are both vestigial and innovative in that they represent modifications of designs from earlier times. Experientially, a circuit on the Nautilus machines is likely to include a sense of both accommodation and exclusion (the weights are set to one's current level of ability, but other patrons can do more, and some movements are unpleasant); and a Nautilus circuit entails both compromises and ambiguities (imperfect movements at times, ill-adjusted equipment) and yet cleanliness and articulation (shiny machines in bright lighting, a smooth performance by the user). In addition, a circuit on these machines cannot help but be boring, impersonal, and redundant in part, owing to the repetitions of the movements, but it is also interesting in its simpleness, thanks to the lively music, colors, or other bodies in the room, and the knowledge that one's physique is changing as a result of the activity.

More than that, a Nautilus circuit unifies the body by helping to mold it into a closer copy of the ideal bodies on health club brochures (and on some of the instructors), but it also fragments the body. Depending upon the health club, there can be a dozen or more machines, one for each group of muscles. Finer distinctions about muscular design are made in this context than in almost any other that people ordinarily encounter.

Having said all of this, I am also aware of a sense in which fitness activities do not fit Venturi's vision. In the passage quoted above, he goes on to proclaim, "I am for messy vitality over obvious unity. I include the non sequitur and proclaim the duality." This is an important part of Venturi's assertion, because the disintegration or disavowal of dualities is generally regarded as a fundamental ambition behind postmodern activity (Collins, 1987:16). Whereas the modernist "celebrates the triumph of the male over the female; the post-Oedipal over the pre-Oedipal; the father's dictionary over the mother's body; meaning over things; the linear over the pluridimensional" (Stimpson, 1985:40),[22] the postmodernist heralds "the defusing of polarities, the short-circuiting of every differential system of meaning, the obliteration of distinctions and oppositions." (Baudrillard, 1980:142; and see Hebdige, 1986:85–86; Huyssen, 1986:216–17).

Taken in that light, the residual modernism of the fitness movement shines through brightly: there is a linearity to the pursuit, epitomized in gradual increases in the number of miles run or pounds lifted or shed; participants speak of moving towards a "more perfect" body; and traditionally masculine values such as strength, endurance, and rational self-control are highly valued. Moreover, perhaps the most fundamental tenet of the fitness ideologies is that the body exists in an either-or state: one is either "in shape" or "out of shape," fat or thin.

In other regards, though, the fitness movement does "proclaim the duality."

Vytautas Kavolis wrote, in "Post-Modern Man," a 1970 paper in *Social Problems* (and to my knowledge the earliest sociological account of postmodernity), "I would define the 'post-modern' personality as one characterized by the sense that *both* polarities of a great many. . . . dilemmas are contained, in an unresolved form, within one's own experience (at least as potentialities), in the organization of one's personality" (445). His list of "dilemmas" included the following: mastery versus impotence (resulting from technological growth); vividness versus numbness (engendered by the media environment); and the "participation of 'specialists'" versus the "alienation of 'innocents'" (deriving from the modern division of labor).

Kavolis concluded his essay with a statement of honest confusion about how (or even whether) the "dilemmas" could be "resolved" (446). But from our vantage point in the late 1980s, we can point to a great deal of activity that has been directed against these polarities of modernity.[23] The most ready examples, unsurprisingly, have been in the arts, in which postmodernist creations are "designed to reconcile contradictions" (Mainardi, 1987:35; and see Jencks, 1977). This they do by combining elements from "high" and "low" art (and high and low tech) in the same work, by de-structing (see Spanos, 1987) rather than formalizing or abstracting, by quoting between genres and eras, and by intermixing male and female body parts, articles of clothing, and other gendered media (see Kent and Morreau, 1985), among other ways.

The manner in which fitness ideologies and practices dissolve polarities (or anyway their warrant to segment experience) is admittedly less self-conscious or intentional than in some art movements. But one need not probe very deeply to see that resolution of the primary "dilemmas" Kavolis mentioned is what fitness programs promise. Fitness promoters pledge that by exercising and eating correctly, one will gain mastery, not just of one's appearance and health, but of one's position in the labor and mate markets (Freedman, 1986: chaps. 7 and 8; Glassner, 1988). And you'll feel alive, in charge, and a full participant in life (e.g., Cooper and Cooper, 1972).

More than that, consider some other principal dualities that the fitness movement promises to undo:

Male and female. Jane Fonda and others have suggested that fitness activities are a route to empowerment for women. Even if such claims prove falsely optimistic (Chapkis, 1986:8–14), the contemporary fitness movement does differ in a significant regard from the body improvement movements of the nineteenth and earlier centuries, and even those of the 1920s. In those cases, prescriptions for men and women differed (Green, 1986), whereas typically the prescriptions for fitness in the 1970s and 1980s are nearly the same for both men and women. Both should exercise in qualitatively the same ways (with the same movements, using the same equipment or games) and in the same quantities, they should eat the same healthful foods, and they should subscribe to the same values, such as naturalness, self-control, and longevity.

Even where male-female distinctions are made early on, soon enough they become blurred. For instance, calcium supplements were targeted to women at first, but cereal and vitamin packages and advertising soon stopped specifying gender. Cholesterol reduction, until lately regarded as a worry primarily for men, is now promoted for the entire population. When concerns about exercise "addiction" and "overuse" injuries surfaced, much attention was paid to women's symptoms (e.g., the disruption of menstrual cycles), but soon enough both genders were encouraged to exercise less intensively.

Inside and outside.[24] Over the past hundred or so years, "[w]ithin consumer culture, the inner and the outer body became conjoined: the prime purpose of the maintenance of the inner body [became] the enhancement of the appearance of the outer body" (Featherstone, 1982: 18). And vice versa: enhancement of the outer body is undertaken in the service of the inner body, as witness magazine articles on fitness that equate an "outer glow" with mental and physical health.

More significant still is the outright merging of outer and inner in some forms of talk about fitness. An advertisement for a cosmetic surgery practice in California (reproduced in Dull and West, 1987) features a photo of an attractive woman and beneath it the caption, "It's important for me to look and feel the best I can. That's why I eat the right foods and exercise. And, that's why I had plastic surgery." In the semantics of fitness, acts that earlier predicated either "vanity" or "health" become interchangeable.

Work and leisure. Correspondingly, the terms of the Protestant ethic articulate in new ways. In modernity, "[w]ork strengthens conscience; leisure facilitates impulse" (Wheelis, 1958, quoted in Kavolis, 1970). Conversely, at the postmodern health club—filled with glimmering machines which disaffirm their modernism by being labor-*making* devices (Jacobs, 1987:60)—leisure is work, impulses are harnessed into repetitions-per-minute, and the conscience, now of the body as much as it is of the soul, is only as strong as its owner's heart and as firm as her thighs.[25]

Just what is the consumer of fitness working towards? Not a singular, rational goal, but a mosaic of physical, emotional, economic, and aesthetic transformations, a pastiche of ends and means. The headline atop the cover of *Working Woman* (October 1986) reads, *"Aiming for the Top! How to Stay Fit & Look Great At Every Age"*—combining in one splash of ink some of the most difficult choices many white middle-class women have been told they must make during the last century or two: beauty versus brains, sexuality versus achievement, health versus fashion, and aging versus attractiveness.

For men also, a modernist distinction par excellence has collapsed under similar pressures: namely, that between work time and work values, on the one hand, and leisure, on the other. Fifty thousand or more American manufacturing and service corporations offer fitness programs for their employees, about twenty thousand of them by means of facilities housed on site. The vast majority of these corporate fitness programs sprang up during the 1970s and 1980s, and some large companies, such as Xerox, Pepsi, Kodak, and Campbell Soup, spent millions on large, state-of-the-art health clubs (Castillo-Salgado, 1984; Howe, 1983; McCallum, 1984). These programs send a clear message to employees: if you are out of shape you give the company a bad image and cost it big money in health care expenses and inefficiency (Crawford, 1978). In the words of an advertisement for the Vertical Club, an executive gym in New York, "The drive for excellence begins from within."

A corollary message, this one not in the glossy brochures urging employees to attend classes on smoking, exercise, blood pressure, and weight loss, is that the space between work and the rest of life has narrowed (Conrad, 1987). Keeping oneself fit is a round-the-clock endeavor.

Mortality and Immortality. Finally, while even the most fervent promoter of fitness would not claim that his or her program will keep you alive forever, they sometimes come close. The fitter you become, the longer you'll live—that's the word from national heart, lung. and cancer organizations, health clubs, weight-loss programs, and those insurance companies that offer reduced rates for people who don't smoke, don't eat the wrong food, and do exercise.

Considering ever-increasing life expectancies, and advances in medicine and biotechnology, one has the chance to live to a very old age—or so goes the logic of the fitness movement.

In addition, during the late 70s and early 80s, some exercise fads eclipsed the gulf between life and death in another way. When marathon running and Fondaesque "go for the burn" aerobics were in vogue, the operative notion was that pain and risk of injury—sometimes severe and life threatening (Stutman, 1986; Solomon, 1985)—were not necessarily bad. They were reinterpreted as signs to the self of the potential for greater pleasure, energy, and good health later in life.

Thanks in part to the fitness movement, and despite various exaggerated reports of its death, the self has not only survived in postmodern culture, but can claim to be in better health than it was during the modern age.

NOTES

1. "Postmodernity then is no longer an age in which bodies produce commodities, but where commodities produce bodies: bodies for aerobics, bodies for sports cars, bodies for vacations, bodies for Pepsi, for Coke, and of course, bodies for fashion—total bodies, a total look" (Faurschou, 1987:72).

2. Another example of such conflation is found in *Jane Fonda's Workout Book* (1981). The first sentence of flap copy describes the book as "the best exercise program designed for women—it offers a whole new approach to health and beauty." By the time the last sentence of that book rolls around, however, "This is a fitness book that really works . . . ," and the words "health" and "beauty" are gone.

3. As Hassan (1987:87) correctly noted, however, the term postmodern was an unfortunate choice. "[I]t denotes temporal linearity and connotes belatedness, even decadence, to which no postmodernist would admit." Perhaps dismodern might have been a better choice, evoking as it does many English words describing the transfiguration of modernity that has taken place over the past couple of decades (disabuse, disfigure, disarm, distract, dissemble, dissolve, disjunct, distort, disproportionate, etc.).

4. There is good reason to believe that the years of postmodernism, at least within the arts, are drawing to a close. In architecture, for example, deconstructivists have succeeded postmodernists as the theorists and designers of choice for the current generation of progressive architects. Deconstructivists overtly reject major principles of postmodernism, including the desirability of balanced symmetry and the use of classical forms. Instead, they want their constructions to embody an uneasiness and disconnectedness which they say characterize contemporary culture (see Giovannini, 1988).

5. Within sociology, the disagreements between symbolic interactionists and the quantified mainstream are frequently illustrative. At stake is which ambition of modernity to hope to rescue. The former want to revivify the true self, the latter, true science (see Glassner and Moreno, forthcoming). Just how successful any of the movements have been—whether in theory, politics, the arts, or body care—is another matter. In many cases these efforts have proven no more successful at moving beyond modernism than has the effort after fitness. In looking back on two decades or so of postmodernism in architecture, Venturi (Venturi and Brown, 1984:104–116) argues that the efforts have been too circumscribed and lacking in richness and diversity. "Postmodernism has, in my opinion, proclaimed in theory its independence from Modernism—from the singular vocabulary and the rigid ideology of that movement—and has sub-

stituted, in practice, a new vocabulary that is different from the old in its symbolism, but similar in its singularity, and as limited in its range, and as dogmatic in its principles as the old" (113). See also Laffey (1987), Ghirado (1984–5), and Habermas (1981).

6. A comparison between modern and postmodern architecture is also apposite here. "Free-standing slabs bathed in sun and air" (von Moos, 1987:81) is a good description both of a fit body of the modernist sort (e.g., the kind the military tries to build on its recruits) and the modern office building (e.g., the World Trade Center or the Seagram Building). On the other hand, the maxim of postmodern architecture—"The building should be a mode of portrayal, not merely a functional tool" (Klotz, 1984:10)—accords well with the view of the contemporary fitness enthusiast, that one should work out and eat properly not just to be healthy or a good citizen, but to look good in public, to attract the favorable attention of significant others, and to make a statement about the type of person you are.

7. The analytic distinction Maines (1978:242) made "between bodies—the physical fact of human existence, and identities—social categories through which people may be located and given meaning in some organizational context" has similarly become less apposite to many people's everyday lives.

8. The quote appears in an autobiographical piece in *Prevention* magazine in which Daddona recalls a time when his weight, blood pressure and level of fatigue went way up.

9. "Unfit," an odd term in common discourse anyway, represents an absence of fitness, not its opposite, and implies various other related particulars, such as small muscles, susceptibility to illness, and other lacks, including usually self-discipline.

10. A more direct relationship between MTV and fitness also deserves notice. Exercise videos and health clubs borrow stylings from MTV, and many people, while exercising at home, watch or listen to MTV.

11. Postmodern society is sometimes defined as "knowledge-based society" (Holzner and Marx, 1979:15), and postmodern creations in architecture and the mass media have been characterized as providing "information rather than experience" (Frampton, 1986:29).

12. In this context, we can better understand what to some observers seems anomalous or hypocritical: that some fitness buffs use drugs such as cocaine. From their own point of view, however, it is precisely because they are fit that they can safely take drugs. Their "systems" are able to handle what would otherwise be dangerous pollution.

13. How a person becomes or stays fit increasingly involves information technology as well. Many health clubs and diet centers recruit and keep members by offering them computerized analyses of their "risk factors" for various diseases and their fat and vitamin intake. And manufacturers of exercise equipment have in recent years managed to include computer video in their machines. A rowing machine produced by Bally (the Pac-man company) places the exerciser in front of a monitor on which is simulated a boat race. One boat is labeled "you," the other "pacer," and "your" goal is to outpace the pacer. The screen also displays the number of calories burned during the race (Jacobs, 1987:60).

14. Jameson actually uses this phrase to characterize postmodernity, but the obvious futurism and historical reference in postmodern art and architecture (see e.g., Trachtenberg, 1985) suggests the situation is more complex. Jameson's observations about postmodernity, while insightful, are, as Balsamo (1987:64) put it, a "modernist account of postmodernism."

15. As Foucault (1984:39–40) notes, however, one must be careful to distinguish the form of appreciation for the new: "Modernity is distinct from fashion, which does no more than call into question the course of time; modernity is the attitude that makes it possible to grasp the 'heroic' aspect of the present moment." Moreover, as Habermas notes, the modernist affection for the new does not omit an interest in the classical, only a borrowing of authority from the past. (And see Venturi and Brown, 1984.)

16. At the level of "popular" postmodern culture, note the popularity of "retro dressing," or the wearing of old clothes (usually along with current accessories, as epitomized by the rock singer Madonna); and note also the common practice in "urban contemporary" music of mixing in refrains from earlier disco and r & b tracks.

17. From the art world comes another striking case in point. J. S. G. Boggs, an artist, draws true-color copies of real currency and then "spends" his drawings in lieu of cash for services, meals and other goods. When his drawing is of a denomination higher than the cost of the item he is purchasing, he receives change in real cash. There is an active secondary market for his drawings as well. Art dealers and collectors buy Boggs's drawings from waiters, sales clerks, and others who have received them (Weschler, 1988).

18. A toy company produced an Oliver North doll in mid-1987. When sales proved disappointing, the firm ripped off the heads of the dolls remaining in its warehouse and replaced them with a head resembling Mikhail Gorbachev. The revised doll was then sold during the Christmas season, just after the Reagan-Gorbachev summit aired on nataional television.

19. I've seen this term credited variously to Fredric Jameson (Hayles, 1987: 28) and Michel Serres (Kroker and Cook, 1987:8).

20. Monika Schnarre, who at age 15 was making hundreds of thousands of dollars as a model, was quoted in People magazine: "How ironic this all is. I'm hired for my looks, and yet it takes them three hours to make me pretty enough to photograph. Isn't that weird?" (And see Goffman [1974:293–300] on how the preparations for a performance come to be parts of reality on a par with the performance itself.)

21. More recently, a gallery in Paris has been selling artists' original copies of famous paintings. The owner of the gallery explained to a reporter for the *Wall Street Journal*: "For 55,000 francs, you feel the same emotion as if you had bought the original" (Kamm, 1988:1).

22. I have taken this quotation out of context. Stimpson's point is not about modernism and postmodernism—she is actually arguing for an inverted modernist context in which the second item in each of her binary oppositions wins out. I reproduce her list because the oppositions themselves seem to me those at issue for my discussion. My understanding of them is at odds, however, with her semiological analysis. For her, the point is that in "our conventional, patriarchal speech" the first items ("the signified") stand over the second

items ("the signifier"). Yet a glance at the list suggests this neat division will not hold up. Is "father's dictionary" necessarily the signified rather than the signifier?

23. Kavolis fails to notice that the developing post-modernist art of the 1960s did address itself, at times, to the "dilemmas" he mentions. Examples can be found in novels by John Barth, Donald Barthelme, and John Hawkes, plays by Sam Shepard and Tom Stoppard, music by Steve Reich and John Cage, dance by Twyla Tharp and Trisha Brown, as well as Venturi's and Michael Graves's buildings (Trachtenberg, 1985:263–92).

24. See Melville (1986:4) and Venturi (1966:71–89) on the significance of this difference for the moderns.

25. In David Riesman's classic argument, consumerism and "workism" were juxtaposed. The distinction provided one of the marks of American cultural modernism, one that fitness and other postmodern constructions deconstruct.

References

Balsamo, Anne. 1987. "Unwrapping the Postmodern: A Feminist Glance." *Journal of Communication Inquiry* 11: 64–72.

Baudrillard, Jean. 1980. "The Implosion of Meaning in the Media and the Information of the Social in the Masses." Pp. 137–148 in *The Myth of Information: Technology and Post-Industrial Culture.* Madison, WI: Coda Press.

———. *1983. Simulations.* New York: Semiotext(e).

———. 1987. *Forget Foucault.* New York: Semiotext(e).

Becker, Marshall H. 1986. "The Tyranny of Health Promotion." *Public Health Reviews* 14: 15–25.

Bell, Daniel. 1978. *The Cultural Contradictions of Capitalism.* New York: Basic.

Bowman, Stanley J. 1985. "Photography." Pp. 177–208 in *The Postmodern Moment,* edited by Stanley Trachtenberg. Westport, CT: Greenwood Press.

Brody, Jane. 1987. "Research Lifts Blame from Many of the Obese." *New York Times,* March 24, C1.

Brown, Beverly, and Parveen Adams. 1979. "The Feminine Body and Feminist Politics." *m/f* 3:39–50.

Bruno, Giuliana. 1987. "Ramble City: Postmodernism and 'Blade Runner.'" *October* 41:61–74.

Castillo-Salgado, Peter. 1984. "Assessing Recent Developments and Opportunities in the Promotion of Health in the American Workplace." *Social Science and Medicine* 19:349–58.

Chapkis, Wendy. 1986. *Beauty Secrets.* Boston: South End Press.

Chen, Kuan-Hsing, ed. 1986. Special issue on MTV. *Journal of Communication Inquiry* 10.

Clarke, Garry E. 1985. "Music." Pp. 157–76 in *The Postmodern Moment*, edited by Stanley Trachtenberg. Westport CT: Greenwood Press.

Collins, James. 1987. "Postmodernism and Cultural Practice: Redefining the Parameters." *Screen* 28:11–26.

Conrad, Peter. 1987. "Wellness in the Workplace: Potentials and Pitfalls of Worksite Health Promotion." *Millbank Quarterly* 65.

Cooper, Mildred and Kenneth Cooper. 1972. *Aerobics for Women.* New York: Bantam.

Crawford, Robert. 1978. "You Are Dangerous to Your Health." *Social Policy* 8:11–20.

———. 1984. "A Cultural Account of 'Health'." Pp. 198–214 in *Issues in the Political Economy of Health Care.* London: Tavistock.

Crimp, Douglas. 1980. "The Photographic Activity of Postmodernism." *October* 15:91–101.

Doubiet, Susan. 1984. "I'd Rather Be Interesting." *Progressive Architecture* 2:65–69.

Dull, Diana and Candace West. 1987. "'The Price of Perfection': A Study of the Relations between Women and Plastic Surgery." Paper presented at the meetings of the American Sociological Association.

Elman, Judith B. 1986. "The Loneliest of the Long-Distance Runners." *Runner's World* 21 (July):34–39.

Ewen, Stuart and Elizabeth Ewen. 1982. *Channels of Desire: Mass Images and the Shaping of American Consciousness.* New York: McGraw-Hill.

Fain, Jean. 1987. "Kathy Smith: Making Fitness Fun for Every Body." *Weight Watchers Magazine*, December, 47–50.

Faurschou, Gail. 1987. "Fashion and the Cultural Logic of Postmodernity." *Canadian Journal of Political and Social Theory* 11:68–82.

Featherstone, Mike. 1982. "The Body in Consumer Culture." *Theory, Culture, and Society* 8:18–33.

Fiske, John. 1986. "MTV: Post Structural Post Modern." *Communication Inquiry* 10:74–79.

Folkins, Caryle H., and Wesley E. Sime. 1981. "Physical Fitness Training and Mental Health." *American Psychologist* 36:373–89.

Fonda, Jane. 1981. *Jane Fonda's Workout Book.* New York: Simon and Schuster.

Foucault, Michel. 1970. *The Order of Things: An Archaeology of the Human Sciences.* New York: Random House.

———. 1977. *Discipline and Punish.* New York: Pantheon.

Frampton, Kenneth. 1986. "Some Reflections on Postmodernism and Architecture." Pp. 26–29 in *Postmodernism*, edited by Lisa Appignanesi. London: ICA Documents.

Freedman, Rita. 1986. *Beauty Bound.* Lexington MA: Lexington Books.

Freund, Peter E. S. 1982. *The Civilized Body.* Philadelphia: Temple University Press.

Frisby, David. 1986. *Fragments of Modernity: Theories of Modernity in the Work of Simmel, Kracauer and Benjamin.* Cambridge, MA: MIT Press.

Ghirardo, Diane. 1984–85. "Past or Post Modern in Architectural Fashion." *Telos* 62:187–196.

Gillick, Muriel R. 1984. "Health Promotion, Jogging, and the Pursuit of the Moral Life." *Journal of Health Politics, Policy, and Law* 9:369–87.

Giovannini, Joseph. 1988. "The Limit of Chaos Tempts A New School of Architects." *New York Times*, February 4, pp. C1 and C12.

Glassner, Barry. 1988. *Bodies.* New York: G. P. Putnam.

Glassner, Barry, and Jonathan Moreno. 1982. *Discourse in the Social Sciences: Translating Models of Mental Illness.* Greenwood, CT.: Greenwood Press.

———. forthcoming. *The Qualitative-Quantitative Distinction.* The Hague: Kluwar.

Goffman, Erving. 1963. *Behavior in Public Places: Notes on the Social Organization of Gatherings.* Glencoe, IL: Free Press.

———. 1974. *Frame Analysis.* New York: Harper and Row.

Goodman, Lenn E. and Madeleine J. Goodman. 1986. "Prevention: How Misuse of a Concept Undercuts Its Worth." *Hastings Center Review* 16:26–38.

Green, Harvey. 1986. *Fit for America: Health, Fitness, Sport, and American Society, 1830–1940.* New York: Pantheon.

Gurin, Joel and T. George Harris. 1987. "Taking Charge." *American Health*, March, pp. 53–57.

Habermas, Jurgen. 1981. "Modernity versus Postmodernity." *New German Critique* 22:3–14.

Hassan, Ihab. 1987. *The Postmodern Turn: Essays in Postmodern Theory and Culture.* Columbus, OH: Ohio State University Press.

Hayles, N. Katherine. 1987. "Text out of Context: Situating Postmodernism within an Information Society." *Discourse* 9:24–36.

Hebdige, Dick. 1986. "Postmodernism and 'The Other Side.'" *Journal of Communication Inquiry* 10:78–98.

Herron, Jerry. 1987–88. "Postmodernism Ground Zero, or Going to the Movies at the Grand Circus Park." *Social Text* 18:61–77.

Hinkson, John. 1987. "Post-Lyotard: A Critique of the Information Society." *Arena* 80:123–55.

Holzner, Burkart, and John H. Marx. 1979. *Knowledge Application: The Knowledge System in Society.* Boston: Allyn and Bacon.

Howe, Christine. 1983. "Establishing Employee Recreation Programs." *Journal of Physical Education, Recreation, and Dance* 54:52–53.

Hughes, John R. 1984. "Psychological Effects of Habitual Exercise." *Preventive Medicine* 13:66–78.

Huyssen, Andreas. 1986. *After the Great Divide: Modernism, Mass Culture, Postmodernism.* Bloomington: Indiana University Press.

Illich, Ivan. 1975. *Medical Nemesis.* New York: Pantheon.

Jacobs, Karrie. 1987. "Making Work." *Metropolis,* November, 58–63 and 95–98.

Jameson, Fredric. 1983. "Postmodernism and Consumer Society." Pp. 111–125 in *The Anti-Aesthetic,* edited by Hal Foster. Port Townsend, WA: Bay Press.

———. 1984. "Postmodernism, or the Cultural Logic of Late Capitalism." *New Left Review* 146:53–92.

Jencks, Charles. 1977. *The Language of Post-Modern Architecture.* New York: Rizzoli.

Kamm, Thomas. 1988. "Are They Copies or Are They Fakes? Art World Diverges." *Wall Street Journal,* January 12:1 and 12.

Kavolis, Vytautas. 1970. "Post-Modern Man: Psychological Responses to Social Trends." *Social Problems* 17:435–48.

Kent, Sarah and Jacqueline Morreau. 1985. *Women's Images of Men.* London: Writers and Readers.

Klotz, Heinrich. 1984. Postmodern Visions: *Drawings, Painting, and Models by Contemporary Architects.* New York: Abbeville.

Kroker, Arthur, and David Cook. 1987. *The Postmodern Scene.* New York: St. Martin's Press.

Kuhn, Annette. 1985. *The Power of the Image.* London: Routledge and Kegan Paul.

Laffey. John. 1987. "The Politics at Modernism's Funeral." *Canadian Journal of Political and Social Theory* 11:89–98.

LaPorte, Ronald E., Stephen Dearwater, et al. 1985. "Cardiovascular Fitness: Is It Really Necessary?" *The Physician and Sports Medicine* 13:145–50.

Lyotard, Jean-Francois. 1984. *The Postmodern Condition: A Report on Knowledge.* Minneapolis: University of Minnesota Press.

———. 1986. "Defining the Postmodern." Pp. 6–7 in *Postmodernism,* edited by Lisa Appignanesi. London: ICA Documents.

McCallum, Jack. 1984. "Everybody's Doin' It: Getting Into the Fitness Business, That Is." *Sports Illustrated,* December 3, 72–86.

McRobbie, Angela. 1986. "Postmodernism and Popular Culture." *Journal of Communication Inquiry* 10: 108–116.

Mainardi, Patricia. 1987. "Postmodern History at the Musée d'Orsay." *October* 41:31–52.

Maines, David. 1978. "Bodies and Selves: Notes on a Fundamental Dilemma in Demography." Pp. 241–66 in *Studies in Symbolic Interaction*, volume 1, edited by Norman K. Denzin. Greenwich, CT: JAI Press.

Mead, George Herbert. 1934. *Mind, Self and Society.* Chicago: University of Chicago Press.

———. 1938. *The Philosophy of the Act.* Chicago: University of Chicago Press.

Melville, Stephen W. 1986. *Philosophy Beside Itself: On Deconstruction and Modernism.* Minneapolis: University of Minnesota Press.

Nash, Jeffrey E. 1980. "Lying About Running: The Functions of Talk in a Scene." *Qualitative Sociology* 3: 83–99.

O'Neill, John. 1985. *Five Bodies.* Ithaca NY: Cornell University Press.

Paoletti, John T. 1985. "Art." Pp. 53–80 in *The Postmodern Moment*, edited by Stanley Trachtenberg. Westport, CT: Greenwood Press.

Ritenbaugh, Cheryl. 1982. "Obesity as a Culture-bound Syndrome." *Culture, Medicine, and Psychiatry* 6 : 347–61.

Sabol, Blair. 1986. *The Body of America.* New York: Arbor House.

Sawchuk, Kim. 1987. "A Tale of Inscription/Fashion Statements." *Canadian Journal of Political and Social Theory* 11 : 51–67.

Schwartz, Hillel. 1986. *Never Satisfied: A Cultural History of Diets, Fantasies, and Fat.* New York: Free Press.

Shabe, John. 1987. "Taking Fitness in Stride." *Syracuse Post Standard*, June 26.

Solomon, Henry A. 1985. *The Exercise Myth.* New York: Harcourt, Brace, Jovanovich.

Spanos, William. 1987. *Repetitions: The Postmodern Occasion in Literature, and Culture.* Baton Rouge: Louisiana State University Press.

Stein, Howard. 1982. "Neo-Darwinism and Survival through Fitness in Reagan's America." *Journal of Psychohistory* 10 : 163–187.

Stimpson, Catherine R. 1985. "The Somagrams of Gertrude Stein." Pp. 30–43 in *The Female Body in Western Culture*, edited by Susan Rubin Suleiman. Cambridge MA: Harvard University Press.

Stone, Gregory P. 1962. "Appearance and the Self." Pp. 86–118 in *Human Behavior and Social Processes*, edited by Arnold M. Rose. Boston: Houghton Mifflin.

Stutman, Fred A. 1986. *Walk Don't Die.* Philadelphia: Medical Manor Books.

Szasz, Thomas. 1966. *The Myth of Mental Illness.* New York: Dell.

Topousis, Tom. 1987. "Walkers Outpace Joggers." *USA Today*, May 28.

Trachtenberg, Stanley, ed. 1985. *The Postmodern Moment: A Handbook of Contemporary Innovation in the Arts.* Westport, CT: Greenwood Press.

Turner, Bryan S. 1984. *The Body and Society.* London: Blackwell.

Venturi, Robert. 1966. *Complexity and Contradiction in Architecture.* New York: Museum of Modern Art.

Venturi, Robert, and Denise Scott Brown. 1984. *A View from the Campidoglio.* New York: Harper and Row.

Venturi, Robert, Denise Scott Brown and Steven Izenour. 1972. *Learning From Las Vegas.* Cambridge, MA: MIT Press.

von Moos, Stanislaus. 1987. *Venturi, Rauch and Scott Brown: Buildings and Projects.* New York: Rizzoli.

Wellbery, David E. 1985. "Postmodernism in Europe: On Recent German Writing." Pp. 229–50 in *The Postmodern Moment,* edited by Stanley Trachtenberg. Westport, CT: Greenwood Press.

Weschler, Lawrence. 1988. "Onward and Upward with the Arts (Boggs—Parts I and II)." *New Yorker,* January 18, 33–56, and January 25, 88–98.

9

People Are Talking:

Conversation Analysis and

Symbolic Interaction

Deirdre Boden

When people come together, they talk. Not always, nor everywhere, but most of the time that's what they do. They talk in bed, on the phone, in the classroom, in the judge's chambers, in the physician's office, in jury deliberations and counselling sessions, on tea breaks and on airplanes, around the dinner table and across the boardroom, in crisis and in comfort. Talk is the stuff, the very sinew, of social interaction. The mundane or momentous talk of people in their everyday world is what conversation analysis studies. Where the fine-grain and fine-tuned rhythm of turns at talk spark, fan, and fuel interpersonal relations, business deals, labor negotiations, trade embargoes, disarmament agreements, there too is the stuff of history.

LANGUAGE AND MEANING

One way of characterizing talk, a favorite of mine, is as language-in-action, and it is here, as thought becomes action through language, that conversation analysis meets symbolic interaction (and vice versa). Symbolic interactionists have long been concerned with language, thought, meaning, shared symbols, and social acts. Even a minor review of these concepts lies beyond the scope of this chapter, but it is worth noting that these ideas form the core of Mead's symbolic and interactional perspective on mind, self, and society, and are at the heart of a general understanding of the symbolic interactionist enterprise. The role of language and meaning is central to all that flows from them; namely that the significant and shared symbols that constitute language give rise to thought, which in turn contributes to the consti-

My thanks for the enthusiastic support of the editors of this volume and the many useful comments of panelists at the SSSI Stone Symposium at which this paper was originally presented. I have especially benefited from the varied comments of Howard Becker, Spencer Cahill, Carl Couch, Anthony Giddens, John Heritage, Douglas Maynard, Michal McCall, and Jack Whalen, though I can hardly have met them in full measure.

tution of the social self, which is, in its turn, possible only through social interaction, and so forth.

The elegance of these formulations turns on the dynamic axis of language and meaning. The very words "language" and "meaning"—particularly the latter—seem to conjure up symbolic interactionism for most American sociologists. Meanings are seen as the products of social interaction, "as creations that are found in and through the defining activities of people as they interact" (Blumer, 1969:5).

There are times, however, when the importance of language to meaning seems more slogan than practice within the field, and language becomes one of those taken-for-granted features of interactionist research. Lately, a number of writers have formulated theories and reviewed materials that would begin to make the connections between language and meaning more concrete (e.g., Perinbanayagam, 1985; Stone, 1982; MacCannell and MacCannell, 1982; Denzin, 1983), though deconstructionism would surely seem something of a cul-de-sac in this regard (cf. Denzin, 1987). Nevertheless, rarely are language and meaning per se objects of symbolic interactionist enquiry; rather they typically serve as resources out of which the essentially shared and social nature of society is conjured. This is rather perplexing given the foundational writings of Peirce and Dewey and Mead. The very writers who gave the world semiotics, abduction, significant symbols, and the social self seem to have spawned later studies in which sign, symbol, and meaning have become rather free-floating concepts adrift from the very behavioral grounding advocated by Mead and that early Chicago School tradition.

Part of the problem is that the very notions of language and meaning are quite abstract and bound up in the very same process we might expect them to elucidate. Both have long occupied modern philosophers and linguists, as well as social scientists, literary critics, writers, artists—indeed anyone who works directly with symbols and signs knows only too well the inherently delicate mediation between symbol and meaning. The poststructural upsurge of interest in discourse and text has both expanded and compounded the problem. Suddenly everything is discourse and there are texts everywhere. Yet we are really only a little closer to being able to provide definitive notions of how language works or how meaning gets done. A blizzard of philosophically erudite phrases from Derrida or Barthes or Foucault produce flurries of insight, to be sure (cf. Lamont, 1987), but an elaborate language game is also in progress. With much the same dense and deeply interwoven philosophical, historical, and cultural concepts that characterized much of critical theory a decade earlier, poststructuralism is about to spin off into intellectual limbo, leaving many of us with an improved French vocabulary and yet another collection of relatively inaccessible volumes to fill our bookshelves and impress our less eclectic friends. This is not, I hasten to add, meant unkindly; much can be learned and has been, both from critical theory and poststructuralist thought.

But the real world is elsewhere, and both symbolic interactionists and conversation analysts know that. It is that shared insight, I would like to suggest, that makes a joint examination of our shared enterprise particularly worthwhile, and particularly at this juncture (or *conjoncture*, to continue the French mood) of intellectual history. Social life needs, as Hughes (1971) insisted, to be studied in situ, and the combined creative forces of symbolic interaction and conversation analysis can expose just that momentary yet recurrent and patterned quality of the world.

I am inclined to agree with Giddens's insistence (1984 passim), for example, that it is through the recurrent and recursive properties of interaction that actors both produce and reproduce social relationships across time and space. Moreover, it is the localized process of social interaction, as Blumer (1969) has characterized it, that reveals those routine activities as a fundamentally collaborative achievement in Garfinkel's (1967) sense. At another level, Collins has recently suggested that what he calls the x factor in ethnomethodology may well prove to be tied to emotion and, more, that "we have to come to grips with the grounding of language not only in cognitive aspects of social interaction but in what may turn out to be its emotional interactional substrate" (1986:1349).

It is hardly a coincidence that major European social theorists have, in the past ten years, turned explicitly to the findings of American micro-sociologists (e.g., Bourdieu, 1982; Giddens, 1976, 1979, 1984; Habermas, 1984) as a way of bringing agency back in from a structuralist chill (see also Ritzer, 1985). Borrowing again from Collins (1986), it is also clear that the boundaries of artificial intelligence cannot be much further expanded without a huge revision in current psychologically and cognitively oriented concepts of so-called intelligent systems (e.g., Suchman, 1987; Irons and Boden, 1988). The "scripts" and "plans" of cognitive theory dissolve as human meets machine (Suchman, 1987), and it is just that problem of shared worlds of meaning, situated action, and joint projects that currently defeats the most sophisticated of interactive software. Issues of relevance, context, temporality, sequentiality, recursivity, and indexicality shape all human interaction.

Only students of the interaction order (Goffman, 1983) can discover and document both the delicacy and durability of that moment-by-moment social order.

LANGUAGE-IN-ACTION

The purpose of this paper is to explore the complementary frameworks of conversation analysis and symbolic interaction. Conversation analysis is, as many know, the creative invention of the late Harvey Sacks. Together with Emanuel Schegloff and Gail Jefferson, Sacks developed a field that, while certainly still small, has had considerable impact in sociology and, almost more, in communications, linguistics, and, to some extent, anthropology. As students of Goffman, both Sacks and Schegloff began to dabble with tape recordings in the early 1960s. Sacks was, first and foremost, interested in getting a handle on direct data of the world, and his orientation was remarkably similar to those earlier ethological urges of Mead. He was concerned with capturing concrete behavior and felt that it is only in the direct study of the world that sociology might be able to build a genuinely *scientific* view of that social environment (Sacks, 1984).

So, one of the charms and fascinations of conversation analysis is that it is highly empirical, grounded firmly in a form of data that can be repeatedly analyzed. The data are always comprised of either audio or video recordings of naturally occurring occasions of ordinary interaction, across any variety of social settings. At the heart of the enterprise is the insistence on observation and analysis that avoids the sort of categorization and idealized description of most social science, whether quantitative or qualitative (Sacks, 1963). Talk is instead offered as primary data of the *world-as-it-happens* (Boden, in press b), a direct handle on the details of the real world, actual events as they happen, such that, as Sacks proposed, observations can be repeated and "anyone else can go and see whether what was said is so" (1984:26). Of particular note here to students of the interaction order is the proposal—offered by both Sacks (1963) and Garfinkel (1967; Garfinkel et al., n.d.)—that in *describing* the world in detail we also come to know profoundly how that world is organized and ultimately what it consists of, again, in all its detail. The interest of conversation analysts is not in language in a linguistic sense but rather in talk as the very heart of social interaction, and in the formal properties of social order or "structures of social action" (Atkinson and Heritage, 1984). The materials just happened to be conversations—given the nature and recent availability of magnetic recording tape in the early 1960s. A better name for the field would, in fact, probably be something like "interactional analysis," as everything in the interaction, from a quiet in-breath to the entire spatial and temporal organization of the scene, may be subject to analysis. The essential difference, for purposes of our current discussion, is on the general insistence on recorded materials in naturally occurring interactional settings as opposed to any retrospectively constructed dialogue or researcher-mediated setting such as interviews or experimental settings.

Twenty-five years later, conversation analysis researchers continue to study a wide variety of recorded materials that encompass both verbal and nonverbal apects of interaction and social setting. The orientation is essentially ethnomethodological, although that is not always explicitly acknowledged. Nevertheless, it is the force of Garfinkel's seminal ideas that drives conversation analytic exploration, in particular his recurrent insistence on the irremediably local production of social life. There is a good deal of internal debate about technical issues of just how best to track conversational phenomena, but a kind of universal fascination with what Garfinkel is fond of calling the "structures of practical action." The more one studies interaction—and the more closely—the greater one's respect for the interactional domain as a kind of primordial site of sociation, to borrow both from Simmel and Schegloff (cf. Rawls, 1987). Indeed, much classic conversation analysis is highly Simmelian, given the concern to uncover the formal properties of interaction.[1]

The primal site of interactional intimacy and interchange is at the heart of the conversation analytic enterprise. Conversational interaction is taken as having a "bedrock" in relation to all other forms of institutional and interpersonal exchange (Heritage and Atkinson, 1984:12).

Talk as Data

Conversation analysis is probably the most micro of all microsociology. While linguists often use made-up examples of talk in their work, and ethnographers routinely reconstruct dialogue from fieldnotes, conversation analysis is always done with actual recordings and, as noted above, materials that have been gathered in natural settings of interaction.[2] The insistence on recordings centers on at least two practical factors: (1) it provides for near-endless reexamination of the primary data, and by anyone, and thus goes a long way to meeting typical issues of "interpretation," and (2) it is, as Heritage points out (1984b:236), quite difficult to imagine the invention by social scientists of data such as the following strip of talk.

```
E:   Oh honey that was a lovely luncheon I shoulda ca:lled
     you s:soo :ner but I: l:- lo:ved it. It w's just
              [           ]  [
M:               .((f)) Oh::: (        )
E:   deli:ghtfu :l
          [   ]
M:           Well I w's gla d    you (came).-
                  [              ]
E:                            'nd yer f: friends 're
     so da:rli:ng, =
M:  = Oh::: : it w'z:
          [     ]
E:          e-that P a:t isn'she a do: :ll?
                              [   ]
M:                            iYe h isn't she pretty,
                  (.)
E:   Oh: she's a beautiful girl. =
M:  = Yeh I think she's a pretty gir l.
                  [   ]
E:                    En' that Reinam'n
              (.)
E:   She SCA:RES me. =
```
                                    (cited in Heritage, 1984b:236)

Neither informant nor ethnographer's reconstruction could hope to capture this detail nor, as Heritage also underlines, could it be heard again and again. The transcripts in this sort of work, developed by Gail Jefferson, are always considered as a technical convenience while the primary data is always the actual talk (see appendix). Most notable for general purposes here is the rather remarkable interactional density available at this level of analysis and transcription.

Conversation analysis has focused, since its inception, on what Heritage characterizes as the "primacy of mundane conversation" (1984b:238), which is to say on ordinary, everyday conversation. The payoff has been high. What linguists and communication specialists had long seen as a rather random and almost chaotic activity turns out to be a profoundly ordered and orderly social organization. Here I do not mean to be redundant; to propose that phenomena are ordered and orderly is the essence of reflexivity, in Garfinkel's (1967) sense—or what Giddens calls the "duality of structure" in structuration theory (1984). Conversational phenomena are *ordered* in that, as we shall see shortly in this chapter, the very structure of turns *shapes* them in sequential and consequential ways. At the same time, talk is *ordering* in that participants collaborate in mobilizing those same ordered properties to achieve meaningful and purposive interaction. In this sense, social order and social structure are not external to action but rather produced *in and through the local structures of interaction.* This is the heart of the interaction order and it is here, I believe, that Goffman, Garfinkel, and Giddens meet.

Conversational turn-taking, for example, has been revealed to be a highly precise and predictable system for structuring interpersonal exchange, a kind of driving mechanism for all interaction. This finding, first demonstrated in the now seminal paper by Sacks and his colleagues in 1974, has held up across a range of languages and cultures such that it now seems quite reasonable to claim that this core machinery for talk transcends both language and culture (Moerman, 1977; Boden, 1983; Besnier, 1989). Turn-taking, moreover, appears to be an utterly central social act so that, however banal it may appear, it merits critical and careful analysis (cf. Collins, 1988).

The turn-taking model proposed by Sacks, Schegloff, and Jefferson (1974) predicts that turn allocation and turn transfer will occur in a recursive cycling series of options which enable precise and timely coordination between interactants (Jefferson, 1973, 1983). As simple as this formulation may appear, the interactional consequences that flow from it are considerable. The structured and structuring mechanism of turn-taking "exerts pressure on the design of individual turns and hence on syntax" (Heritage, 1985:2). Moreover, the central operation of the turn-taking system has both enabling and constraining consequences for the overall interaction (Sacks, Schegloff, and Jefferson, 1974; C. Goodwin, 1979; Schegloff, 1979; Levinson, 1983).

The early work of Sacks has led by now to a wide range of findings in the organization of talk, including such familiar features as greetings, questions/answers, invitations, topic initiations and transitions, laughter, interruptions, and so forth. A full review of these studies is hardly germane here,[3] but it may be useful to note two central theoretical assumptions in all conversation analytic work, and two clear strains in current research. The organizational features of conversation are treated as structures in their own right and are taken to operate— like other social structural factors—independently of specific actors, psychological dispositions, or attributions of particular individuals. That is not to say, of course, that there isn't variation across individuals, but rather that these conversational structures are "context free." Secondly and simultaneously, the structures of talk are assumed to be "context sensitive" in the sense that their instantiation at particular moments and in particular contexts, as well as at specific points in interactional time, constitutes that moment and shapes that interaction (see also Wilson, 1982; Giddens, 1984; Boden, in press a). Again, this is not to say that much talk does not run off as routine and non-problematic, but that "routine" is itself an interactional accomplishment, as both ethnomethodologists and symbolic interactionists have long known (see also Maynard, 1984; Schegloff, 1986, 1987; Wilson, in press).

Conversation analysts have long been interested in the systematic ways in which one turn (or turn component) predicates the next in sequential and interactionally consequential ways. Schegloff (1980), for example, has demonstrated the systematic and thereby highly stable manner in which interactants project a question by saying, in effect, "Can I ask you a question?" Conventional social science logic would find such an analysis trivial, assuming that what would follow such an opening gambit would be the question itself. Instead, in finely accomplished ways, what follows is *another* "preliminary" as actors routinely then produce a further frame of reference, typically a context for the question that follows. Schegloff went on to note that the organization of "preliminaries" in conversation—to a question, an offer, a story, a denial, and so forth—shows how the "sequential machinery" of turn-taking is, through and through, an interactional accomplishment. Moreover, hearers are clearly oriented to this projected organization. It is, I would suggest, in this way that meaning—as a cognitive construct—becomes empirically available for analysis. What Heritage calls the intersubjective architecture of talk (1984b:284) provides a "framework in which speakers can rely on the *positioning* of what they say to contribute to the *sense* of what they say as an action" (1984b:261, emphasis in original). This is, with more analytic precision, Blumer's general notion that social interaction entails a fitting together of lines of action such that group life can be brought off as joint action. Moreover, as Heritage has also forcefully argued, conversational structures are additionally context *shaping* and context *renewing* in that they both organize the local flow of interaction and thereby also create the renewed conditions for further exchange. Indeed, it is reasonable to argue that it is through just such structured and structuring properties of interaction that social order is possible at all.

Current research in conversation analysis moves along two intertwined and complementary strands. Basic research continues into the fine-grained structures of talk, analyzing both the analytic and formal properties of turns and their connective tissues such as pauses, uhms, overlaps, and chuckles, as well as the myriad nonvocal and gestural displays that accompany the briefest of face-to-face exchange (Pomerantz, 1984; Heritage, 1984a; Schegloff, 1986; Jefferson, Sacks, and Schegloff, 1986; Wilson and Zimmerman, 1986; Houtkoop-Steenstra, 1987). The organization of more topic-related features have also begun to receive the same analytic attention, though it must be noted that that very density of interactional detail noted earlier makes the establishment of apparently simple issues like topic boundaries very tricky indeed (Maynard, 1980; Button and Casey, 1984; Maynard and Zimmerman, 1984; de Fornel, 1986, 1987; Boden and Bielby, 1986; Bergmann, 1987).

The second stage of work that has emerged in the past ten years or so has moved researchers into a more varied range of settings of talk and interaction and, in the process, into a variety of different occasions of turn-taking as well. Some of the earliest work was Zimmerman and West's (1975) on gender differences in conversation (see also West and Zimmerman, 1983, 1987), which West later extended in her research on doctor-patient interaction (1984). Medical settings have become a considerable area of research more generally (Heath, 1981, 1984, 1986; Frankel, 1984; ten Have, 1987, in press), as have legal and judicial settings (Atkinson and Drew, 1979; Atkinson, 1982; Lynch, 1982; Maynard, 1984, 1988), and a variety of other institutional areas such as classrooms, learning disability clinics, crisis intervention services, and so forth (e.g., McHoul, 1978; Mehan, 1979; Maynard and Marlaire, 1987). Research has also expanded into organizational and work settings (Zimmerman, 1984; Meehan, 1986; Anderson, Hughes, and Sharrock, 1987; Whalen and Zimmerman, 1987; Suchman, 1987; Boden, in press a) and into areas utilizing media materials as data (Greatbatch, 1982; Atkinson, 1984; Molotch and Boden, 1985; Heritage and Greatbatch, 1986; Clayman, 1988; Halkowski, 1988).

Throughout all, researchers working with everyday conversational materials have uncovered a veritable gold mine of "structures of social action" (Atkinson and Heritage, 1984); precise and patterned procedures for producing talk that reveal, in their instantiation, the sort of fine-grained order in the social world that so amazed early naturalists in the nineteenth century as they began to systematically observe the natural environment. This is, I believe, the fascination of talk for anyone who has taken the time to slow down the spinning world of interaction and watch the effects. And, they *are* "effects" in that it is the essential reflexivity and indexicality of language-in-action that produces that density of interaction alluded to above. The structures of social action studied in this manner are locally managed mechanisms that simultaneously structure and transform the interaction.

Close analysis of everyday conversation reveals just that coordination of action Mead and Blumer were so sensitive to, and locates it precisely in the orientation of one actor to another in the most pervasive of all social acts. Language and meaning come together as talk. It is, as Schegloff suggests, through analyzing discourse as an achievement rather than a text that we can discover "the contingency of real things" (1982:89). Moreover, it is by treating language-in-action as a topic of enquiry that we can begin to trace out just how thought becomes action through language, and thus learn rather precisely what "meaning" comes to mean in and through interaction. Talk is, I am suggesting, language-in-action. Thus I am proposing that the symbolic interaction that is *thought*, in Mead's sense, becomes quite concretely available, both for analysis and further theorizing, through the fine-grained activities of talk in interaction.

TRACKING THE INTERACTION ORDER

Language and meaning are practical matters. That is to say, academic theorizing apart, they present and resolve pressing and omnipresent problems in everyday human intercourse. There is a temptation to characterize much of daily life as "ritual" or "routine," and much of the very language of social science contributes to this notion. Yet a return to Mead reminds us that each social act is produced in a continuous present in terms of a never-to-be-arrived-at future. Habit, to be sure, plays a part, but the process of meaning is ongoing, varied, and indeterminate. It is that realtime and contingent flavor of social life that is captured at the level of talk.

In a recent study of organizational life (Boden, in press a), I was interested in the reflexive relation of organizational structure and conversational interaction. Talk in organizations paces the business of the day, and I have been interested in tracking the interactive and interdependent nature of talk and task in producing and reproducing that abstract object we call "the organization"—both within and beyond the boundaries of the firm itself. Organizational members, their clients, and suppliers, for example, spend a considerable amount of interactional energy coordinating activities in time and space while, at the same time, their very talk is itself a microcosm of that synchrony.

```
Rhonda:  Thizziz = Rho:nda.
                    (0.2)
Bill:    .hh Hi Rhonda!  Bi::ll    here?
                                  [    ]
Rhonda:                           Hi::  Bill?
Bill:    Retu::rning (.) not Marco's (0.2) but Ro::n's
         call?
Rhonda:  Right.  Jus'a minnit.
                    ((caller on hold: 6.5 secs))
Ron:     Hullo:   ::?
                  [  ]
Bill:             Hi  Ron.   Sorry I didn'git back t'ye,
Ron:     'Kay.  D'ja = talk = t'- (.) Jo::hn?
Bill:    Yeah = an = I = go:t the figures
                    (0.3)
Ron:     Oh. (0.2) Alrea::dy?
Bill:    Yeah.
Ron:     N'ka::y (0.3) ya  wanna come u::p?
                          [  ]
Bill:                     .h                Ri:ght.
Ron:     'Ka::y, I'm here?
Bill:    Ri:ght = bye.


                    ((click))
```

This strip of interaction is assuredly routine, produced in and through the flow of talk, yet it is hardly automatic since each turn shapes the next in ways that, while patterned, cannot be abstractly pinpointed. A feature both of interaction and of the world is that it is sequential, not merely serial. The world unfolds, as Garfinkel has often noted, on a "once through" basis, with each moment shaping the next in consequential ways. Each moment is both new and old; old in that it contains and reproduces existing features of the world, yet new in that this particular moment has just been reached, under just these conditions, just now, with just certain information to hand, just certain actors involved, just those, no more. Bill, Ron, and Rhonda work together every day, moving from the twenty-fourth to the twenty-fifth floors of an office building in search of figures, files, and the occasional friendly face. But *how* that day and those routines are constituted and reconstituted is the essence of organizational life.

Rhonda's opening line "self-identifies" with "Thizziz = Rho:nda" and frames this call as intraorganizational, i.e., an internal communication between frequent and familiar interactants (Boden, in press a). Bill responds with a greeting and self-identification, getting an overlapped return greeting and thus completing two canonical rounds of telephone openings (Schegloff, 1968). Bill's "reason for the call" is similarly located in the typical next slot, where it is the caller who provides a warrant for the call; he announces a temporal and organizational issue, namely that his is a "return" call, a response, not to Marco, but to Ron, thereby embedding a number of organizational relationships and commitments in a single economical turn at talk. Note, too, the interweaving of temporal frames such as "returning" a call, waiting "jus'a minnit," apologizing for not getting "back t'ye," and having the figures "alrea::dy?" These formulations also involve coordination of actors and activities that are critically contingent on such realtime accommodation, as is Ron's demand, "D'ja = talk = t'- (.) Jo::hn?" and Bill's locally produced understanding that such a contact had to do with "the figures"—that is to say, not any figures but a shared and oriented-to set of numbers that each understands and whose current possession precipitates a next organizational task. These coordinated issues are, in turn, also organized around further understandings about mutual availability and the need for copresence in time and space, so that having the figures results in an invitation from Ron and an offer of being "here." Importantly, for this discussion of the interactional achievement of meaning through language-in-action, Bill marks both invitation and offer with an unambiguous and unelaborated affirmative, and their short exchange is terminated.

Action and meaning, at this level of analysis, reveal that their negotiation is a highly local affair. It is joint action, in Blumer's sense, but more. Their talk and tasks are mutually elaborative in a turn-by-turn manner. They are not just talking "about" work; that work is, and will continue to be, produced as talk. Organizational members routinely produce multiple levels of activities that are reflexively and simultaneously tied in and through their talk. Take, for example, the following fragment from a multiparty meeting.

```
Dean:    We scre:wed up agai::n.  We didn' a::sk f'r that
         material- we a:sked f'r it last year (.) la:te in
         pie ce ri    ght?
              [     ]
Matt:          Yeah.
         The fe::llowship people again,
Jim:     S'there uh March fiftee:nth dead li:ne?
                                    [    ]
Matt:                               Ye::s.
Jim:     Tha's  sad  we'll  have a::ll- all these people's
         [[     ]    [    ]
Jean:    .h:::       of all-
Jim:     = applications  (.) by the time (you need 'em)
              [                                       ]
Dean:              MAY I MA:KE
         (.) thuh following suggestion?
         [                               ]
Matt:    WE CAN DA::NCE around the March   fiftee:nth . . .
```

The "topic" of this exchange between four university administrators
might be described as "fellowships" or perhaps "fellowship deadlines,"
but with the dean's opening gambit the organizational stage is set for a
round of interdepartmental accommodations. The dean and Jim represent the graduate school who "screwed up again." Matt is from the
office of financial aid. As Jim laments the fact that, practically speaking and despite the technical deadline of March 15, their office will
have needed materials by the time they are needed, the dean initiates
a suggestion and, faster on his conversational feet, Matt offers to
"dance" around the deadline. Such is the stuff of bureaucratic life, but
note the degree to which the very accomplishment of accommodation
is an interactional one produced in and through the ordering and overlapping of turns at talk. Note too that the temporal formulations are
not in any way loosely "socially constructed" but rather precisely produced as interdepartmental *and* interactional collaboration. It is in
this way, I believe, that the business of talk constitutes the business of
the day (Boden, in press a). The connection between talk as structure
and structure *through* talk is a tightly coupled phenomenon.

Organizations are ubiquitous settings of modern society. Such organizations are often viewed by sociologists as abstract entities per-
sisting in time and space, setting agendas, pursuing goals, making
decisions, expanding, contracting, collapsing, resurging. They are seen
as having existence and momentum above and beyond the individual.

And so they do. But when an organization such as the New York Stock Exchange dives precipitously in a single trading day, it is to the traders on the floor, the analysts at their computers, the account executives at their phones, and the institutional buyers in fern-filled offices across the country that we look. It is their actions, impressions, conversations, rumors, and reactions that constituted so-called Black Monday in October 1987. Even the programmed trading that *may* have triggered the volume trading of the day is the result of earlier conversations and impressions, rumors of currency and commodity shifts, talk of inflation, and so forth. People *are* a central part of all organizations, and their talk is the interactional material out of which those organizations are constituted.

Indeed, one of the recurring features of all organizations is the stories and myths through which the daily activities and long-range actions of firms are understood. These stories are often mistakenly treated as a kind of culture and studied abstractly and acontextually. But stories are part and parcel of talk. They draw their strength and carry their message in interaction.

TELLING STORIES

It is interesting that Erving Goffman experienced a linguistic turn of his own in his latter years, inspired and also apparently irritated by the work of his former students (e.g., Schegloff, 1988). In *Forms of Talk* particularly, he recommends firmly that "microanalysis of interaction lumber in where the self-respecting decline to tread" (1982:2), namely into the realm of talk, and goes on to offer a number of useful approaches to that study. Among them, he correctly observes that we spend a good deal of our talking-time telling stories. People in their everyday intercourse tell stories all the time, as Sacks and others have pointed out (Sacks, 1972, 1974; Jefferson, 1978; Boden and Bielby, 1983; Maynard, 1988). This too has parallels in symbolic interactionist enquiry in that it provides a way of moving further along the important tack of letting subjects tell their own narratives (see McCall and Wittner, this volume). They do. All the time. It is just a matter of sitting back and letting the world happen—with a tape recorder or video camera running.

In McCall and Wittner's essay (this volume) on life histories, for example, storytelling groups studied by McCall provide a way of examining how people discover new meaning in their lives and their shared location in history. In some recent ethnographic and conversation analytic work, I spent time hanging out in an English senior center in west London and in a coffee shop on what I call "High Street" in Palo Alto located near a medical center, a favorite drugstore, and the local senior center. In earlier research (Boden and Bielby, 1983, 1986), we found a great deal of narrative in the everyday talk of the elderly and among strangers provides a remarkable display of spontaneously generated life history. These stories are, however, *part* of the talk, rather than some special interlude.

```
Ben:    And uh-
Erma:   .hh Well when- (.) when I:: lived there in this
        liddle German community .h uh FARMING  community
                                [              ]
Ben:                            .hh Oh yea:h
Erma:   = and uh- (.) th- the only way we could get out of
        there was by TRAIN  and it-  it was on the branch
                          [     ]
Ben:                      Ye::s?
Erma:   = line of the MK and T .h:: we called it the KATIE,
        it was  uh-  Missouri    Kansas an  TEXas  line and
              [    ]                       [       ]
Ben:          Yes                         Yeah
Erma:   = we- we  uh-
              [   ]
Ben:              Do   they still have that railroad?  I
        think  it's call- They do?
              [                  ]
Erma:          YE:S I thi:nk so    I think  so
                                          [    ]
Ben:                                      Yeah  I
        'member cuz I RODE that one uh-
Erma:   And the County Seat was Gai::nesville  and uh
                                            [      ]
Ben:                                        Oh yes
Erma:   = the County Seat and that- if we wanted to-
        t'go to the County Seat we hadda either go by
        bug- horse an' BUGGY o:r .h
                              [   ]
Ben:                          Uh!
```

In this "life as narrative" (cf. Gergen and Gergen, 1983; Bruner, 1987) interaction, old people establish identity and explore shared history in a highly collaborative manner, often interweaving several layers of public history with quite detailed accounts of private lives lived across long spans of time and space. Analytically Ben and Erma can be seen, in one sense, to compete for the topical floor, but in terms of their shared storytelling we argued that they are also, significantly, contrasting past with present in a constructive and coconstitutive manner (Boden and Bielby, 1986). The result is, for the researcher, rather compelling insights into the role of the past in the present lives of the elderly, a role that turns out to be both interactive and positive rather than a "living" in the past. Thus, as we also suggested (Boden and Bielby, 1983), the past is a *resource* out of which present lives are made meaningful and interactionally active.

My more recent research in and around senior centers suggests a similar pattern, although here—in settings of food preparation, card playing, and eating—talk and task in the present interplay with narratives of the past in a more complex manner. The pattern of marking shared historical periods persists as present-day events are contrasted with stories told out of past events. In this fragment, Edith is making tea in the back of the London senior club as Bess struggles to open a package (packet) of cookies (bickies, as in biscuits).

```
Edith:  . . . an' 'e tol' me- he to::ld me no' t' take 'm
        wif'outuh cuppa tea:::?
                    (1.7)
        ((sound of electric kettle clicking off—
        plastic wrapping noise, voices in background))

Edith:  He said ne:vuh t'ta::ke 'm wi- withou:t uh cuppa.
Bess:   Ye:h.
Edith:  A::n' a:h do::n' (0.2) nei:ther.  Here!  Le'me 'elp
        you:: wif that pa cket?
                        [    ]
Bess:                   O:h  a:wrrigh' the:n?
        ((sound of wrapping paper))
Edith:  Like my A:nd rew?
                    [   ]
Bess:               Hm  hmm,
Edith:  When 'e was li'ttle?
Bess:   Yeh.
Edith:  'E had a::wf'lly bad bronchi::tis? =
Bess:                                   =Hmm,
Edith:  'e did. An' the doctuh sai::d-  There y'a::re, tha's
```

               done i:t?   Those bickies look evuh so goo: :d?
                    [   ]   [   ]
   Bess: (Yeh)   Mm.
               Right then.
                    [   ]
   Edith: Thuh   doctor said 'e was to 'ave those bi::g
               ta:blets with tea as well.   They were ever so bi::g,
               an' 'e was ever so lihhle, an it was during the wa::r?
   Bess: Oh ye::h, hmhmm?
   Edith: An' we wuz livin' in Battersea, so I . . .

               ((story continues))

   Stories are intriguing, though tricky, conversations to study analytically, particularly as their sequential production mimics though does
not mirror the sequence of events being captured. Stories, as Sacks
(1974, 1978) has demonstrated, are artful both in their telling and in
what is told. They fit into an ongoing conversation as they unfold in
real time, and contain their own intricate and consequential structure.
They are staged, both in their sequentially produced elements and in
the story they track. They are also carefully located interactionally as,
above, Edith's announcement to Bess about taking large tablets with
tea builds into a wartime story of when her son was young and they
lived in Battersea. Storytellers are often, as Maynard has noted, "part
of the narratives they present" (1988:452), and this has important implications for the way both stories and tellers can be understood.
   Maynard's own work demonstrates the rather subtle ways in which
storytellers engaged in third-party narratives can become *part* of the
narrative and thus demonstrate their position vis-à-vis the story. More
generally, my own point is that all storytellers reveal aspects of self
and other in the way stories are told and the relative stance they take
in relation to the narrative (e.g., Whalen and Zimmerman, 1985).
Stories are thus not "just" tales but active and interactive productions which, particularly when examined on video, reveal collaborative qualities of verbal and nonverbal displays of participation both
by speaker and recipient (M. Goodwin, 1982; C. Goodwin, 1984).
   In the above strip of interaction, Edith has been telling a story about
a recent visit to her doctor, a story that has been contextually cued by
the joint activity of making tea. The doctor, she says, told her not to
take her medication "withou:t uh *cuppa*." This instruction is then
summarized in the claim: 'A::n' a:h *do::n*' (0.2) nei:ther." The local
activity of struggling with wrapping, an increasing daily problem for

the elderly whose dexterity is decreasing as packaging is becoming ever more complicated, produces an inserted *"Here!* Le'me 'elp you::."* Again, we can observe, in fine detail, that localized production of joint action characterized by Blumer, as talk, task, and topic are managed. The medication story is then built into a wartime story of Edith's son Andrew and his bronchitis, in a deft yet typical telling of past and present (see also Boden and Bielby, 1986).

Indeed the very activity of "telling" turns out to be a rather precise and coordinated act. Jefferson, for example, has developed this vein of research in a particularly elegant examination of how people tell troubles in everyday life (Jefferson, 1980).

The telling of a trouble revolves around maintaining both the routine features of the conversation and discourse identity while inserting a more intense focus—the trouble—and then returning to business as usual. Jefferson proposes that trouble-telling has a kind of trajectory that moves interactants from the routine to the trouble and back. Of interest here is that the close-up techniques of conversation analysis have not only an illuminating but also an animating quality for microanalysis in that they both track the interaction order and rather graphically trace its fundamentally interactional ordering, bringing to the analytic surface the dynamic structure of the interaction order itself.

History as Talk

Jefferson's examination of trouble-telling points to a further feature of conversational interaction that has only begun to be explored by researchers in the area, namely the sequential aspects of interaction across long stretches of talk (Jefferson, 1980; Heritage, 1985; Button, in press) and across interactions (Boden, in press a). In my own organizational work, I had become concerned with whether the sequential quality of interaction could be used to understand the constitution of institutions across time. This is a recurring problem for organizational analysis (Hall, 1987), one which has been forcefully theorized by Giddens in recent years (1979, 1984, 1987) as well as by Foucault, (1977; see also Glassner, 1982) but rather rarely demonstrated empirically.

Temporality and duration are central to both ethnomethodology and symbolic interaction (Glassner, 1982). There is a temptation to consider the work of Garfinkel and Sacks, for instance, as "merely" concerned with the details of structure in action. Yet this would be a fundamental misreading of their work because it is in the mutual elaboration of structure in action (and vice versa) that social organization is possible at all. That interpenetration of action and structure is, in turn, essential to understanding the embeddedness of micro in macro and macro in micro (e.g., Alexander et al., 1987; Alexander, 1988; Collins, 1987, 1988; Fine, 1987; Boden, n.d.). Indeed it points, as Giddens is fond of insisting, to the futility of such distinctions, a "division of labour [that] leads to consequences that are at best highly misleading" (1984:139).

In this light, I have recently become interested in the possibility of tracking history through talk and thereby revealing, in the fullness of verbal interaction, the *production* of history, both objectively and subjectively. That is, as a sequence of events in time and a sequentially achieved series of intersubjectively located events in the lives of real people. Given Hall's illuminating discussion (this volume) on the relation of historical considerations to more general issues in symbolic interaction, a final section on what I call "history as talk" may further ground this brief excursion into the dense world that is everyday talk.

I have been focusing, for my ethnomethodological study of history, primarily on a single series of telephone calls that occurred between John F. Kennedy and the governor of Mississippi on a single weekend in 1962 that came to be called "the Mississippi crisis" or the "insurrection at Ole' Miss."[4] The materials are audio recordings made at the White House, and now in the archives of the Kennedy Presidential Library, along with extensive documents of the incident, its immediate precursors, subsequent consequences, historical assessments, and so forth.

A fragment of these materials quickly captures the flavor of this rather new type of historical record. The crisis at the University of Mississippi involved the registration of James Meredith as the first black to attend an institution of higher learning in that deeply traditional state. The confrontation is recognised by historians as the most significant crisis in federal-state authority since the close of the American Civil War a century earlier. That drama and those aspects of history were clearly not lost on Jack Kennedy and his brother as attorney general as they managed events from the White House that long weekend. Furthermore, the interactional data, comprised of a sequence of telephone calls and a limited number of snatches of meeting conversation in the Oval Office, catch and document that sense of crisis in a highly analyzable way. The following "moments of history" take place about halfway through the weekend of crisis, in the afternoon of Sunday, September 30, 1962. Earlier calls between President Kennedy and Governor Barnet display a distinct kind of negotiation between the two leaders, one marked by Kennedy's willingness to tolerate the governor's attempts to avoid cooperation, an avoidance that is as much interactionally produced and reproduced as it is legally located in the governor's official stance vis-à-vis a federally mandated court order to register Meredith. The president is providing an account of why the governor must keep in close touch with the White House. The governor breaks in to announce the death of a state trooper, victim of a sniper's bullet, who had earlier been accompanied to a hospital.

```
JFK:   Y'see we don'- we got an hour t'go::: an' that's not
       u:h- we- we may not ha::ve an hour  what with this-
                                         [          ]
Gov:                                       Uh- this man
       this man has jus' died
JFK:   Did he die?
Gov:   Yes sir
         [   ]
JFK:       Whi ch one?  State police?
Gov:   Tha's the State Police
JFK:   Yea:h, well you see we gotta get order up there an'
       that's what we thou::ght we  were gonna  ha:ve =
                                   [            ]
Gov:                                 Mistuh
       = Pre::s'dent PLEA::SE why don't you uh- can't you give
       an order up there to remo::ve Mer'  dith
                                        [   ]
JFK:                                      HOW  CAN I REMO::VE
       HIM GOVernor when there's a- a ri::ot in the street an'
       he may step out of that building an' something ha::ppen
       to him?  I can't remove him under tho::se conditions.
                         (1.0)
Gov:   U::::h-                 but-but- but we can-
         [[        ]            [
JFK:   Y'go-   let's get o::rder     up there an' then we can do
       something  about Meredith
                 [               ]
Gov:               we can        sur::rou::ound it with
       plenty 'v offi::cials
JFK:   Well we've got to get somebuddy up there now to get
       order, and stop the firing and the shooting.  Then we-
```

you and I will ta::lk on the phone about Meredith
                    (0.2)
        But firs' we gotta get o::rder
    [[   ]
  Gov: A::rright   I'll- I'll ca:ll an'
        tell"em to get every- every official they ca::n?

The governor's announcement is notable in numerous ways that lie outside the current scope of this discussion, but it is worth highlighting a few ways in which the sequential shape of these turns consequentially shapes the action of these historical moments, social action that both structures and is structured by the unfolding events. In routine conversation, the governor's announcement of a death would project an immediate assessment by his interactant (Pomerantz, 1984). But the president's first move here is a clarification request, "Did he die?" followed by more specificity, "Which one? State police?" concluded with a token acknowledgment and a disagreement marker, "Yea:h, well." He then shifts the topic back to his own earlier point of the need to establish order at the campus at Oxford. The governor again breaks in with a plea for a very different sort of order, one that would achieve his goal of removing Meredith from the campus and, preferably, far from the state of Mississippi. The notion of "order" thus proceeds at several levels. It is through *sequentially produced*, rather than structurally located, power that the president's definition overrides the governor's version, not just in this closing sequence of the telephone conversation, but across the long-distance interactions that continue deep into that night in 1962. By the next morning, the president's concern for the situation, assessed largely through these telephone calls both to Governor Barnet and through an open telephone line to his own staff on the Oxford campus, has resulted in the arrival of over 5000 national guards from nearby Memphis, and quietly at 9:00 a.m. James Meredith registered at Ole' Miss, to graduate a year later. The rest, as they say, is history.

This meeting of history and one of the newest subfields of sociology underlines, I believe, another important area of shared ground between symbolic interactionists and conversation analysts. The latter's more focused concern for the sequential details of action is complemented by symbolic interactionist interest in recurrent patterns of collective activity (e.g., Becker, 1982, 1986). Historical crises occur neither in a tidy research vacuum, nor are they structurally determined in such a way as their outcome is inevitable. Rather they are the result of particular people coming together (or not) in temporally located and sequentially organized ways (cf. Collins, 1988). Meredith, Kennedy, and Barnet occupied structural positions unlikely to produce an intersection in any social scientist's model of such events. Yet people *do* make history, and how they do it under conditions, both material and interactional, outside their choosing is the stuff of sociology and history. Series and sequence are, as Hall (this volume) notes, the objects of historical enquiry. To capture them sociologically as talk can be the conversation analyst's contribution—at least in the area of contemporary history where recorded and video materials are becoming increasingly available.

CONCLUSION

It has been my goal in this chapter to suggest that the friendly paths of symbolic interaction and conversation analysis come together at the intersection of language and meaning. Through characterizing talk as language-in-action, I have suggested that *where thought becomes action through talk* we may find that crossroads. Symbolic interactionists and conversation analysts travel together more broadly along a route that examines the intertwining of meaning, shared symbols, joint action, and social order.

Thus, at that larger intersection of agency and structure, sociologists generally may expect to find both symbolic interactionists and conversation analysts. Both are centrally concerned with temporality, with duration, with action, and with, as it were, the pulse of society. In this ability to trace the measured and thereby measurable pace of social life, we have much to offer the often arbitrarily collapsed categories and aggregate abstraction of most quantitative sociology. Methodologists are fond of characterizing much social research as having a "snapshot" quality—capturing a cross-sectional moment of society. But this is really hopelessly inaccurate. Most sociology captures no moment at all, but rather the latent and leftover traces of past action, past emotion, past cognition—inaccurately remembered, recorded, or measured. The considerable virtue of the shared enterprise of symbolic interaction and conversation analysis is a steady yet animated view of the world-as-it-happens.

APPENDIX

The transcription notation used by conversation analysts was developed by Gail Jefferson. It attempts, using a standard typewriter or computer keyboard symbols, to capture for the eye the way the talk is heard by the ear. Transcripts are always analyzed together with relevant audio or video materials and are not intended as substitutes for the data they capture. The transcripts in this chapter have been simplified for presentation purposes. For more extensive discussion, see Atkinson and Heritage (1984:ix–xvi).

A: Ye s, two. [ ] B: Oh goo :d.	Brackets indicate the point at which simultaneous speech starts and ends.
A: How- [[ ] B: When did you hear?	Utterances starting together are indicated by double left brackets.
A: Hello::= B: =Hi.	When there is no audible gap between one utterance and the next, equal signs are used.
(0.8)	Numbers in parentheses indicate elapsed time in tenths of seconds.
(.)	A dot in parentheses indicates a slight gap, typically less than one-tenth of a second.
A: *Right*.	Italic indicates emphasis in delivery.
B: HOW MUCH?	Capital letters indicate that a word or phrase is louder than the surrounding talk.
A: So:::	Colons indicate that the immediately prior syllable is prolonged or "stretched"; the number of colons denote, approximately, the duration.
A: We added to-	A hyphen represents a cutoff of the immediately prior word or syllable.
A: Sure. B: Issues, C: Ca:mpus?	Punctuation marks are used to capture characteristics of speech delivery rather than grammatical notation. period = downward contour comma = sustained contour question mark = rising contour
.hh::	A dot-prefixed *h* indicates an in-breath; without a dot, exhalation.
Heh-heh-huh-huh	Laughter particles
(h)	An *h* in parentheses denotes breathiness or a plosive delivery.
('r something)	Empty parentheses or items enclosed in single parentheses incidate transcribers doubt of a hearing.
((cough)) ((ring)) ((loud bang))	Double parentheses are used to enclose a description of some phenomenon that characterizes the talk or the scene.

Notes

1. I am indebted to Gary Alan Fine for this insight.

2. There are a few exceptions to this claim, most notably in the work of West and Zimmerman, who, in part of their studies of gender and interruption, used quasi-experimental settings (e.g., West and Zimmerman, 1983; see also Boden and Bielby, 1983, 1986).

3. For excellent reviews of basic findings in conversation analysis and recent research directions, see Heritage, 1984b (chapter 8) and Heritage, 1985. Levinson (1983) also has an insightful introduction to the field in his general discussion of pragmatics (see also Conein, 1985; Zimmerman, 1988; Zimmerman and Boden, in press).

4. The larger study, "History as Talk," will attempt to locate this central series of telephone calls within a larger analytic framework, using a range of audio and video, and conventional archival sources available through the John F. Kennedy Presidential Library in Boston.

REFERENCES

Alexander, Jeffrey. 1988. *Action and Its Environment.* New York: Columbia University Press.

Alexander, Jeffrey, et al. 1987. *The Micro-Macro Link.* Berkeley: University of California Press.

Anderson, Robert J., John A. Hughes, and Wesley Sharrock. 1987. "Executive Problem Finding: Some Material and Initial Observations." *Social Psychology Quarterly* 50(2):143–59.

Atkinson, J. Maxwell. 1982. "Understanding Formality: Notes on the Categorization and Production of 'Formal' Interaction." *British Journal of Sociology* 33:86–117.

———. 1984. *Our Masters' Voices: The Language and Body Language of Politics.* London: Methune.

Atkinson, J. Maxwell, and Paul Drew. 1979. *Order in Court.* London: Macmillan.

Atkinson, J. Maxwell, and John Heritage, eds., 1984. *Structures of Social Action: Studies in Conversation Analysis.* Cambridge: Cambridge University Press.

Becker, Howard S. 1982. *Art Worlds.* Berkeley: University of California Press.

———. 1986. *Doing Things Together.* Evanston: Northwestern University Press.

Bergmann, Jörg. 1987. *Klatsch: Zur Sozialform der diskreten Indiskretion.* Berlin: Walter de Gruyter.

Besnier, Niko. 1989. "Information Withholding as a Manipulative and Collusive Strategy in Nukulaelae Gossip." *Language and Society* 18:315–41.

Blumer, Herbert. 1969. *Symbolic Interaction: Perspective and Method.* Englewood Cliffs, NJ: Prentice Hall.

Boden, Deirdre. 1983. "Talk International: An Analysis of Conversational Turn-Taking and Related Phenomena in Seven Indo-European Languages." Paper presented at the annual meetings of the American Sociological Association, Detroit.

———. In press a. *The Business of Talk: Organizations in Action.* Cambridge: Polity Press.

———. In press b. "The World as It Happens: Ethnomethodology and Conversation Analysis." Pp. 185–213 in George Ritzer, ed., *Frontiers in Social Theory.* New York: Columbia University Press.

———. N.d. "Islands of Sociology: Beyond the Micro-Macro Debate." Unpublished ms. Department of Sociology, Washington University.

Boden, Deirdre, and Denise D. Bielby. 1983. "The Past as Resource: A Conversational Analysis of Elderly Talk." *Human Development* 26(4):308–19.

———. 1986. "The Way It Was: Topical Organization in Elderly Conversation." *Language and Communication* 7(1):73–89.

Bourdieu, Pierre. 1982. *Le Sens Practique.* Paris: Editions Minuit.

Bruner, Jerome. 1987. "Life as Narrative." *Social Research* 54(1): 11–32.

Button, Graham. In press. "Conversation-in-a-Series." In Deirdre Boden and Don H. Zimmerman, eds., *Talk and Social Structure.* Cambridge: Polity Press.

Button, Graham, and Neil Casey. 1984. "Generating Topic: The Use of Topic Initial Elicitors." Pp. 167–90 in J. Maxwell Atkinson and John Heritage, eds., *Structures of Social Action: Studies in Conversation Analysis.* Cambridge: Cambridge University Press.

Clayman, Stephen E. 1988. "Displaying Neutrality in Television News Interviews." Paper presented at the Midwest Sociology Society annual meetings, Minneapolis.

Collins, Randall. 1986. "Is 1980s Sociology in the Doldrums?" *American Journal of Sociology* 91:1336–55.

———. 1987. "Interaction Ritual Chains, Power, and Property: The Micro-Macro Connection as an Empirically Based Theoretical Problem." Pp. 177–206 in Jeffrey Alexander et al., *The Micro-Macro Link.* Berkeley: University of California Press.

———. 1988. "The Micro Contribution to Macro Sociology." *Sociological Theory* 6(2):242–53.

Conein, Bernard. 1985. "L'Enquete Sociologique et l'Analyse du Langage: Les Formes Linguistiques de la Connaissance Sociale." Pp. 6–30 in *Arguments Ethnomethodologiques: Problemes d'Epistemologie en Sciences Sociales III.* Paris: E.H.E.S.S.

Denzin, Norman K. 1983. "Interpretive Interactionism." Pp. 129–46 in G. Morgan, ed., *Beyond Methods.* Beverly Hills: Sage.

———. 1987. "On Semiotics and Symbolic Interactionism." *Symbolic Interaction* 10(1):1–19.

Fine, Gary Alan. 1987. "On the Macrofoundations of Microsociology: Order, Meaning, and Comparative Context." Paper presented at the Stone-SSSI Symposium, Urbana, IL.

de Fornel, Michel. 1986. "Pre-sequences and Topical Organization in

Conversation." Paper presented at the International Conference on Talk and Social Structure, University of California, Santa Barbara.

———. 1987. "Remarques sur l'Organisation Thématique et les Séquences d'Actions dans la Conversation." Pp. 15–36 in Bernard Conein, ed., *Lexique et Faits Sociaux*. Lille: Presses Universitaires de Lille.

Foucault, Michel. 1975. *Surveiller et Punir: Naissance de la Prison*. Paris: Editions Gallimard.

Frankel, Richard. 1984. "From 'Sentence' to 'Sequence': Understanding the Medical Encounter through Microinteractional Analysis." *Discourse Processes* 7:135–70.

Garfinkel, Harold. 1967. *Studies in Ethnomethodology*. Englewood Cliffs, NJ: Prentice Hall.

Garfinkel, Harold, Michael Lynch, Eric Livingston, and Douglas Macbeth. N.d. "Respecifying the Natural Sciences as Discovering Sciences of Practical Action." Department of Sociology, University of California, Los Angeles.

Gergen, Kenneth J., and Mary M. Gergen. 1983. "Narratives of the Self." Pp. 251–73 in T. R. Sarbin and K. E. Scheibe, eds., *Studies in Social Identity*. New York: Praeger.

Giddens, Anthony. 1976. *New Rules of Sociological Method*. London: Macmillan.

———. 1979. *Central Problems in Social Theory*. Berkeley: University of California Press.

———. 1984. *The Constitution of Society*. Berkeley: University of California Press.

———. 1987. "Time and Social Organization." Pp. 140–65 in Anthony Giddens and Jonathon Turner, eds., *Social Theory Today*. Stanford: Stanford University Press.

Glassner, Barry. 1982. "An Essay on Iterative Social Time." *Sociological Review* 30:668–81.

Goffman, Erving. 1981. *Forms of Talk*. Philadelphia: University of Pennsylvania Press.

———. 1983. "The Interaction Order." *American Sociological Review* 48(1):1–17.

Goodwin, Charles. 1979. "The Interactive Construction of a Sentence in Natural Conversation." Pp. 97–121 in George Psathas, ed., *Everyday Language: Studies in Ethnomethodology*. New York: Irvington.

———. 1984. "Notes on Story Structure and the Organization of Participation." Pp. 225–46 in J. Maxwell Atkinson and John Heritage, eds., *Structures of Social Action: Studies in Conversation Analysis*. Cambridge: Cambridge University Press.

Goodwin, Marjorie. 1982. "Instigating: Storytelling as Social Process." *American Ethnologist* 9:799–819.

Greatbatch, David. 1982. "The Turn-Taking System for British News Interviews." Unpublished mimeo. Department of Sociology, University of Warwick, U.K.

Habermas, Jurgen. 1984. *The Theory of Communicative Action.* Vol. 1: *Reason and the Rationalization of Society.* London: Heineman.

Halkowski, Timothy. 1988. "The Interaction of Gaze and Talk in a Congressional Inquiry: The Social Accomplishment of Answers." Unpublished mimeo. Department of Sociology, University of California, Santa Barbara.

Hall, Peter. 1987. "Interactionism and the Study of Social Organization." *Sociological Quarterly* 28(1):1–22.

ten Have, Paul. 1987. *Sequenties en Formuleringen: Aspecten van de Interactionele Organisatie van Huisarts-Spreekuurgesprekken.* Amsterdam: University of Amsterdam Press.

———. In press. "Assymetry in Doctor-Patient Interaction." In Deirdre Boden and Don H. Zimmerman, eds., *Talk and Social Structure.* Cambridge: Polity Press.

Heath, Christian. 1981. "The Opening Sequence in Doctor-Patient Interaction." Pp. 71–90 in Paul Atkinson and Christian Heath, eds., *Medical Work: Realities and Routines.* Farnborough, U.K.: Gower.

———. 1984. "Talk and Recipiency: Sequential Organization in Speech and Body Movement." Pp. 242–65 in J. Maxwell Atkinson and John Heritage, eds., *Structures of Social Action: Studies in Conversation Analysis.* Cambridge: Cambridge University Press.

———. 1986. *Speech and Body Movement in Medical Encounters.* Cambridge: Cambridge University Press.

Heritage, John. 1984a. "A Change-of-State Token and Aspects of Its Sequential Placement." Pp. 299–345 in J. Maxwell Atkinson and John Heritage, eds., *Structures of Social Action: Studies in Conversation Analysis.* Cambridge: Cambridge University Press.

———. 1984b. *Garfinkel and Ethnomethodology.* Cambridge: Polity Press.

———. 1985. "Recent Developments in Conversation Analysis." *Sociolinguistics* 15(1985):1–18.

Heritage, John, and J. Maxwell Atkinson. 1984. Introduction to J. Maxwell Atkinson and John Heritage, eds., *Structures of Social Action: Studies in Conversation Analysis.* Cambridge: Cambridge University Press.

Heritage, John, and David Greatbatch. 1986. "Generating Applause: A Study of Rhetoric and Response at Party Conferences." *American Journal of Sociology* 92:110–57.

Houtkoop-Steenstra, Hanneke. 1987. *Establishing Agreement: An*

Analysis of Proposal-Acceptance Sequences. Amsterdam: University of Amsterdam.

Hughes, Everett C. 1971. *The Sociological Eye*. Chicago: Aldine.

Irons, Larry, and Deirdre Boden. 1988. "Ethnomethods and Expert Systems: Knowledge Acquisition as a Matter of Practice." Paper presented at the Midwest Sociology Society meetings, Minneapolis.

Jefferson, Gail. 1973. "A Case of Precision Timing in Ordinary Conversation: Overlapping Tag-Positioned Address Terms in Closing Sequences." *Semiotica* 9:47–96.

———. 1978. "Sequential Aspects of Storytelling in Conversation." Pp. 219–48 in Jim Schenkein, ed., *Studies in the Organization of Conversational Interaction*. New York: Academic Press.

———. 1980. *Final Report to the (British) SSRC on the Analysis of Conversations in Which "Troubles" and "Anxieties" Are Expressed*. Report HR 4805/2.

———. 1983. "On Exposed and Embedded Correction in Conversation." *Studium Linguistik* 44:58–68.

Jefferson, Gail, Harvey Sacks, and Emanuel A. Schegloff. 1986. "Notes on Laughter in the Pursuit of Intimacy." Pp. 152–205 in Graham Button and John Lee, eds., *Talk and Social Organization*. Bath: MultiLingual Matters.

Lamont, Michele. 1987. "How to Become a Dominant French Philosopher: The Case of Jacques Derrida." *American Journal of Sociology* 93(3):584–622.

Levinson, Steven. 1983. *Pragmatics*. Cambridge: Cambridge University Press.

Lynch, Michael. 1982. "Closure and Disclosure in Pre-trial Agreement." *Human Studies* 5(4):285–318.

MacCannell, Dean, and J. F. MacCannell. 1982. *The Time of the Sign*. Bloomington: Indiana University Press.

McHoul, A. W. 1978. "The Organization of Turns at Formal Talk in the Classroom." *Language in Society* 7:183–213.

Maynard, Douglas W. 1980. "Placement of Topic Change in Conversation." *Semiotica* 30:263–90.

———. 1984. *Inside Plea-Bargaining*. New York: Plenum.

———. 1988. "Narratives and Narrative Structure in Plea Bargaining." *Law and Society Review* 22(3):449–81.

Maynard, Douglas W., and Courtney Marlaire. 1987. "The Interactional Substrate of Educational Testing." Paper presented at the annual meetings of the American Anthropological Association, Chicago.

Maynard, Douglas W., and Don H. Zimmerman. 1984. "Topical Talk, Ritual, and the Social Organization of Relationships." *Social Psychology Quarterly* 47:301–16.

Meehan, Albert J. 1986. "Record-Keeping Practices in the Policing of Juveniles." *Urban Life* 15:70–102.

Mehan, Hugh. 1979. *Learning Lessons: Social Organization in the Classroom.* Cambridge, MA: Harvard University Press.

Moerman, Michael. 1977. "The Preference for Self-Correction in a Tai Conversational Corpus." *Language* 53(4):872–82.

Molotch, Harvey L., and Deirdre Boden. 1985. "Talking Social Structure: Discourse, Dominance, and the Watergate Hearings." *American Sociological Review* 50:273–88.

Perinbanayagam, Robert. 1985. *Signifying Acts.* Carbondale: Southern Illinois University Press.

Pomerantz, Anita. 1984. "Agreeing and Disagreeing with Assessments: Some Features of Preferred/Dispreferred Turn Shapes." Pp. 57–101 in J. Maxwell Atkinson and John Heritage, eds., *Structures of Social Action: Studies in Conversation Analysis.* Cambridge: Cambridge University Press.

Rawls, Ann. 1987. "The Interaction Order Sui Generis: Goffman's Contribution to Social Theory." *Sociological Theory* 5:136–43.

Ritzer, George. 1985. "The Rise of Micro-sociological Theory." *Sociological Theory* 3:88–98.

Sacks, Harvey. 1963. "Sociological Description." *Berkeley Journal of Sociology* 8:1–16.

———. 1972. "On the Analyzability of Stories by Children." Pp. 325–45 in John Gumperz and Dell Hymes, eds., *Directions in Sociolinguistics.* New York: Holt, Rinehart and Winston.

———. 1974. "An Analysis of the Course of a Joke's Telling in Conversation." Pp. 337–53 in R. Bauman and J. Sherzer, eds., *Explorations in the Ethnography of Speaking.* Cambridge: Cambridge University Press.

———. 1978. "Some Technical Considerations of a Dirty Joke." Pp. 249–69 in Jim Shenkein, ed., *Studies in the Organization of Conversational Interaction.* New York: Academic Press.

———. 1984. "Methodological Remarks." Pp. 21–27 in J. Maxwell Atkinson and John Heritage, eds., *Structures of Social Action: Studies in Conversation Analysis.* Cambridge: Cambridge University Press.

Sacks, Harvey, Emanuel A. Schegloff, and Gail Jefferson. 1974. "A Simplest Systematics for the Organization of Turn-Taking in Conversation." *Language* 50:696–735.

Schegloff, Emanuel A. 1968. "Sequencing in Conversational Openings." *American Anthropologist* 70:1075–95.

———. 1979. "Identification and Recognition in Telephone Openings." Pp. 23–78 in George Psathas, ed., *Everyday Language: Studies in Ethnomethodology.* New York: Irvington.

————. 1980. "Preliminaries to Preliminaries: 'Can I Ask You a Question?'" *Sociological Inquiry* 50:104–52.

————. 1982. "Discourse as an Interactional Achievement: Some Uses of 'Uh Huh' and Other Things That Come between Sentences." Pp. 71–93 in Deborah Tannen, ed., *Analyzing Discourse: Text and Talk*. Georgetown University Round Table on Languages and Linguistics. Washington, DC: Georgetown University Press.

————. 1986. "The Routine as Achievement." *Human Studies* 9(2–3). Special issue on Interaction and Language Use, edited by Graham Button, Paul Drew, and John Heritage.

————. 1987. "Between Macro and Micro: Contexts and Other Connections." Pp. 207–34 in Jeffrey Alexander et al., eds., *The Micro-Macro Link*. Berkeley: University of California Press.

————. 1988. "Goffman and the Analysis of Conversation." Pp. 89–135 in Paul Drew and Anthony Wootton, eds., *Erving Goffman: Exploring the Interaction Order*. Cambridge: Polity Press.

Stone, B. L. 1982. "Saussure, Schutz, and Symbolic Interactionism: A Constitution and Interpretation of Signitive Behavior." Pp. 91–106 in Norman K. Denzin, ed., *Studies in Symbolic Interaction*. Greenwich, CT: JAI Press.

Suchman, Lucy. 1987. *Plans and Situated Action: The Problem of Human-Machine Interaction*. Cambridge: Cambridge University Press.

West, Candace. 1984. *Routine Complications: Troubles in Talk between Doctors and Patients*. Bloomington: Indiana University Press.

West, Candace, and Don H. Zimmerman. 1983. "Small Insults: A Study of Interruptions in Cross-Sex Conversations between Unacquainted Persons." Pp. 86–111 in Barrie Thorne, Cheris Kramarae, and Nancy Henley, eds., *Language, Gender, and Society*. Rowley, MA: Newbury House.

————. 1987. "Doing Gender." *Gender and Society* 1(2):125–51.

Whalen, Marilyn R., and Don H. Zimmerman. 1985. "Telling Trouble: Citizen Calls to the Police." Paper presented at the annual meeting of the Society for the Study of Social Problems, New York.

————. 1987. "Sequential and Institutional Contexts in Calls for Help." *Social Psychology Quarterly* 50(2):172–85.

Wilson, Thomas P. 1982. "Qualitative vs Quantitative Methods in Social Research." Mimeo. Department of Sociology, University of California, Santa Barbara. Published in German in *Kolner Zeitschrift für Soziologie und Socialpsychologie* 34 (1984):487–508.

————. In press. "Social Structure and the Sequential Organization of Interaction." In Deirdre Boden and Don H. Zimmerman, eds., *Talk and Social Structure*. Cambridge: Polity Press.

Wilson, Thomas P., and Don H. Zimmerman. 1986. "The Structure of Silence between Turns in Two-Party Conversation." *Discourse Processes* 9:375–90.

Zimmerman, Don H. 1984. "Talk and Its Occasion: The Case of Calling the Police." Pp. 201–8 in Deborah Schiffrin, ed., *Meaning, Form, and Use in Context: Linguistic Applications.* Georgetown University Roundtable on Language and Linguistics 1984. Washington, DC: Georgetown University Press.

———. 1988. "On Conversation: The Conversation Analytic Perspective." *Communication Yearbook* 11:406–32.

Zimmerman, Don H., and Deirdre Boden. In press. "Talk and Social Structure." In Boden and Zimmerman, eds., *Talk and Social Structure.* Cambridge: Polity Press.

Zimmerman, Don H., and Candace West. 1975. "Sex Roles, Interruptions, and Silences in Conversation." Pp. 105–29 in Barrie Thorne and Nancy Henley, eds., *Language and Sex: Difference and Dominance.* Rowley, MA: Newbury House.

Contributors

KATHRYN PYNE ADDELSON is professor of philosophy at Smith College.

HOWARD S. BECKER is MacArthur Professor of Arts and Sciences at Northwestern University.

DEIRDRE BODEN is assisant professor of sociology at Washington University, St. Louis.

ADELE E. CLARKE is assistant professor of sociology at the University of California, San Francisco.

ELIHU M. GERSON is director of the Tremont Research Institute, San Francisco.

SAMUEL GILMORE is assistant professor of sociology at the University of California, Irvine.

BARRY GLASSNER is professor of sociology at the University of Connecticut.

JOHN R. HALL is professor of sociology at the University of California, Davis.

MICHAL M. McCALL is associate professor of sociology at Macalester College.

MARY JO NEITZ is associate professor of sociology at the University of Missouri, Columbia.

JUDITH WITTNER is assistant professor of sociology, Loyola University, Chicago.

Index